ADOLESCEN
PREJUDIC

**Published in cooperation with the
Anti-Defamation League of B'nai B'rith**

Charles Y. Glock, Robert Wuthno
e Allyn Piliavin, and Metta Spe

ADOLESCENT PREJUDICE

Adolescent Prejudice

Charles Y. Glock, Robert Wuthnow
Jane Allyn Piliavin, Metta Spencer

1817

HARPER & ROW, PUBLISHERS

NEW YORK   EVANSTON   SAN FRANCISCO   LONDON

Volume Seven in a series based on
the University of California Five-Year Study of Anti-Semitism
in the United States
being conducted by the Survey Research Center
Charles Y. Glock, Program Coordinator,
under a grant from the Anti-Defamation League of B'nai B'rith

ADOLESCENT PREJUDICE. Copyright © 1975 by Anti-Defamation League of B'nai B'rith. All rights reserved. Printed in the United States of America. No part of this book may be used or reproduced in any manner whatsoever without written permission except in the case of brief quotations embodied in critical articles and reviews. For information address Harper & Row, Publishers, Inc., 10 East 53rd Street, New York, N.Y. 10022. Published simultaneously in Canada by Fitzhenry & Whiteside Limited, Toronto.

FIRST EDITION

Library of Congress Cataloging in Publication Data
Main entry under title:

Adolescent prejudice.
   (Patterns of American prejudice series ; v. 7)
   Includes bibliographical references and index.
   1. Prejudices and antipathies. 2. Adolescent
psychology. I. Glock, Charles Y. II. Series.
BF575.P9A35 1975   301.45'1'042   74–15824
ISBN 0–06–011567–X

75 76 77 78 79 10 9 8 7 6 5 4 3 2 1

To Karen Muhonen

Contents

Acknowledgments

To acknowledge by name everyone who has contributed to this volume would require credits of a magnitude approximating that of many a film epic or stage triumph. To collect, codify, and process the research instruments on which the book is based involved work being done by close to 300 people if we don't count our subjects, and almost 5,000 if we do. Among these expediters were supervisors from the staff of the National Opinion Research Center at the University of Chicago, who oversaw the collection of the data, several hundred teachers in three schools systems, who helped in the administration of the questionnaires, about sixteen coders at the Survey Research Center who edited the returns and made them suitable for computerization, four keypunch operators, who transferred the data into machine-readable form, an unknown number of data processing personnel on the staffs of the Computer Center and the Survey Research Center at the University of California, Berkeley, who over the years helped the unfolding of the results, and the teenagers who generously and conscientiously answered our questionnaires. To all these people, our sincere appreciation for the assistance, paid and unpaid, they provided.

Among those whose help ought to be acknowledged by name are the school superintendents, the members of the school boards, and the principals of the schools in the three communities where the study was done. For reasons which are explained later, they choose to remain anonymous. Their cooperation was crucial to the project, and we regret not being able to acknowledge publicly our deep gratitude for the time and effort they gave to make the arrangements necessary to allow the project to proceed.

The enabling funds were provided by the Anti-Defamation League of B'nai B'rith. We are indebted to the League and especially to its program director, Oscar Cohen, not only for financial support, but for the goodwill, friendship, and encouragement they extended to us at every step of the way.

M. Brewster Smith, now vice chancellor for social sciences at the University of California, Santa Cruz, conceived the project on' which this book is based and was instrumental in bringing Jane Piliavin to Berkeley to direct it. He served as senior consultant while the project was being designed and executed and was a participant in the early stages of analysis. Dr. Smith is also author and co-author of earlier publications emanating from the project.

We are also indebted to David Stein, now on the faculty of Yeshiva University in New York. As a research assistant on the project, he was extremely helpful in early analytic work. Professor Stein is also author and co-author of earlier project publications.

This book could not have been produced without Karen Muhonen, and our gratitude to her is unbounded. She took responsibility for all the computer work to produce the statistical tables, for their formats, and for overseeing the production of the complete book manuscript. Our dedication of the book to her can only partly express our indebtedness to her.

We should also like to thank Rod Fredrickson, Margaret Baker, Ann Finlayson, Patsy Fosler, George Lavender, John Lawson, Don Trummell, Frank Many, and Harvey Weinstein of the Survey Research Center for their programming help.

William Nicholls, executive officer of the Survey Research Center, was responsible for the construction of the homophily and heterophily indexes used in the analysis. He was also extremely helpful in assisting on other measurement problems.

Because it is not common, especially in the social sciences, for a book to have as many authors as this one, it is appropriate perhaps to identify our own contributions. In assigning authorship we have sought to recognize those who have made a significant intellectual contribution to the book, without requiring that this include participation in the actual writing of the manuscript.

The analysis reported on in the book and the writing of the manuscript were done by Glock and Wuthnow. Glock established the structure of the book, oversaw the analysis, and produced the initial drafts of the Introduction and Chapters 1, 4, 6, and 7. Chapters 2, 3, and 5 and Appendixes A and B were drafted initially by Wuthnow. Given the extensive revisions these initial drafts have gone through subsequently, it is difficult now to say just who is responsible for what. The analysis and writing are best judged as a truly collaborative effort.

Piliavin's contribution is the production of the data on which the book is based. She designed the project, oversaw its execution, and was responsible for carrying it through the early stages of analysis. Piliavin's ideas are omnipresent, and her design of the project has been a major influence in shaping the analysis. Also significant is the early analytic work she was able to complete before leaving Berkeley.

Spencer's contribution is derivative of her having worked closely with the senior author on both the present and more general analysis of the data (which will produce an additional monograph to be authored by Spencer). Many of Spencer's ideas advanced during this period of collaboration have influenced the writing of the manuscript. Co- authorship affords appropriate recognition of her contribution.

Our book has been long in coming, and some comment is called for on the relevancy for the seventies of data collected in the sixties—1963, to be exact. Insofar as there has been change in the incidence of prejudice in the school systems studied, our analysis obviously cannot reflect them. Primarily, however, our book is concerned with accounting for adolescent prejudice, not with describing its extent. The accounting, we believe, is as relevant to an understanding of prejudice today as ten years ago, and unless remarkable advances are made toward the elimination of prejudice, the relevancy is likely to remain for the future as well.

Our book has been preceded by the following publications based on the same data.

Stein, David D., Jane Allyn Hardyck, and M. Brewster Smith, "Race and Belief: An Open and Shut Case," *Journal of Abnormal and Social Psychology,* 1:4 (April, 1965), 281–89.

Stein, David D., "The Influence of Belief Systems on Interpersonal Preference: A Validation Study of Rokeach's Theory of Prejudice," *Psychological Monographs,* 80:8, 1966.

Smith, M. Brewster, "The Schools and Prejudice: Findings," in Charles Y. Glock and Ellen Siegelman (eds.), *Prejudice, U.S.A.,* New York: Praeger, 1969, 112–35.

Smith, M. Brewster and Jane Allyn Piliavin, "The Schools and Prejudice: Findings," Anti-Defamation League pamphlet, 1970.

The book will be followed by an additional monograph by Metta Spencer, "Race and Youth."

Introduction

This book has its origins in a grant from the Anti-Defamation League of B'nai B'rith to the University of California for a study of anti-Semitism and other forms of prejudice in contemporary America. The grant, given without strings except for the subject of the study, left it to the university to decide how best to pursue the inquiry.

The size of the grant—$500,000—made it possible to study prejudice from a number of perspectives. Among those chosen was the investigation of the phenomenon as it manifests itself among youth, more specifically adolescent youth.[1]*

The choice was made partly because very little is known about adolescent prejudice. There have been scattered studies[2] but no substantial attempt to measure the incidence and sources of prejudice in this age group. The choice was also made because of a concern that the results of the inquiry should contribute to the reduction of prejudice in society. A study of adolescent prejudice, it was felt, might provide a basis to improve the ability of schools to exert leverage more effectively in the control of prejudice.

Once embarked on this course, further decisions were very quickly called for. What specifically was to be the focus of the inquiry? What questions did we want to answer? What theory, if any, did we want to test? And how exactly was the study to be done?

From the outset we decided against giving attention to all forms of prejudice and elected to focus primarily on anti-Semitism as called for by the terms of the grant and incidentally on racial prejudice. In addition, several of us had had a long-standing interest in anti-Semitism and had done previous

* Notes begin on page 213.

research on it. We chose to examine racial prejudice as well to allow for contrasting the patterning of the two forms of prejudice among adolescents.

At the time our study began, there was a need, as there continues to be, for accurate nationwide descriptive information on the nature and incidence of prejudice among youth. Such information collected repeatedly on a periodic basis would be tremendously helpful in guiding a national effort to combat prejudice. But such efforts obviously must be grounded in knowledge, not only of how extensive the problem is, but also of what its causes are.

Our dilemma was that we shared an interest in both kinds of problems but saw no way effectively to explore both within our resources and within a single inquiry. The descriptive question would be best served by a study calling for data to be collected from a substantial national sample of the adolescent population. However, such a study presented tremendous practical problems in light of the obvious desirability of combining information collected from teenagers with data obtained from school records. Moreover, such a design even if practical was not particularly conducive to examining the more analytic questions we wanted to address.

In the end, we opted for a more analytic design because we saw no way within our resources to undertake a descriptive study of national scope and because the causal questions were judged to be more important than the descriptive ones, particularly given our interest in having the results contribute to the control of prejudice. The cure for prejudice, it was felt, is more likely to lie in knowing its causes than in knowing its incidence, if one cannot know both.

The basic question to be addressed is what accounts for prejudice *and* its absence? Why is it that by the time of adolescence some youngsters have absorbed the prejudices that persist in the culture? In turn, and of equal importance, how is it that other teenagers manage to avoid being prejudiced?

There was no prospect, it was recognized, to answer these questions completely in a single study to be conducted at only one point in time. Still we wanted the study to make a contribution to answers. In particular, we wanted to learn what difference it makes to the development or the prevention of prejudice that teenagers of different religious and racial backgrounds study together in the same schools.

The continuing issue of school integration makes the latter question especially salient. Some knowledge has been accumulated about the effects of racial integration on school performances.[3] We are still uninformed essentially about the positive or negative effects of integration on relations between the races. The effect of intergroup contact is also an important question in the study and discussion of anti-Semitism. What is the effect of a Jewish presence on anti-Semitism?

The prevailing imagery in these questions is that interreligious and interracial contact breaks down prejudices by falsifying religious and racial stereotypes, by creating opportunities for friendship across religious and racial lines, and by generating norms of tolerance. Evidence to this effect is at most spotty and rooted mostly in correlations that do not indicate whether it is contact which produces prejudice or the absence of prejudice which produces contact.[4] It seemed to us of both practical and theoretical importance to try to find out.

To deal with both the general and special questions about prejudice, a research design was formulated calling for contrasting the patterns of prejudice among adolescents in three communities. We wanted the communities to be as much alike as possible with respect to such factors as scale of living, type of employment, and nearness to metropolitan area, but given our special interest in anti-Semitism, to vary in the proportion of Jewish teenagers in their school populations. Ideally, we wanted one community where there were no Jews in the schools, another where they constituted a substantial minority, and a third where they made a majority. In this way, we would be able to investigate the effects of a Jewish presence on anti-Semitism.

We also wanted the communities to have a black presence so as to allow examination of the relationship between the extent of interracial contact and racial prejudice. To optimize our ability to study anti-Semitism, however, we felt that the communities ought not to vary in the proportion of black teenagers in their school populations. We recognized that this would mean sacrificing an exploration of the size of a black presence on racial prejudice, but our resources did not allow extending the study to the larger number of communities such exploration would have called for.

Aside from enabling the study of contextual effects, conducting the study in three communities was also seen as conducive to identifying root causes of anti-Semitism that operate whether Jews are present or not. To find particular factors to be producing or reducing prejudice uniformly in all three communities would be strong evidence, we felt, of their wider generalizability.

The design, it was recognized, would not produce evidence on the *incidence* of prejudice that could be generalized accurately to any larger population. Still, information for three American communities about how much prejudice exists among adolescents and what form it takes is more information than we now have about adolescent prejudice.

Matching model with reality is always difficult in social research, and our experience was no exception. Some problems were met in identifying communities meeting the criteria of racial and religious mix and comparability set by the design. Few school systems are racially and religiously integrated in the ways our original design called for. Compounding these problems was the additional and formidable one of gaining the necessary cooperation.

Cooperation meant a substantial disruption in regular classroom routine that many school districts, we discovered, were unwilling to allow. The study also turned out to be more sensitive politically than we had anticipated. Considerable resistance was encountered because school boards saw the subject matter of the study and our approach as controversial and productive of possible community conflict.

While these fears proved ungrounded in the communities in which the study was eventually undertaken, they did necessitate a compromise in the research design simply because we ran out of communities that would have enabled us to implement it exactly. More by good fortune than by design, the three communities finally settled upon did provide the desired inter-religious variation in their school populations. The proportion of Jews in the three school populations varied from 43 percent to 23 percent to less than 1 percent. We also succeeded in getting equivalence in the relative number of black teenagers in the three school populations. As it turned out, the proportion of black students in the three communities ranged from 14 percent to 16 percent.

We were unsuccessful, however, in gaining equivalence in the three communities in other respects; they differed from one another considerably more than we had wanted in size, population characteristics, nearness to metropolitan area, etc. This made the task of trying to isolate the effect of a Jewish presence or its absence on anti-Semitism more difficult.

However, the variation improved the study's ability to look more generally into the sources of adolescent prejudice, and enhanced the confidence that can be placed in generalizing from uniform findings in the three communities.

Because anonymity had to be promised to secure cooperation, we are obliged to use pseudonyms to identify the three communities. Having in mind that the names chosen ought to convey something about each community's character, they have been called Commutertown, Oceanville, and Central City.

All three communities are within 200 miles of New York City. Commutertown, with a population of about 75,000, is a well-to-do New York City suburb in which over half of the employed males have sales, managerial, professional, or other white-collar occupations. The average income, therefore, is well above the national average and unemployment is low. The percentages of nonwhite and of foreign-born are both quite high, reflecting the nearness of the community to New York. Even with these population segments, both of which tend to make up the lower economic echelons in most communities, Commutertown is highly prosperous and is considered to be a desirable place to live and to work. It is Commutertown in which 43 percent of the student population is Jewish.

Central City is probably a good deal more "representative" of small American cities than is Commutertown. Situated a good distance from New York City, it is an independent city, not a suburb or even a closely bound satellite of a larger metropolitan area. The nonwhite and foreign-born populations are quite small (8.8 percent and 2 percent, respectively), and the proportion of Jewish students in the schools is less than 0.5 percent. Central City is a less affluent community than Commutertown. Less than one-third of the employed males are in white-collar occupations; median family income is near the national average, as was the rate of unemployment at the time of our study. Educational level is relatively low on the average, the lowest of the three communities in the study. Central City's population of 55,000 represented a slight decline from the previous population count, an indication that the core city is losing more well-to-do citizens to the suburbs.

From the viewpoint of its school population, Oceanville cannot be considered to be one community. Students at Oceanville High School come from Oceanville proper and from several surrounding small municipalities. Oceanville and the communities that feed its high school are on the seacoast and the whole area is famed as a resort. The population of Oceanville and Beach Township combined is 26,000. Oceanville has a substantial nonwhite population (40 percent) and a small foreign-born minority. Median family income in Oceanville proper is below the national average but income in the feeder communities is considerably higher, almost as high as Commutertown. There are substantially more blue-collar workers in Oceanville proper, as might be expected, than in the surrounding communities. The effect on the high school population is to produce a heterogeneous mix of students from different ethnic, religious, and income groups. The proportion of Jewish students in the feeder schools and the high school itself is 23 percent.

A statistical summary of selected characteristics of the three communities derived from the census and other sources is included in Table 1. We shall have more to report by way of background information on the three communities as we proceed.

The data collected in the three communities comprise the responses to three-part questionnaires by all students enrolled in the 8th, 10th, and 12th grades of all public schools. There was only one high school in each community, and all 10th- and 12th-grade students in the study were attending it. The 8th graders came from two feeder schools in Commutertown,

Table 1   SELECTED CHARACTERISTICS OF THE THREE COMMUNITIES

	Commutertown	Central City	Oceanville
Population (approx.)	75,000	55,000	26,000
Percent nonwhite	13.7%	8.8%	40.1%
Percent foreign-born	13.5%	2.0%	8.9%
Median school years completed, male	12.4	9.2	9.4
Median family income	$8,131	$5,933	$5,016
% of families with income less than $3,000 a year	9.5	14.5	24.0
% of males over 14 years of age in labor force who are unemployed	3.3	6.0	10.4

one in Oceanville and environs, and three in Central City. The questionnaires were self-administered in three sittings over a three-week period under the supervision of staff from the National Opinion Research Center, to whom the task was subcontracted. In total, 1,886 usable questionnaires were obtained in Commutertown, 1,045 in Oceanville, and 1,700 in Central City.[5] It will be more appropriate to report on the content of the questionnaires in the context of reporting our findings. Suffice it here to say that they were directed to measuring the extent of prejudice and to collecting auxiliary data about its sources. In addition to questionnaires administered to schoolchildren, teachers in the three school systems were also asked to complete questionnaires about their impressions of the nature and extent of prejudice in the schools.[6]

This report on the results of the inquiry begins with a description of the nature and extent of anti-Semitism in the three communities. The social location and causes of this form of prejudice are then analyzed in depth, after which racial prejudice is taken up primarily to assess how much correspondence exists in the findings for the two forms of prejudice.

1 Attitudes, Feelings, and Patterns of Friendship

Consensus among observers about the height of a person or about a person's weight is likely to be arrived at readily. There may be quibbling about precision—how many ounces to round off weight, for example—but given an accurate measuring stick or scale, disagreement can be quickly resolved. On other attributes it is not so easy to get agreement—for instance, how friendly they are, or how good-looking, or how smart. People are prone, of course, to make judgments about such personal attributes but, compared to height and weight, the criteria for judging are considerably less precise and as many opinions are likely to be expressed as people making them.

Anti-Semitism belongs to the second class of attributes. There is no absolute way to decide whether someone is anti-Semitic. Judgments depend on what one means by anti-Semitism and here, unlike height and weight, there is no universally agreed-upon standard. Anti-Semitism not only means different things to different people but can be manifested in more than a single way.

Any study of anti-Semitism, consequently, faces a special problem of measurement. A study of anti-Semitism among adolescents has the additional problem of deciding whether the phenomenon manifests itself differently among youth than it does among adults.

Our study adopted several rather than a single approach to detect anti-Semitism among teenagers. None of the approaches constitutes a radical departure from those used in other studies. Indeed, one of the findings of early qualitative interviews conducted in preparation for the study was that youth mirrored adults in their expression of this prejudice. As with adults, anti-Semitism is expressed in negative beliefs about Jews, in negative feelings toward them, and in a willingness to countenance and abet anti-Jewish

discriminatory behavior.[1] The profile of anti-Semitism among youth—
that is, the way that negative beliefs, feelings, and actions combine—may
be different from that for adults but the ingredients are essentially the same.

We designed our questionnaires to try to tap the belief, feeling, and behavioral components of anti-Semitism. How this was done and what was
learned about the nature and distribution of beliefs about and feelings and
behavior toward Jews are the subjects of this chapter.

Beliefs About Jews

Ask an adolescent to express himself about Jews, we discovered in our
preliminary interviews, and all sorts of imagery quickly pour out. Sometimes negative and sometimes positive, the comments are almost always
full and articulate. Only rarely do youth respond that they don't know anything about Jews. It doesn't matter very much whether a youngster knows or
has ever met anyone who is Jewish. He still has something to say.

The content of adolescent imagery is influenced markedly by the time-
worn shibboleths of the past. Indeed, the traditional stereotypes virtually set
the boundaries for conversation as teenagers remark on what they know
about Jews, what they imagine them to be like, and how they feel about
them. However much anti-Semitism may be indicated by the imagery,
youth's familiarity with old saws about Jews—pro and con—is testimony to
how deeply these have become imbedded in American culture.

Because traditional stereotypes dominated the conversation in our preliminary interviews, in the structured part of the inquiry a format was
adopted of confronting youngsters with such stereotypes and asking them
about the extent of their agreement with them. The stereotypes used were
culled out of the preliminary interviews. Items that had been used in other
studies of anti-Semitism were also adopted. Both positive and negative
stereotypes were included and phrased in ways to avoid the possibility of
creating a response set.[2]

Some stereotypes were added that have not been especially associated
with anti-Semitism in the past. Such atypical items, for example, as "Jews
are often sloppy and unconcerned about their personal appearance" or "are
rather loose in their moral standards and behavior" were included as a way
to see whether those with a negative imagery are prone to extend it un-
reservedly to accept anything "bad" that might be said about Jews.

As the instrument was being constructed, it occurred to us that it might
make a difference in responses whether the referents of the stereotypes asked
about were adult Jews or Jewish teenagers. Persuaded that there might be
such a difference and that it would be of interest to know what it is, the

Items	Identification	
	Teenage Form	*Adult Form*
(Jewish teenagers) are frequently in trouble with school authorities and the police; often break rules and laws.	Troublemakers	
(Jews in general) are frequently in trouble with the police and other authorities; are not very law-abiding.		Troublemakers
(Jewish teenagers) try to push into groups where they are not really wanted.	Pushy	
(Jews in general) try to push into groups or neighborhoods where they are not really wanted.		Pushy
(Jewish teenagers) (Jews in general) are sincerely religious on the whole.	Religious	Religious
(Jewish teenagers) are quite different from other students in what they do and stand for.	Different	
(Jews in general) are quite different from others in what they do and stand for.		Different
(Jewish teenagers) are likely to be untrustworthy; lie and cheat more often than others.	Untrustworthy	
(Jews in general) are likely to be somewhat dishonest in their dealings with others.		Untrustworthy
(Jewish teenagers) avoid forcing their beliefs and wishes on other students; are not bossy.	Bossy	
(Jews in general) avoid forcing their beliefs and wishes on others; are not bossy.		Bossy
(Jewish teenagers) (Jews in general) are likely to be selfish; concerned only for themselves or their own group.	Selfish	Selfish
(Jewish teenagers) (Jews in general) are unfriendly; do not mix with others; go around only with their own group.	Unfriendly	Unfriendly

Items	Identification	
	Teenage Form	*Adult Form*
(Jewish teenagers) (Jews in general) are quite intelligent and well informed; think clearly about things.	Intelligent	Intelligent
(Jewish teenagers) are very concerned with getting good grades; are always working for A's.	Ambitious	
(Jews in general) are very concerned with making a lot of money; are "money-mad."		Greedy
(Jewish teenagers) (Jews in general) often dress in a loud and flashy way.	Gaudy	Gaudy
(Jewish teenagers) think they are better than other students; easily develop a superiority complex.	Conceited	
(Jews in general) think they are better than other people; easily develop a superiority complex.		Conceited
(Jewish teenagers) have too much to say about what goes on in school; run pretty much everything.	Powerful	
(Jews in general) have too much power in business and politics in this country.		Powerful
(Jewish teenagers) give up on hard problems easily; never seem to try very hard in school.	Quitters	
(Jews in general) expect "something for nothing"; are not willing to work for what they want.		Lazy
(Jewish teenagers) have quite a lot of athletic ability.	Athletic	
(Jews in general) support movements and groups that are working for equal rights for everyone.		Civil rightists
(Jewish teenagers) are often sloppy and unconcerned about their personal appearance.	Sloppy	
(Jews in general) do not keep their property and possessions in good condition.		Sloppy

Items	Identification Teenage Form	Adult Form
(Jewish teenagers) (Jews in general) are rather loose in their moral standards and behavior.	Immoral	Immoral
(Jewish teenagers) have a lot of school spirit; know what's going on around school and take part in activities.	School spirit	
(Jews in general) participate a good deal in community affairs; are active and interested citizens.		Responsible citizens
(Jewish teenagers) often try to "get ahead" by "buttering up" the teachers.	Sly	
(Jews in general) are inclined to be more loyal to their own groups than they are to America.		Disloyal
(Jewish teenagers) (Jews in general) are loud and show-offy; will do almost anything to gain recognition or draw attention to themselves.	Vain	Vain

study design was modified so that half of the subjects in each school district were asked to respond to the stereotype items having "Jewish teenagers" in mind with the other half being asked whether they agreed or not that "Jews in general" are as the stereotypes allege them to be.

In the end, twenty stereotypes were asked about in the two forms of the questionnaire. Seven of these were worded in exactly the same way, eight were modified slightly to make them appropriate to the referent, and five were independent, meaning that they were completely different in the two questionnaire forms. The stereotypes asked about are reported above with notations inserted wherever an item was modified for, or different in, the adult version. Next to each item we have inserted a key word or phrase which will be used hereafter as a short-hand identification.

The responses to these items were tabulated with several preconceptions in mind. To begin with, it was anticipated that responses would reveal at most a modest amount of hostility toward Jews. Given the mounting evidence of a reduction in attitudinal anti-Semitism in the United States,[3] it seemed reasonable to expect that the decline would have reached its nadir among adolescents and that they would be even less prone to hostile responses than their elders.

It was also expected that what adolescents imagine Jews to be like would be more favorable in Commutertown and Oceanville, the two communities where there are a substantial number of Jews in school, than in Central City where there are virtually none. There were no grounds to anticipate that our findings would in any way contradict the consistent results of other studies of an association between greater contact and less prejudice.

As between white and black teenagers, we judged that blacks would probably express more hostility. Other studies have shown low economic status to be associated with prejudice, and we knew that the families of black students in our samples were economically poorer on the average than the families of white students.[4]

Finally, it was expected that there would be a more favorable response in all three communities, but particularly in Commutertown and Oceanville, to teenage than to adult Jews. Teenagers, it was assumed, would be more ready to identify with other teenagers than with adults, especially in settings where there are a substantial number of Jewish youngsters to identify with.

The results for white non-Jewish teenagers who responded to the teenage form of the questionnaire are presented in Table 2. The table shows the proportion of respondents in each community who agreed that each statement was descriptive of Jewish teenagers.[5] The stereotypes have been ordered to distinguish between those accepted by a majority of respondents (51 percent or more), those accepted by a substantial minority (26 percent to 50 percent), and those accepted by a smaller minority (25 percent or less). Stereotypes which are unambiguously negative in tone have been asterisked. Stereotypes without an asterisk are those which are "seemingly" positive or neutral. We say seemingly in recognition that for an anti-Semitic teenager a conception of Jews as intelligent or as ambitious or as different might be invidiously rather than positively or neutrally interpreted.

The general portrait of adolescent attitudes revealed by Table 2 upsets several of our preconceptions. Judging from the degree of acceptance of outrightly negative stereotypes, there remains, contrary to expectations, a substantial proportion of youth who are willing to give lip service to the anti-Semitic stereotypes of old. Indeed, some of these stereotypes win allegiance from a majority of respondents and most have the support of more than a third of the respondents in two of the three communities.

Not only does Table 2 reveal more hostility than expected, it also disconfirms the prediction that the most anti-Semitism would be found in the community in which there are virtually no Jews. To the contrary, youngsters in Central City, the community without a Jewish presence, prove to be consistently less willing to accept negative stereotypes and about as willing to attribute positive traits to Jewish teenagers as are their counterparts in the two communities where Jews are present.

With one exception, the least accepted stereotypes in all three communities are those which are not elements in historic anti-Semitism and which were inserted in the battery of items as controls. It has rarely been contended even by virulent anti-Semites that Jews tend to be trouble-

Table 2 ACCEPTANCE OF STEREOTYPES OF JEWISH TEENAGERS BY WHITE NON-JEWISH ADOLESCENTS

	Commutertown	%	Oceanville	%	Central City	%
Majority stereotypes (accepted by 50% or more)	Intelligent	77	Intelligent	82	School spirit	76
	School spirit	76	Ambitious	79	Intelligent	75
	Ambitious	74	School spirit	69	Ambitious	67
	*Powerful	70	Religious	61	Religious	67
	*Conceited	70	*Conceited	61	Athletic	50
	*Vain	66	*Sly	60		
	*Selfish	60	*Vain	58		
	*Sly	58	*Powerful	55		
	*Bossy	52	*Selfish	55		
	*Unfriendly	50				
Stereotypes held by a substantial minority (accepted by from 25% to 49%)	*Gaudy	49	*Bossy	48	Different	43
	*Immoral	48	*Pushy	44	*Conceited	35
	Different	43	Different	43	*Bossy	34
	*Pushy	42	*Unfriendly	39	*Vain	33
	Religious	40	*Gaudy	38	*Pushy	32
	Athletic	33	Athletic	36	*Selfish	32
	*Troublemakers	25	*Immoral	33	*Sly	31
	*Untrustworthy	25	*Untrustworthy	25	*Gaudy	29
					*Immoral	28
					*Powerful	26
					*Unfriendly	25
Minority stereotypes (accepted by less than 25%)	*Quitter	17	*Sloppy	16	*Troublemaker	24
	*Sloppy	16	*Quitter	15	*Sloppy	22
			*Troublemaker	13	*Quitter	22
					*Untrustworthy	18
Mean proportion accepting outrightly negative stereotypes		43%		37%		26%
N =	(388)		(301)		(667)	

* Stereotypes judged to be outrightly negative.

makers, to be sloppy, or to give up easily. Depicting the Jew as untrustworthy, as willing to lie and cheat more than others, has been part of the traditional anti-Semitic syndrome. Relatively, however, this stereotype gains little acceptance as characterizing Jewish teenagers today although, in absolute terms, it is not inconsequential that the item gained acceptance by 25 percent, 25 percent, and 18 percent, respectively, in the three samples.

The stereotypes that gain greatest acceptance in all communities and most especially in Commutertown and Oceanville are mostly those concerned with Jewish superiority and success. Such traits are readily granted to Jewish youngsters in all three communities. Substantial majorities see Jews as intelligent and ambitious. These apparently positive attributes are accompanied, however, by other beliefs which suggest that teenagers are made uncomfortable, if not outrightly hostile, by Jews doing well. This tendency is especially marked in the communities where there is a Jewish presence. There, a majority conceive of Jewish teenagers as thinking they are better than other students (conceited), as having too much to say about what goes on in school (powerful), as forcing their beliefs and wishes on other students (bossy), as often trying to get ahead by buttering up teachers (sly), as being selfish and concerned only for themselves (selfish), and as being loud and show-offy (vain). In all three communities, the positive attributions are made by a majority. Invidious allegations are least frequently accepted in Central City; indeed, unlike Commutertown and Oceanville, no negative stereotypes are accepted by a majority in Central City.

Since the major purpose of this chapter is description rather than explanation, consideration of whether the presence of Jews in Commutertown and Oceanville accounts for these rather startling differences will be postponed until later. It is evident, however, that these unexpected results, flying in the face of other research and by now common belief, add a significant new dimension to the analytic problems of the inquiry.

So far we have been reporting on adolescent attitudes toward Jewish teenagers. It will be recalled that equivalent samples in each school were asked about Jews in general rather than Jewish teenagers. The results are reported in Table 3. Once again, outrightly negative items have been asterisked.

All in all, the attitude profile toward Jews in general is very similar to that toward Jewish teenagers. There is again a ready acceptance of positive stereotypes. In all communities, a majority conceive of Jews as intelligent, as sensitive about civil rights, as active participants in community affairs, and as sincerely religious.

As with attitudes toward teenagers, however, such seemingly positive images are not sufficient to derail or forestall unfriendly ones. In all three communities, there is widespread acceptance of negative stereotypes. Once again, the support is somewhat greater in Commutertown and Oceanville than in Central City where only one negative attribution gains majority support and that by only one percentage point.

Looking at details, it is again negative images associated with Jewish superiority and success which produce majority acceptance in Commutertown and Oceanville. Jews are seen as very concerned about making money (greedy), as thinking they are better than other people (conceited), as loud and show-offy (vain), and as selfishly concerned only for themselves (selfish).

Table 3 ACCEPTANCE OF STEREOTYPES OF JEWS IN GENERAL
BY WHITE NON-JEWISH ADOLESCENTS

	Commutertown	%	Oceanville	%	Central City	%
Majority	Intelligent	77	Intelligent	77	Religious	76
stereotypes	Good citizens	76	Good citizens	71	Intelligent	74
(accepted by	*Greedy	69	*Greedy	66	Good citizens	69
50% or more)	*Conceited	67	Religious	62	Civil rightist	68
	Civil rightist	62	Civil rightist	61	Different	54
	*Vain	59	*Selfish	61	*Greedy	51
	*Selfish	59	*Conceited	57		
	Religious	55	*Vain	52		
	*Bossy	50	*Bossy	52		
Stereotypes held	Different	49	Different	49	*Disloyal	45
by a substantial	*Immoral	46	*Disloyal	41	*Bossy	41
minority (ac-	*Gaudy	45	*Unfriendly	40	*Conceited	40
cepted by from	*Powerful	45	*Untrustworthy	39	*Selfish	39
25 to 59%)	*Disloyal	45	*Pushy	38	*Vain	36
	*Unfriendly	43	*Lazy	37	*Untrustworthy	36
	*Lazy	40	*Powerful	36	*Lazy	33
	*Untrustworthy	35	*Gaudy	34	*Powerful	32
	*Pushy	34	*Immoral	31	*Immoral	31
					*Gaudy	29
					*Pushy	28
					*Unfriendly	27
Minority	*Sloppy	21	*Sloppy	11	*Troublemakers	24
stereotypes	*Troublemakers	18	*Troublemakers	11	*Sloppy	21
(accepted by						
less than 25%)						
Mean proportion						
accepting out-						
rightly negative						
Stereotypes		45%		40%		34%
N =	(397)		(318)		(702)	

* Stereotypes judged to be outrightly negative.

Table 4   RELATIVE ACCEPTANCE OF STEREOTYPES OF JEWISH
TEENAGERS AND JEWS IN GENERAL BY WHITE
NON-JEWISH TEENAGERS

	Commutertown	%	*Oceanville*	%	*Central City*	%
Stereotypes more frequently attributed to Jewish teenagers than to Jews in general						
Difference of more than 10 percentage points	*Powerful	25	*Powerful	19		
Difference of 6 to 10 percentage points	*Pushy *Vain *Unfriendly *Troublemakers	8 7 7 7	*Pushy *Vain	6 6		
Stereotypes more frequently attributed to Jews in general than to Jewish teenagers						
Difference of more than 10 percentage points	Religious	15	*Untrustworthy	14	*Untrustworthy Different	18 11
Difference of 6 to 10 percentage points	*Untrustworthy Different	10 6	Different *Selfish	6 6	Religious *Bossy *Selfish *Powerful	9 7 7 6
Stereotypes attributed about equally to Jewish teenagers and Jews in general						
Less than 5 percentage point difference	Intelligent *Conceited *Gaudy *Immoral *Sloppy *Selfish *Bossy		Intelligent *Conceited *Gaudy *Immoral *Sloppy Religious *Bossy *Troublemakers *Unfriendly		Intelligent *Conceited *Gaudy *Immoral *Sloppy *Troublemakers *Vain *Pushy *Unfriendly	

* Stereotypes judged to be outrightly negative.

Least support in all communities is given to attributing sloppiness or troublemaking to Jews in general. These stereotypes, it will be recalled, were also among the least likely to be attributed to Jewish teenagers.

As Table 4 shows, it makes very little difference for most items asked equivalently in the two forms of the questionnaire whether the referent is Jewish teenagers or Jews in general. By town the slight differences are in the direction of Commutertown and Oceanville youngsters being more favorably disposed to Jews in general whereas Jewish teenagers are more favorably viewed in Central City. In all three communities, Jews in general are more likely than Jewish teenagers to be judged untrustworthy. Otherwise, the most compelling difference is the greater tendency in Commutertown and Oceanville to see Jewish teenagers as having more power in school than to see Jews in general as having too much power in business.

Despite these differences, the experiment failed to produce anywhere near the magnitude of difference anticipated. On hindsight, this might be because adult Jews tend to be viewed relatively the same as Jewish teenagers. It may also be the result of youngsters not connoting "Jews in general" to mean, as we intended, adult Jews.

Earlier we remarked that the sheer amount of hostility which these white non-Jewish teenagers express against Jews seems surprisingly large. Some perspective is given to that observation when we compare the teenagers' attitudes to those of an adult sample of the national population of the United States. The adult data were collected shortly before our own in connection with another volume in the Patterns of American Prejudice Series.[6] Although the questions in the two studies were not worded exactly alike, a number of them were similar enough to warrant comparing results. The comparison is reported in Table 5.

In all comparisons save one, teenagers show considerably more hostility than do adults despite the fact that the teenage items tend to be worded somewhat less harshly than the questions asked of adults. Indeed, on the one item where teenagers show more tolerance (seeing Jews as unfriendly and sticking together too much), less harsh wording rather than greater teenage tolerance may account for the less hostile teenage response.

Obviously it is not justifiable to generalize from these community samples to the country as a whole. Yet, considering that these communities are presumably in more "enlightened" areas of the country, there is little basis for wishful thinking that the national picture would prove to be better.[7]

There has been considerable discussion, more since our data were collected than before, about black attitudes toward Jews. The overtly anti-Semitic stance of some militant black leaders and the seemingly positive response from their followers have produced concern that anti-Semitism is on the rise in the black community. Research has neither wholly confirmed nor disconfirmed these fears.[8] There is no evidence that the black population on the whole is any more anti-Semitic than the white population. A finding from a nationwide study that younger blacks are more likely to be anti-Semitic than their elders has been partly the basis for assertions that black anti-Semitism is on the rise. Among whites, our evidence to the contrary, youth are found to be less anti-Semitic than their elders.[9]

Our own inquiry cannot contribute to the discussion on whether or not anti-Semitism among blacks is on the rise. It is possible, however, to com-

Table 5   BELIEFS ABOUT JEWS AMONG NON-JEWISH ADOLESCENTS AND A NATIONAL SAMPLE OF NON-JEWISH ADULTS COMPARED

National Sample of Adults % Agree		Teenage Samples from Present Inquiry % Agree		
		Commuter-town	Ocean-ville	Central City
Jews have too much power in the U.S.	11%	Jews in general have too much power in business and politics in this country.		
Jews have too much power in the business world.	29%		45%	36%	32%
Jews don't care what happens to anyone but their own kind.	26%	Jews are likely to be selfish, concerned only for themselves or their own group.	59%	61%	39%
Jews are not just as honest as other businessmen.	28%	Jews in general are likely to be somewhat dishonest in their dealings with others.	35%	39%	36%
Jews are more loyal to Israel than to America.	30%	Jews in general are likely to be more loyal to their own group than to America.	45%	41%	45%
Jews stick together too much.	52%	Jews in general are unfriendly, do not mix with others, go around only with their own group.	43%	40%	27%
N =	(1,913)		(397)	(318)	(702)

pare the incidence of hostility in the black and white teenage populations in our samples. (The comparisons will be made for the teenage questionnaire only. The results using the adult form are about equivalent.)

Looking first at the profile of black attitudes (see Table 6), the patterning of responses is roughly similar to that already seen for white non-Jewish teenagers, although among blacks there is a muting of hostile attitudes in Commutertown and especially in Oceanville.

Like white youngsters, a majority of black teenagers endorse the positive and neutral stereotypes. In all communities, a majority think of Jewish teen-

Table 6 ACCEPTANCE OF STEREOTYPES OF JEWISH TEENAGERS BY BLACK ADOLESCENTS

	Commutertown	%	Oceanville	%	Central City	%
Majority	Intelligent	77	School spirit	75	Intelligent	76
stereotypes	Ambitious	76	Ambitious	72	School spirit	74
(accepted by	School spirit	76	Intelligent	68	Ambitious	68
50% or more)	*Selfish	59	Religious	59	Athletic	60
	*Powerful	59	Different	51	Religious	58
	*Conceited	53	*Powerful	50		
	*Sly	53				
	Religious	51				
Stereotypes held	Different	49	*Bossy	49	Different	49
by a substantial	*Immoral	44	Athletic	49	*Bossy	41
minority (ac-	*Vain	36	*Conceited	47	*Selfish	38
cepted by from	*Gaudy	35	*Sly	46	*Sly	33
25 to 49%)	*Unfriendly	34	*Selfish	45	*Unfriendly	31
	Athletic	34	*Vain	45	*Pushy	28
	*Bossy	32	*Immoral	39	*Conceited	28
	*Troublemakers	29	*Unfriendly	34	*Vain	29
	*Pushy	26			*Immoral	29
					*Powerful	27
Minority stereo-	*Sloppy	24	*Pushy	25	*Gaudy	24
types (accepted	*Untrustworthy	21	*Gaudy	25	*Troublemakers	23
by less than	*Quitter	14	*Sloppy	21	*Sloppy	23
25%)			*Quitter	17	*Quitter	18
			*Troublemakers	16	*Untrustworthy	17
			*Untrustworthy	16		
Mean proportion accepting outrightly negative stereotypes		37%		34%		28%
N =		(121)		(71)		(119)

* Stereotypes judged to be outrightly negative.

agers as intelligent, ambitious, religious, and school-spirited. The larger the
Jewish presence in a community, the more frequently hostile stereotypes
are endorsed, although community differences are smaller among black than
among white youngsters. Images of Jews as having too much power in
school, as being selfish, conceited, and sly gain majority support among
Commutertown blacks. These attributes are less widely endorsed in Oceanville though a majority uphold them, and least accepted in Central City.

The differences between black and white responses are more sharply
delineated in Table 7, which reports the percentage-point difference in the
response of the two racial groups to each item. In Commutertown and to a
slightly lesser extent in Oceanville, the difference between black and white
responses is particularly marked on those items that reflect envy of Jewish

Table 7 RELATIVE ACCEPTANCE OF STEREOTYPES OF JEWISH
TEENAGERS BY BLACK AND BY WHITE NON-JEWISH ADOLESCENTS

	Commutertown	%	Oceanville	%	Central City	%
Stereotypes more frequently attributed to Jewish teenagers by white adolescents						
Difference of more than 10 percentage points	*Vain	30	*Pushy	19		
	*Bossy	20	Intelligent	14		
	*Conceited	17	*Conceited	14		
	*Unfriendly	16	*Sly	14		
	*Pushy	16	*Gaudy	13		
	*Powerful	11	*Vain	13		
Difference of 6 to 10 percentage points			*Selfish	10	Religious	9
			*Untrustworthy	9	*Conceited	7
			Ambitious	7		
Stereotypes more frequently attributed to Jewish teenagers by black adolescents						
Difference of more than 10 percentage points	Religious	11	Athletic	13		
Difference of 6 to 10 percentage points	Different	6	Different	8	Athletic	10
	*Sloppy	8	*Immoral	6	*Bossy	7
			School spirit	6	Different	6
					*Selfish	6
					*Unfriendly	6

Stereotypes attributed to Jewish teenagers about equally by white non-Jewish and by black adolescents			
Difference of 5 percentage points or less	Intelligent Ambitious School spirit *Selfish *Quitter Athletic *Sly *Immoral *Troublemakers *Untrustworthy	*Quitter *Troublemakers Religious *Powerful *Unfriendly *Sloppy *Bossy	Intelligent Ambitious School spirit *Quitter *Sly *Immoral *Troublemakers *Untrustworthy *Powerful *Sloppy *Pushy *Vain *Gaudy

* Stereotypes judged to be outrightly negative.

success and a tendency to downgrade it. Whites in both communities are consistently the more critical. Indeed, in these communities, any tendency for blacks to be more accepting of stereotypes than whites is confined almost exclusively to favorable or neutral stereotypes.

The tendency in Commutertown and Oceanville for white teenagers to be consistently more hostile than black youngsters on items bearing on Jewish success is not repeated in Central City. There, the results are essentially the same for both whites and blacks. Except for blacks showing a greater tendency to conceive of Jews as bossy, on no item is the percentage point difference greater than ten.

These findings do not warrant complacency about the extent of anti-Semitism among black teenagers. Clearly, too much hostility is revealed for it to be written off as inconsequential. At the same time, the results do not support a conclusion that a particular problem of attitudinal anti-Semitism exists among young blacks.

This exploration of teenage attitudes toward Jews was begun with four expectations in mind. Not one of these was proved correct. Contrary to them, there remains (1) a significant amount of hostility toward Jews among these adolescents, (2) the hostility appears to be greater rather than less the larger the Jewish presence in a school setting, (3) hostility toward Jewish teenagers is, if anything, greater than toward Jewish adults, and (4) black teenagers show less hostility than do white non-Jewish youth. Attempts to explain these disconfirmations and, more generally, to account for the conditions generating hostility and those muting and derailing it will be subjects of subsequent chapters. For now, we will further explore the nature and incidence of anti-Jewish prejudice by examining indications of its expression in feelings about Jews rather than beliefs about them.

Feelings About Jews

Two approaches were adopted to assess teenagers' feelings about Jews. A version of the social distance scale was administered to judge the extent and conditions under which non-Jewish youngsters were willing to associate with Jews. Second, respondents were simply asked: "If you have just met a person and the only thing you know about him is that he is Jewish, what would your immediate reaction be? Would you feel quite friendly, a little friendly, nothing either way, a little unfriendly, or quite unfriendly?"

The form of the social distance measure was one which called on respondents to say whether they would be willing or unwilling to associate with Jews in a number of social situations varying in the amount of intimacy involved. The assumption underlying the measure, obviously, is that the more anti-Semitic a youngster is, the less willing he will be to be involved in situations in which he comes in close contact with Jews.

We expected to find less social distance in Commutertown and Ocean-ville than in Central City on more or less the same grounds as we anticipated less attitudinal anti-Semitism. The opportunity to get to see and to know Jewish teenagers would have the effect, we thought, of making closer relationships more acceptable. It was also expected that less social distance would be shown by non-Jewish whites than by blacks, simply because of the absence of racial barriers among whites.

In formulating the social distance questions, we conceived, as for the attitudinal batteries, that it would make a difference whether the referent were a teenage or an adult Jew. Consequently, the same half of the samples who had been asked to answer the attitudinal battery having Jewish teenagers in mind were now asked to do the same in answering the social distance items. In the other half of the samples, the referent was "Jews in general."

It was also thought that the social status of the referent might be a factor in his being accepted. To check on this, we asked respondents to first say how much they would be willing to associate with a lower-status

Jewish teenager (or Jewish adult). The question was then repeated asking about willingness to associate with a higher-status Jew. (This procedural decision, as we shall shortly see, had some unanticipated consequences.)

The results were largely the same for the samples asked about Jewish teenagers and the samples asked about Jews in general. Consequently, the report here is confined to the results for the former samples.

In the teenage form of the questionnaire, the lower-status referent was described as "a student in the vocational program who is white, Jewish, and is getting failing grades." "A student in the college preparatory program who is white, Jewish, and is getting B's" was the description of the higher-status referent. For both the referents, respondents were asked whether they would be willing to:[10]

> Sit next to this person in class?
> Work on a committee at school with this person?
> Have this person as one of your speaking acquaintances?
> Go to a party to which this person was invited?
> Eat lunch with this person at school?
> Have this person as a member of your social group or club?
> Have this person as a close personal friend?
> Invite this person home to dinner?
> Have this person date your sister?

Table 8 reports the social distance exhibited by white non-Jewish adolescents to a more academically ambitious and successful Jewish teenager.

More or less consistently with other studies that have used social distance measures, acceptance is greater the less intimate the relationship called for. Thus, there is least resistance to sitting next to a successful Jewish student in class and most resistance to having him date one's sibling. Except for dating, the majority of students in all three school systems are willing to countenance all other forms of social contact asked about. There remains a substantial minority, however—between 25 percent and 35 percent—who would not be willing to have a Jew as a close friend or to invite him home.

There is no precise way to decide whether these students exhibit more or less social distance than attitudinal hostility toward Jewish teenagers. From a crude comparison of Table 8 with Table 2 on attitudes, it appears that there is more hostility than social distance. There appears to be a willingness to interact with Jews even when one feels hostile toward them.[11]

The results for the three communities are remarkably similar. For example, the rank order correlations of the items between Commutertown

Table 8   SOCIAL DISTANCE TO A HIGH-STATUS JEWISH TEENAGER
AMONG WHITE NON-JEWISH ADOLESCENTS

Percent unwilling to have successful Jewish student:	Commutertown %	Rank Order	Oceanville %	Rank Order	Central City %	Rank Order
Date sibling	54.2	1	56.6	1	58.2	1
Home to dinner	31.9	2.5	25.0	4	31.0	2
As close friend	31.9	2.5	26.7	2	26.3	3
Member of social club	28.3	4	26.4	3	19.4	4
To lunch	19.8	5	11.1	6	12.7	6
At party	18.0	6	14.6	5	18.5	5
On same committee	17.7	7	10.2	7	9.3	8
As speaking acquaintance	13.5	8	8.2	8	11.6	7
Sit beside in class	10.3	9	5.1	9	4.9	9
Mean percent	25.0		20.4		21.3	
N =	(388)		(301)		(667)	

and Oceanville is 0.86, between Commutertown and Central City 0.87, and between Oceanville and Central City 0.95. Moreover, for only one item of the battery the percentage point difference between the three communities exceeds 10, and other smaller differences form no consistent pattern that would reveal one community more socially distant than another. The mean percentage social distance scores for the three communities are also quite close: 25.0 for Commutertown, 21.9 for Oceanville, and 22.1 percent for Central City.

The similarity of the three communities conflicts with the prediction that a Jewish presence would reduce gross social distance. It is also, of course, inconsistent with the earlier finding that a Jewish presence is related to greater attitudinal hostility toward Jews. To separate the descriptive from the analytic portions of the inquiry, efforts to explain the lack of a community difference in social distance despite a substantial difference in attitude will be made later.

So far, we have been reporting white non-Jewish teenagers' social distance to a college-bound, academically successful Jewish student. Respondents were also asked what social relationships they would be willing to engage in with an academically less ambitious and less successful Jewish student. The comparison was introduced into the research design to judge how social status would affect social distance rather than as a further measure of anti-Semitism *per se.* The results, therefore, reveal more about social class prejudice than they do about anti-Semitism. Nevertheless, to gain a general orientation to the social situations in the three school systems, it is helpful to determine how much social class prejudice there is.

Judging from the results, there is quite a lot. In all three communities, on every item greater social distance is shown to the low-status than to the high-status referent and the differences are generally substantial (see Tables 9 and 10). Particularly startling is the discrepancy between willingness to work with a high- and a low-status Jewish student on a school committee. On a whole range of items involving close social contact, the low-status referent meets considerably greater resistance than the high-status one.

There are no startling differences in response in the three communities. The rank order correlation between Commutertown and Oceanville is 0.80, between Commutertown and Central City it is 0.88, and between Oceanville and Central City, 0.80. The mean percentage score on the social distance items for Commutertown is 42.9, for Oceanville 42.6, and 46.6 for Central City. In this comparison, Commutertown reveals itself the least prejudiced. The differences are not significant, however, nor is the patterning of responses in the three communities.

There may be an element of anti-Semitism in the startling differences in

Table 9 SOCIAL DISTANCE TO A LOW-STATUS JEWISH TEENAGER AMONG WHITE NON-JEWISH ADOLESCENTS

Percent unwilling to have low-status Jewish student:	Commutertown %	Rank Order	Oceanville %	Rank Order	Central City %	Rank Order
Date sibling	73.6	1	76.1	1	78.0	1
As close friend	56.8	2	54.8	2	57.5	2.5
Home to dinner	52.1	3	50.9	5	54.6	4
On same committee	50.0	4	53.6	4	49.3	5
Member of social club	49.7	5	54.1	3	57.5	2.5
To lunch	27.5	6.5	26.7	6	28.1	8
As speaking acquaintance	27.5	6.5	22.3	8	38.0	6
Sit beside in class	26.4	8	24.1	7	24.6	9
At party	22.8	9	20.9	9	31.8	7
Mean Percentage	42.9		42.6		46.6	
N =	(388)		(301)		(667)	

the response to the high- and low-status referent. That social class prejudice is more at work is indicated by the response of the Jewish students in Commutertown and Oceanville to the two batteries (see Table 11).

Virtually all Jewish respondents express a willingness to interact in all situations with a fellow Jewish student of high status, but not with one of low status. In Commutertown, for example, 58 percent of the Jewish students would be unwilling to have a brother or sister date the low-status referent, 43.5 percent would not want him as a close friend, and 31.6 would not want to work with him on the same committee. The equivalent figures in Oceanville are 55.8 percent, 45.3 percent, and 43.0 percent. As might be expected, Jewish teenagers on all items show less social distance to the

Table 10   RELATIVE SOCIAL DISTANCE TO HIGH- AND TO LOW-STATUS JEWISH TEENAGER AMONG WHITE NON-JEWISH ADOLESCENTS

Higher-status favored over lower-status Jewish teenager (in percentage points)	Commutertown		Oceanville		Central City	
More than 40			Work on committee	43.4		
36–40					Member of same club Work on committee	38.1 40.0
31–35	Work on committee	32.3			Close friend	31.2
26–30			Close friend Member of same club	28.1 27.7	Speaking acquaintance	26.4
21–25	Close friend Member of same club	24.9 21.4	Home to dinner	25.9	Home to dinner	23.6
16–20	Home to dinner Date sibling Sit beside in class	20.2 19.4 16.1	Date sibling Sit beside in class	19.5 19.0	Date sibling Sit beside in class	19.8 19.7
11–15	Speaking acquaintance	14.0	To lunch Speaking acquaintance	15.6 14.1	To lunch At party	15.4 13.3
6–10	To lunch	7.7				
0–5	At party	4.8	At party	6.3		

Table 11 SOCIAL DISTANCE TO LOW- AND HIGH-STATUS
JEWISH STUDENTS AMONG JEWISH TEENAGERS

Percent unwilling to have Jewish student:	Commutertown		Oceanville	
	High-Status Referent	Low-Status Referent	High-Status Referent	Low-Status Referent
Date sibling	5.2%	57.7%	3.5%	55.8%
As close friend	0.2%	43.5%	0.0%	45.3%
On same committee	1.0%	31.6%	0.0%	43.0%
Home to dinner	1.7%	32.8%	0.7%	34.1%
Member of social club	0.7%	29.4%	0.0%	30.4%
Sit beside in class	0.2%	16.3%	0.7%	15.5%
To lunch	0.0%	14.0%	0.0%	9.2%
As speaking acquaintance	0.2%	12.4%	0.0%	9.8%
At party	0.2%	10.6%	0.0%	8.5%
N =	(436)		(146)	

low-status referent than do non-Jewish teenagers. Nevertheless, the substantial Jewish rate of rejection is evidence that social class prejudice is a major element in the response of both Jewish and non-Jewish teenagers.

Black youngsters, we predicted, would exhibit more social distance from Jews than non-Jewish whites because the racial barrier compounds the religious one. Blacks do and don't, it turns out. When the Jewish referent is of high status, black youngsters do show more social distance than whites on the average in Oceanville and Central City. The relationship is reversed, however, in Commutertown. When the referent is of low status, in all three communities black respondents show less social distance than their white counterparts. These findings are summarized in Table 12, which uses in place of the social distance items a scale of social distance whose construction is described in Appendix A.[12]

Table 12 SOCIAL DISTANCE TO LOW- AND HIGH-STATUS JEWISH
STUDENTS AMONG BLACK AND NON-JEWISH ADOLESCENTS

Mean Social Distance Scores*	Commutertown	Oceanville	Central City
High-status referent			
Blacks	1.71	1.84	1.96
Whites	1.81	1.62	1.65
Low-status referent			
Blacks	2.16	2.29	2.34
Whites	2.45	2.50	2.66
Blacks (number)	(107)	(69)	(111)
Whites (number)	(374)	(295)	(655)

* Scores range from 1 to 5.0; the higher the score, the greater the social distance.

Perhaps the greater social distance that white students in Commutertown feel toward a high-status Jew is an indication of greater anti-Semitism on their part. The differences revealed in all other comparisons seem more revealing of differences in social class prejudice than in anti-Semitism between whites and blacks. Black teenagers, it is evident, feel relatively more comfortable with an academically less successful person. Whites, in Oceanville and Central City at least, feel relatively more at ease with the successful referent. These differences are relative, however. In both racial groups, the high-status referent is preferred over the low-status one.

Looking at the results for black adolescents, on the average the social distance expressed is least in Commutertown and greatest in Central City. This conforms to the original prediction that a Jewish presence would be associated with less anti-Semitism.

Illuminating as these results are in showing how social class prejudice can affect social distance, they make questionable the utility of social distance as a measure of anti-Semitism *per se*. Youngsters can harbor rather deep hostility toward Jews without this having a negative impact on willingness to associate with them. The "some of my best friends . . ." phenomenon is apparently at work here.

But aggravating a basic weakness in the measure is the innovation of the distinction between high- and low-status referents. This turned out to reveal a surprising amount of social class prejudice among teenagers. Its unanticipated effect was to contaminate social distance as a measure of anti-Semitism; it is not possible to dissociate how much of what is being expressed is a result of social class prejudice and how much is due to anti-Semitism. For this reason, social distance will not be used as a major measure of anti-Semitism in later phases of the analysis though there will be occasion from time to time to refer to the measure as a check on other results.

The other means used to measure the feeling component of anti-Semitism was the responses to the question asking teenagers how friendly they would feel toward meeting a person about whom the only thing they knew was that he was Jewish. The responses of non-Jewish white youngsters to this question (see Table 13) show them to be on the friendly side. Relatively few—15.5 percent in Commutertown, 9.7 percent in Oceanville, and 9.3 percent in Central City—responded that they would feel either a little or quite unfriendly. Feelings of friendliness tend to be muted, however; more in each town say they would feel a little, rather than quite, friendly. Moreover, a substantial minority feel nothing either way. The differences by community are not sharp although they are in the direction of more hostility being expressed the larger the Jewish presence.

Table 13   INITIAL RESPONSE TO MEETING A JEWISH TEENAGER
AMONG NON-JEWISH WHITE AND BLACK ADOLESCENTS

White Non-Jewish Response

Feelings	Commutertown	Oceanville	Central City
Quite unfriendly	7.1% ⎱ 15.5%	4.7% ⎱ 9.7%	4.1% ⎱ 9.3%
A little unfriendly	8.4 ⎰	5.0 ⎰	5.2 ⎰
Nothing either way	26.7	26.3	23.3
A little friendly	35.3	36.7	43.5
Quite friendly	22.5	27.3	23.9
N =	(382)	(300)	(657)

Black Response

Feelings	Commutertown	Oceanville	Central City
Quite unfriendly	2.6% ⎱ 5.2%	4.4% ⎱ 7.3%	6.0% ⎱ 9.4%
A little unfriendly	2.6 ⎰	2.9 ⎰	3.4 ⎰
Nothing either way	23.3	27.9	13.8
A little friendly	43.1	39.7	51.7
Quite friendly	28.4	25.0	25.0
N =	(116)	(68)	(116)

Among black teenagers, the opposite is the case. The tendency toward expressing unfriendliness is greatest in Central City and least in Commutertown. Whites are more likely than blacks to respond in an unfriendly way in both Commutertown and Oceanville. In Central City, the proportion expressing unfriendly feelings is about the same, but blacks are considerably less likely to avoid taking a position by not responding in either way.

Patterns of Intergroup Friendship

Of the three components of prejudice—beliefs, feelings, and behavior—the most difficult to measure is behavior. There are seldom opportunities to observe prejudice being acted upon and, when there are, the means to collect systematic evidence on all participants are rarely available. In the usual survey, the best that can be done is to ask respondents how they would act in hypothetical situations in which behaving in a prejudiced way is an alternative. One element of nonhypothetical behavior that we are able to measure is friendship with Jews.

Friendship between members of different racial or religious groups is not an absolute sign of the absence of prejudice. Indeed, the claim of friendship is a mask that the prejudiced sometimes adopt. Other things being equal, however, it seems a reasonable inference that the probability of prejudice is less where friendship exists.

Friendship is partly a matter of opportunity, of course, and of the three communities, in only one—Central City—was the possibility of Jewish/non-Jewish friendships virtually nil. In both Commutertown and Oceanville the substantial number of Jews in the student body provided ample opportunity for the formation of such friendships. A sign of the persistence of prejudice is their frequency.

The procedure adopted was to ask all students to tell us the names of other students in their grades in school whom they go around with most often. Boy respondents were asked to name boys, and girl respondents girls, and a limit of five was set on the number who might be named. Respondents were not asked to supply any other information about their friends except their names. Since we had information on the universe of students in each grade, it was possible to discover the religion, among other things, of each student's friends.

From this information, the extent to which non-Jewish students chose Jews as friends was then calculated. The measure we used—the heterophily index (see Appendix A for details)[13]—is one which takes into account the difference in opportunity to make Jewish friends, given their relatively greater number in Commutertown than Oceanville.

Heterophily scores run from +1 to −1. A score of 0 means that there is no difference between the observed number of choices given and the number of choices one would expect purely by chance. Positive scores indicate over-choice relative to chance, and a score of +1 means that *all* the choices of the chooser group were given to the other group in question; in the present instance, it would mean that all one's friends are Jewish. Contrariwise, negative scores indicate under-choice, and an index of −1 means that none of the choices of the choosing group was given to Jewish teenagers.

The heterophily scores (Table 14) show the relative tendency of black and non-Jewish white teenagers to choose Jews as friends. The figures have been computed for Commutertown and Oceanville only. Given the small number of Jews, doing so for Central City would be meaningless.

Non-Jewish youngsters in Commutertown and Oceanville show a disposition to avoid friendships with their Jewish classmates. Blacks are the

Table 14   CHOOSING JEWS AS FRIENDS

(Heterophily scores for black and non-Jewish white teenagers)

	Commutertown	Oceanville
Heterophily scores of:		
Blacks	−0.82	−0.89
Non-Jewish whites	−0.41	−0.41

least likely to have such friendships. However, this reflects more a general absence of friendships between white and black teenagers rather than a special tendency for black non-Jewish adolescents not to became friends with Jews. Black heterophily scores with respect to non-Jewish white youngsters are as high as for Jewish teenagers in Oceanville ($-.90$ as compared to -0.89) and almost as high in Commutertown (-0.73 as compared to -0.82).

Heterophily scores are influenced by how much homophily a group exhibits, homophily being the extent to which friendship choices are limited to one's own group. Before attempting to interpret the heterophily scores, it is useful to see how frequently within-group choices occur. Table 15 reports the homophily scores for each of the subgroups reported in Table 14. For comparison, homophily scores for Jewish teenagers are also presented.

Table 15   WITHIN-GROUP CHOICES AS FRIENDS

(Homophily scores for black, non-Jewish white, and Jewish teenagers)

	Commutertown	Oceanville
Homophily scores of:		
Blacks	+0.78	+0.90
Non-Jewish whites	+0.53	+0.58
Jews	+0.68	+0.55

The homophily scores are all positive, signifying a tendency toward within-group friendships in all three subcommunities. Relatively, black teenagers are the least likely to form friendships outside their own group. This is true in both Commutertown and Oceanville. As between Jewish and white non-Jewish teenagers, the former are more prone to within-group friendships in Commutertown. In Oceanville, however, there is, if anything, a slightly greater tendency for non-Jewish whites to be ethnocentric in their friendship choices.

Tables 14 and 15 are perhaps more revealing of the results of prejudice than of its incidence. Making friends with others who are different religiously or racially is a choice which prejudice militates against among the victims of prejudice as well as among its purveyors.

Conclusions

Our initial descriptive examination of teenage anti-Semitism produced a fair share of surprises and in the process raised some tougher analytic questions than we had anticipated. Among the surprises, the most disturbing was the sheer amount of hostility toward Jews expressed by teenagers. That so many negative stereotypes received majority or near majority support is indicative of a kind of tenacity in this form of prejudice which we, at least, had not anticipated. The most enigmatic of the findings is undoubtedly the evidence that hostility toward Jews, if not social distance, is greater the larger the Jewish presence in a community. This is so contrary to what is ordinarily assumed and what other investigators have found as to make explaining it a fundamental task of the inquiry. The greater hostility to teenage than to adult Jews in two of the three communities can also be counted among the unexpected findings, as can the results that black youngsters exhibit less hostility and in certain respects less social distance toward Jews than do white non-Jewish adolescents. A surprising and significant incidental finding was the evidence showing the power of social class to affect social distance. Social class prejudice of this kind has been examined only rarely by social scientists. If our results are any gauge, the neglect clearly needs to be corrected. Because they came out as we might have predicted, the results on intergroup friendships seemed the least enlightening of the discoveries; still it was comforting to end up with this indication of not everything being out of place.

2 The Social Context of Adolescent Prejudice

This chapter begins the task of trying to account for the prejudice uncovered in our inquiry. What leads some youngsters by the time of adolescence to harbor hostility and unfriendly feelings toward Jews? Why do others grow up in the same communities without the taint of anti-Jewish prejudice? What accounts for the greater hostility in the communities with a substantial Jewish presence? What influence for good or bad do the schools have on the path which young people follow?

Past work by other investigators of these questions advances various theories to account for prejudice. By and large, these are not specific to anti-Semitism nor to adolescents. Rather, they constitute efforts to explain prejudice in all its manifestations in populations at large.

These theories are at odds in where they locate the root causes of prejudice.[1] Some see the source of prejudice in the human psyche, the result of some psychological impairment. Others state that prejudice is not the result of some impairment but of an individual's capacity for cognitive reasoning. From this viewpoint, prejudice persists because people are not armed with the powers of reasoning and the education to recognize and combat it. Prejudice has been conceived by others as having primarily cultural rather than individual roots. What counts most in deciding the incidence of prejudice is how much it is countenanced and reinforced in the subculture in which the individual is reared and which serves as his primary reference group.

However much the theories differ in other respects, there exists underlying agreement as to where in the social structure prejudice is most likely to be found. Implicitly, if not always explicitly, most theories of prejudice postulate that the chances of prejudice decline the more an individual is privileged in his social arrangements. Or, stated oppositely, prejudice and social deprivation tend to go together.

Social scientists are prone to quibble about what constitutes social deprivation, not unlike people disagreeing in everyday life about whether someone is worse or better off compared to somebody else. In every society known to man, individuals differ in how their personal attributes are generally evaluated by others and by their access to the rewards which the society has to bestow. Relative to others, people may be deprived economically in terms of how much money they have, socially in terms of the status, power, and prestige they enjoy, or culturally in terms of education and such attributes as interest in art, music, drama, and politics. Being relatively deprived in one way does not necessarily mean that one is also deprived in other ways. Generally speaking, however, there tends to be a high correlation between the kinds of deprivation.

Virtually all studies of prejudice that have examined its association with indicators of deprivation have found the association to be positive, and this has been true whatever the basic theoretical stance of the investigator. That agreement has bred disagreement is because the factor or factors postulated as being the root causes of prejudice—e.g., personality deficiencies, cognitive malfunctioning, cultural shallowness—have also been found to be associated with deprivation. No one has succeeded in identifying the causal sequence to everyone else's satisfaction. Thus, it not only remains an issue whether prejudice is more satisfactorily explained as a result of personality, cognitive, or cultural deficiencies; but there is also disagreement as to where social deprivation fits into the picture. Is psychological impairment a consequence of social deprivation so that the causal chain is from social deprivation to psychological impairment to prejudice? Are personality deficiencies at birth a source of both social deprivation and prejudice? Similarly, if cognitive or cultural factors are postulated as primary, where does social deprivation fit? Is it a cause or a consequence of cognitive or cultural deficiency?

Our study, conducted as it was at one point in time, provides no means to resolve, even for our subjects, controversy about the causal sequence leading to prejudice. To tease out this developmental process in any detail would require observing youngsters from infancy to at least adolescence and probably beyond. With our data, however, we are able to determine whether the association between prejudice and social deprivation, as found in studies of adults, also holds up for adolescents. We are also in a position to explore whether adolescent prejudice is more a result of psychological impairment, cognitive deficiency, or cultural deprivation. Moreover, unlike other studies, and with respect specifically to anti-Semitism, we are able to investigate the effects of a Jewish presence on anti-Semitism.

We propose to address these tasks in turn, examining first the association between prejudice and social deprivation and next exploring the efficacy of several general theories of prejudice to explicate adolescent anti-Semitism. The effects of a Jewish presence will occupy our attention in Chapter 4. (We shall pursue these analyses for the time being using only the data on white non-Jewish teenagers.[2]) In Chapter 5, we shall determine whether the findings on anti-Semitism also hold for racial prejudice. Chapter 6 is addressed to an overview of all our findings. In the final chapter, we shall give some attention to the role of the school in prejudice formation and reduction.

A Measure of Anti-Semitism

Constructing a measure of anti-Semitism is not an altogether unambiguous task. Given the several ways in which anti-Semitism may be revealed—in belief, in feelings, and in behavior—and the variety of indications within each of these dimensions which warrant the attribution of anti-Semitism, it would seem offhand that no one measure will suffice, but rather that the phenomenon must be investigated from a number of vantage points based on different modes of measurement. Such a course, however, would soon prove cumbersome and repetitious and, because of the high degree of association between different indications of anti-Semitism, it is unnecessary. A preferable strategy, and the one we have adopted, is to select one measure for extensive exploration, introducing others at critical junctures along the way to make sure that crucial findings are not an artifact of the measure used.

Our options being set by the data we have collected, we have chosen to concentrate primarily on anti-Semitic belief. Given the limitations of our data, a measure based on negative beliefs is clearly preferable to one grounded in negative feelings since our indications of the latter are contaminated, as noted in the previous chapter, by the introduction of a status referent in the attempts to measure social distance.

A measure based on behavior might seem, at first glance, preferable to a measure of either anti-Semitic belief or feeling since discrimination is perhaps the most damaging form of anti-Semitism. It is worse for Jews to be excluded from school activities, shunned by potential friends, and in other ways ostracized than for them to be stereotyped in negative ways. But concentration on a behavioral measure of anti-Semitism poses the dilemma that it excuses those who display no anti-Semitism merely because they haven't an opportunity. Behaviorally, Central City teenagers are virtually free of anti-Semitism, even though a significant minority of them give strong indications of being anti-Semitic in other ways.

In some respects negative beliefs are not only the most practical indicator of anti-Semitism for our purposes, but also perhaps in an adolescent context the most serious form of prejudice to examine. As will be seen later, whether teenagers transcend being prejudiced or not is highly related to their cognitive capabilities. Thus it is entirely possible that beliefs are the key factor producing negative feelings and actions. Indeed, some evidence from studies of younger children suggests that negative beliefs develop at an early age, even before they are understood, with negative feelings and discriminatory actions following later.[3] But this process, it is to be recognized, is far from simple or settled. Consequently, while concentrating on a measure of anti-Semitic belief, caution and good sense suggest that other indications of anti-Semitism not be ignored.

The data available for measuring teenagers' beliefs about Jews is constituted by their responses to the stereotype battery reported on in the previous chapter. That battery called for teenagers to indicate their relative agreement or disagreement with twenty statements descriptive of what Jews are allegedly like. The battery included both positive and negative statements and produced considerable variation in response.

Eight items were chosen to form a summary measure of anti-Semitism:

> Jewish teenagers (Jews in general) are likely to be selfish—concerned only for themselves or their own group. (Selfish)
> Jewish teenagers (Jews in general) are unfriendly; do not mix with others; go around only with their own group. (Unfriendly)
> Jewish teenagers (Jews in general) often dress in a loud and flashy way. (Gaudy)
> Jewish teenagers (Jews in general) think they are better than other students (people); easily develop a superiority complex. (Conceited)
> Jewish teenagers (Jews in general) try to push into groups (groups or neighborhoods) where they are not really wanted. (Pushy)
> Jewish teenagers (Jews in general) are rather loose in their moral standards and behavior. (Immoral)
> Jewish teenagers (Jews in general) are loud and show-offy; will do almost anything to gain recognition or draw attention to themselves. (Vain)
> Jewish teenagers (Jews in general) are frequently in trouble with school authorities and the police (police and other authorities); often break rules and laws (are not very law-abiding). (Troublemakers)

Two procedures were used in selecting these items. First, a factor analysis of all twenty stereotype items discussed in Chapter 1 was conducted to determine whether the items are measures of the same thing, and if not, to identify possible subfactors. The results of this analysis are presented in detail in Appendix A.[4] In brief, there indeed seemed to be only one major factor underlying the items. Consequently, those items that correlated most highly (at least 0.50) with this factor were chosen. From these items only those worded equivalently on both the teenage and the adult forms of the questionnaire were retained, making it unnecessary in most of the ensuing analysis to present separate figures for each form.

To combine the eight items into a single summary measure, a numeric score ranging from 1 to 7 was first assigned to each item, depending on the teenager's response: 1 for a "strongly disagree" answer: 7 for a "strongly agree" answer, with other scores assigned accordingly.[5] Then the average of these eight scores was computed to provide a summary score reflecting the amount of anti-Semitism held by each teenager. Higher scores indicate higher degrees of anti-Semitism; lower scores indicate lesser amounts.

It should be noted that the eight items finally selected as a measure of anti-Semitism are all unequivocally negative. Positive stereotypes, such as "intelligent," or "religious," are not included; nor are there any ambiguous items, such as "Jews are different" or "Jews are ambitious." At least four of the items are stereotypes that have been historically applied to Jews: "conceited," "vain," "selfish," and "unfriendly." These, we have seen, are widely accepted in our sample of teenagers—by a majority, in fact, in the two towns with Jews. Several other items, such as "troublemakers," are less often used to characterize Jews, but when they are, as is the case for a significant minority in our sample, they seem to represent a particularly hostile (or at least deeply confused) attitude. The effect of our factor analysis, moreover, is to show that these items are highly correlated with the more prevalent anti-Semitic stereotypes. In sum, the eight items vary widely in the ease with which they are accepted. Moreover, they are not all mild stereotypes that might receive superficial assent, thereby overestimating the actual prevalence of anti-Semitism in the three towns. We would not expect many youth to score highly on this summary measure, but those who do can confidently be said to display anti-Semitism at an undeniably acute level.

The proportions of white non-Jewish students in each of the three communities receiving each score on the summary anti-Semitism index is reported in Table 16. The proportions receiving higher scores on the scale are largest in Commutertown and smallest in Central City, with Oceanville in between. For example, 16 percent in Commutertown, 12 percent in Oceanville, and 6 percent in Central City score extremely high (6 or 7) on the scale. This pattern holds both for those who have clearly anti-

Semitic scores and those who on the average at least fail to reject anti-Semitic stereotypes: the proportion scoring 4 to 7 is 66 percent in Commutertown, 53 percent in Oceanville, and 41 percent in Central City.

Table 16   ANTI-SEMITISM BY COMMUNITY FOR WHITE NON-JEWISH ADOLESCENTS

Anti-Semitism		Commutertown	Oceanville	Central City
High	7	3.3%	1.6%	1.1%
	6	13.1%	10.0%	5.1%
	5	24.0%	18.8%	13.1%
	4	25.3%	22.9%	21.6%
	3	17.9%	24.7%	26.0%
	2	10.2%	14.7%	23.4%
Low	1	6.2%	7.4%	9.6%
Total		100.0%	100.0%	100.0%
N =		(755)	(612)	(1,331)

This pattern is consistent with that observed in Chapter 1 when each of the stereotype items was examined separately, thus enhancing our confidence in the scale. If the burden of our analysis is to focus on this measure, however, its validity must be tested further. It must be shown to be associated with other negative stereotypes, negative feelings, and negative actions.

Table 17 shows the relationship between the summary index of anti-Semitism and viewing Jews as too powerful. This view, traditionally a key component of anti-Semitic ideology, was one of the most prevalent stereotypes in each town, ranging from 70 percent in Commutertown and 55 percent in Oceanville to 26 percent in Central City. It was excluded from the summary measure, however, since it was worded differently on the teenage and adult forms of the questionnaire. Looking at Table 17, it is evident that the summary index predicts responses to this item on both the adult and teenage forms with a high degree of accuracy. The relationship is both strong and consistent.

It is appropriate here to comment on the use of terms such as "strong" and "consistent" and, more generally, on the conventions that will be used throughout the analysis in discussing tabular relationships. Table 17, as will virtually all subsequent tables, presents the relationship between the two items at issue in *cross tabular* form; in the form of a summary measure of association, Goodman and Kruskal's *gamma*, and in the form of *chi square* (χs). The principal reason for using three procedures is simply that they report different things about relationships and in combination, therefore, tell us more than any one alone or any two in combination.

Gamma is most useful in affording an easy indication of the strength of a relationship and of its direction, whether positive or negative.[6] Gammas can run from −1 to +1 although it is unusual for them in social research to be greater than ±0.50. There are no strict nor commonly agreed upon criteria for distinguishing weak from moderate from strong relationships. For the present analysis, we shall, as a general rule of thumb, consider gammas of ±0.35 or greater to be "strong," gammas at ±0.20 to ±0.34 to be "moderate," and those between ±0.10 and ±0.19 as "weak." If a gamma falls below ±0.10, we shall consider that an indication of the absence of an association. Thus in Table 17, we would say that all the relationships are strong.

In a crude way, cross tabulations also afford a measure of the strength of a relationship. At least, they make evident whether or not a relationship exists and, if so, some indication of its size is afforded by examining the relative size of the figures in adjacent and in extreme cells. For the present analysis, however, we shall rely primarily on gammas to provide a measure of strength.

Cross tabulations will be relied on to judge the form of a relationship,

Table 17 PROPORTION VIEWING JEWS AS TOO POWERFUL BY SCORE ON INDEX OF ANTI-SEMITISM FOR WHITE NON-JEWISH ADOLESCENTS

Percent viewing Jews as too powerful among those whose score on the index of anti-Semitism was:

Respondents to:	Low 1	2	3	4	5	High 6	7	Gamma	Xs
Adult Form									
Commutertown	7%	14%	26%	36%	66%	90%	100%	0.640	0.001
	(27)	(42)	(62)	(98)	(80)	(40)	(13)		
Oceanville	0%	4%	26%	36%	66%	86%	*	0.640	0.001
	(23)	(51)	(77)	(72)	(53)	(28)	(5)		
Central City	5%	9%	23%	47%	59%	77%	*	0.609	0.001
	(62)	(151)	(182)	(148)	(86)	(43)	(8)		
Teenage Form									
Commutertown	5%	22%	61%	71%	88%	91%	100%	0.589	0.001
	(19)	(32)	(69)	(89)	(97)	(57)	(11)		
Oceanville	0%	26%	45%	66%	78%	82%	*	0.550	0.001
	(22)	(38)	(74)	(67)	(60)	(33)	(5)		
Central City	5%	5%	8%	37%	74%	83%	*	0.696	0.001
	(64)	(157)	(161)	(136)	(88)	(24)	(7)		

* Too few cases for stable percentage.

whether linear or some other form, and if linear, whether or not the linearity is "consistent." By "consistent" we mean that each successive increase (or decrease) on one variable produces a corresponding increase (or decrease) on another variable. For example, in Table 17 the proportion of those in Commutertown scoring 1 on the summary index who think Jews are too powerful (looking at the adult form) is 7 percent; this proportion rises consistently to 14 percent among those scoring 2, to 26 percent among those scoring 3, and then to 36, 66, 90, and 100 percent with each further increase on the summary index.

Although the two tend to vary together, consistency is not synonymous with the strength of a relation. Strong relations can be nonlinear and inconsistent, and consistent relations can be weak ones. Consequently, the wisest course is to consider both the form and strength of relationships.

Understandably, we shall make more of relationships that are both strong and consistent than those that are only strong or only consistent. It also follows, however, that relations having one or the other of the two attributes will be judged more worthy of attention than relations having neither.

Chi square, the third procedure to be followed in reporting relationships, tells us, as the other two procedures do not, about the statistical significance of the relation: what the chances are that the relation might have occurred by chance rather than be a true relationship. We shall consider a relation significant where the probability of its having occurred by chance is 0.05 or less.

Since chi square is very much influenced by the number of cases being entered into a cross tabulation or gamma, there will be occasions where associations are found to be strong and consistent but not statistically significant and vice versa. In such instances, we shall put more weight on the former than the latter kinds of relation for reasons we shall try to make evident as we proceed. Generally speaking, we shall follow the convention of commenting on the significance of relationships only when they are *not* significant at the 0.05 level.

Table 18 illustrates these conventions as well as demonstrating further the validity of the summary index of anti-Semitism. Stereotyping Jews as "sloppy" was excluded from the summary measure because it is worded differently on the two forms. It presents a slightly different test of validity than viewing Jews as too powerful because it is one of the least accepted items in each town. Accepting the belief that Jews are "different" presents another test of our measure since it is not necessarily a negative item and did not score as highly as the other items on the factor analysis. Table 18 shows that the relationships between the summary index and each of these items are strong and for the most part consistent.

We are also interested in knowing how well the measure of anti-Semitic belief predicts anti-Semitic feelings. Of course, there is never a perfect correspondence between one's cognitive processes and his reactions at a more emotive level, but some relationship is to be expected. At the minimum, those with more negative feelings about Jews should also possess negative beliefs, and vice versa. It will be remembered from the previous

Table 18　VALIDATION ITEMS BY ANTI-SEMITISM FOR WHITE NON-JEWISH ADOLESCENTS

Percent viewing Jews as "sloppy" among those whose score on the index of anti-Semitism was:

Respondents to:	Low						High	Gamma	Xs
	1	2	3	4	5	6	7		
Adult Form									
Commutertown	7%	2%	14%	18%	27%	39%	92%	0.362	0.001
	(28)	(43)	(64)	(101)	(81)	(41)	(12)		
Oceanville	0%	0%	12%	3%	18%	39%	*	0.470	0.001
	(23)	(52)	(77)	(73)	(55)	(28)	(5)		
Central City	5%	4%	14%	24%	42%	65%	*	0.586	0.001
	(63)	(152)	(181)	(148)	(86)	(43)	(8)		
Teenage Form									
Commutertown	0%	3%	7%	9%	22%	32%	64%	0.387	0.001
	(19)	(32)	(69)	(87)	(96)	(56)	(11)		
Oceanville	0%	5%	8%	20%	22%	30%	*	0.394	0.001
	(22)	(37)	(74)	(66)	(60)	(33)	(5)		
Central City	3%	4%	11%	33%	58%	58%	*	0.618	0.001
	(62)	(160)	(162)	(135)	(88)	(24)	(7)		

Percent viewing Jews as "different" among those whose score on the index of anti-Semitism was:

Adult Form	1	2	3	4	5	6	7	Gamma	Xs
Commutertown	7%	18%	30%	46%	74%	80%	100%	0.566	0.001
	(28)	(45)	(64)	(101)	(81)	(40)	(14)		
Oceanville	22%	29%	36%	54%	67%	86%	*	0.476	0.001
	(23)	(52)	(76)	(72)	(55)	(28)	(5)		
Central City	27%	28%	50%	71%	80%	91%	*	0.488	0.001
	(63)	(152)	(183)	(148)	(86)	(44)	(8)		
Teenage Form									
Commutertown	0%	6%	13%	48%	55%	75%	100%	0.569	0.001
	(19)	(32)	(69)	(86)	(97)	(57)	(11)		
Oceanville	18%	11%	35%	39%	62%	79%	*	0.490	0.001
	(22)	(37)	(74)	(67)	(60)	(33)	(5)		
Central City	14%	22%	40%	62%	64%	78%	*	0.473	0.001
	(63)	(159)	(162)	(135)	(88)	(23)	(7)		

* Too few cases for stable percentage.

chapter that two measures of anti-Semitic feelings are available to test this expectation. The first is the question which asked simply, "If you have just met a person and the only thing you know about him is that he is Jewish, what would your immediate reaction be—would you feel quite friendly, a little friendly, nothing either way, a little unfriendly, or quite unfriendly?" The relationship between this question and the summary measure of anti-Semitic belief is presented in Table 19. Clearly there is a strong correspondence between the two. In all three towns those who say they would feel "unfriendly" or "quite unfriendly" are consistently more common among those scoring higher on the summary scale than those scoring lower. In fact, there is nearly as strong a relationship between our summary measure of anti-Semitic belief and this measure of anti-Semitic feeling as there was in Tables 17 and 18 between our summary measure and other belief items. This finding suggests that the various dimensions of anti-Semitism are sufficiently similar that our analysis of one is likely to yield similar conclusions when applied to others.

Table 19   HOSTILITY TO JEWS BY SCORE ON ANTI-SEMITISM INDEX FOR WHITE NON-JEWISH ADOLESCENTS

Percent hostile to Jews among those whose score on the anti-Semitism index was:

	Low 1	2	3	4	5	High 6	7	Gamma	Xs
Commutertown	0% (47)	0% (75)	4% (134)	10% (188)	18% (175)	43% (95)	54% (24)	0.407	0.001
Oceanville	0% (45)	3% (90)	3% (150)	8% (139)	23% (114)	31% (61)	* (9)	0.446	0.001
Central City	0% (127)	2% (312)	5% (340)	9% (286)	25% (173)	35% (68)	47% (15)	0.399	0.001

* Too few cases for stable percentage.

The relationship between negative feelings and scores on our measure of negative belief can also be tested through the use of the social distance scales discussed in Chapter 1. A high score of 4 or 5 on either of these scales indicates unwillingness to engage in even the most casual interaction. Table 20 reveals that teenagers' scores on both social distance scales are highly related to their scores on the summary measure of anti-Semitic belief. The proportions unwilling to interact with Jews become larger with each successive increase in anti-Semitic belief. In Commutertown, for example, only 15 percent of those scoring lowest (1) on the scale are unwilling to interact with Jews, but this proportion rises to 64 percent among those scoring highest (7). The close connection between each of these indicators of prejudiced feelings and mean scores of anti-Semitic belief, then, is further evidence that the latter may be taken as a general measure of anti-Semitism.

Table 20   SOCIAL DISTANCE BY SCORES ON ANTI-SEMITISM INDEX FOR WHITE NON-JEWISH ADOLESCENTS

Percent whose social distance to low-status Jews is high among those whose score on the anti-Semitism index was:

	Low						High		
	1	2	3	4	5	6	7	Gamma	Xs
Commutertown	15%	14%	26%	41%	45%	60%	64%	0.333	0.001
	(46)	(76)	(130)	(183)	(173)	(94)	(25)		
Oceanville	18%	21%	28%	44%	52%	59%	*	0.367	0.001
	(44)	(85)	(149)	(131)	(109)	(61)	(9)		
Central City	15%	28%	39%	47%	59%	65%	71%	0.321	0.001
	(126)	(309)	(339)	(284)	(173)	(68)	(14)		

Percent whose social distance to high-status Jews is high among those whose score on the anti-Semitism index was:

	Low						High		
	1	2	3	4	5	6	7	Gamma	Xs
Commutertown	2%	8%	10%	21%	31%	50%	68%	0.473	0.001
	(47)	(75)	(133)	(178)	(173)	(91)	(25)		
Oceanville	2%	5%	7%	23%	34%	38%	*	0.514	0.001
	(45)	(86)	(150)	(131)	(109)	(60)	(9)		
Central City	3%	8%	17%	21%	42%	42%	60%	0.487	0.001
	(126)	(308)	(338)	(284)	(172)	(67)	(15)		

* Too few cases for stable percentage.

It is also of importance to know how strongly anti-Semitic belief is related to anti-Semitic behavior. We have just seen that hypothetical behavior as measured by social distance questions is highly associated with the summary measure, but what of actual behavior; that is, friendship patterns? Since this question is taken up in some detail in Chapter 4, it would be repetitious to give a complete answer here. Suffice it to say that friendship patterns are related to prejudiced beliefs.

Thus, the summary measure holds up against any criteria by which it is judged. It is composed of items that have "face validity" (appear to be anti-Semitic) and are highly intercorrelated. It predicts with a reasonable degree of accuracy other belief items not included in the scale. And it is closely related to other forms of anti-Semitism, such as hostility, social distance, and friendship choices. The measure would appear, therefore, to be a fitting instrument for pursuing an examination of the sources of adolescent anti-Semitism.

The Social Location of Adolescent Prejudice

The task set for this chapter is to establish the social location of adolescent prejudice. Specifically, we want to test the proposition that anti-Semitism flourishes in settings of social deprivation and is relatively absent in contexts of social privilege. This has been a consistent finding of studies of prejudice among adults. We want to discover whether it holds also for adolescent youth.

Inequality is as much a quality of adolescent as of adult society. Scarce rewards which adolescents themselves have to bestow as well as rewards which come from the adult world are distributed quite unequally throughout the teenage population. Some youngsters have all the money they need and more; others have none or close to it. Respect and social standing in teenage life are the privileges of some while others are stigmatized and denied substantial social status. Power, too, is variously distributed as are opportunities for future privileges beyond adolescence.

To some extent social rewards are distributed unevenly to encourage achievement of one kind or another. This is especially true of rewards coming from the adult world. Academic honors are an example as are the granting or withholding of privileges by parents to encourage academic achievement. Teenagers, too, are prone to distribute rewards they control as a means to honor achievement, as, for example, the accolades given the successful athletic hero or the power bestowed on the student leader.

But, as in the adult world, social rewards are also distributed arbitrarily and even invidiously. Achievement notwithstanding, the chances are still that social rewards will be more available to a teenager who is white than to one who is black, or to a boy more than to a girl, or to a youth whose parents are well-to-do and prestigious than to one whose parents are poor and of low social status. Similarly, those with less appealing appearances and personalities are apt to find themselves disdained or excluded from opportunities open to others. Indeed, being privileged or disprivileged in such ascribed characteristics has much to do with the "quality" of teenagers' achievements and how they are judged. Often a regard for highly esteemed ascribed characteristics opens opportunity for achievement which is denied the less highly regarded.

Moreover, achievement breeds achievement and success, success. The child who succeeds is rewarded enough to achieve more while the unsuccessful child is unlikely to be motivated enough to try.

The net effect is to produce an adolescent world of considerable inequality with the majority of youngsters experiencing social deprivation of greater or lesser intensity relative to a highly privileged few.

There are several reasons why we might expect deprivation to be associated with prejudice among teenagers as it is among adults. For one, an important determinant of social standing among adolescents is the socioeconomic status of their parents. Coming from an economically deprived home not only all too often causes a youngster to be regarded less highly by his peers, but also strongly influences his ability to compete for other privileges, such as academic success and the educational opportunities that follow.[7] Since adults of lower socioeconomic standing are more likely to be prejudiced, and since parents typically, whether consciously or unconsciously, transmit their prejudices to their children, we would expect relatively deprived adolescents to be prejudiced in part simply because of their parents' prejudices.

Perhaps the most important reason for expecting deprivation to be associated with prejudice among teenagers, however, is that—just as with adults —their social status determines their cultural exposure. Leaving aside any variations in the values they have learned from their parents, youths with motivation and abilities to perform well in school are typically affected more deeply by sophisticated understandings of social life and arguments in favor of democratic values, both of which militate against prejudices they may hold. Moreover, academic success, coupled with economic privilege, channels youth on to higher academic training where the cognitive processes that maintain prejudice are, hopefully, eroded further.

There is good reason, then, to expect deprivation and prejudice to be related among teenagers. On the other hand, it can be argued that this relationship—if it exists at all—may not be as strong among teenagers as among adults. For one thing, some adults are highly educated while others are extremely deprived, having little or no formal education. Such great differences produce wide variations in the amounts of prejudice held. Among the teenagers in our study, in contrast, practically everyone of the same age had the same amount of education. Thus, one of the most important ways in which adults may be deprived relative to their peers was not a factor among these adolescents. Similarly, age plays an important role when comparing adults since the elderly, often bypassed by the mainstream of modern culture, are frequently more willing to assent to prejudiced views. Among adolescents (at least in the age range covered by our sample), however, age can hardly be taken as an indication of privilege or deprivation.

Prejudice and deprivation may not be associated among youth for yet another reason. Teenagers may manifest prejudice simply because they are confused. Somewhere, perhaps at home, they have heard negative stereotypes expressed, but elsewhere, perhaps at school, they have been exposed to different views. Regardless of the deprived or privileged status they occupy, they have not yet been locked into one cultural milieu as they may be when they grow older. They assent to prejudiced beliefs, but these views have not yet become deeply embedded. Moreover, these beliefs may not yet have come to fulfill an emotive need to scapegoat and vent aggression. This outlet may not yet have been linked with minority groups. Thus, the deprived among teenagers may not hold negative beliefs either as consistently or as adamantly as their counterparts among adults. Rather than being highly associated with deprivation, then, prejudice may depend more on friendship patterns, idiosyncratic characteristics of personality, or even mood.

That adolescent prejudice should be related to deprivation, then, is a proposition that must be tested empirically. On the one hand, arguments derived from studies of adult prejudice suggest that there should be a relationship; on the other hand, there are also counter arguments. Fortunately, our data allow ample testing of this relationship.

Testing the Relationship of Deprivation and Prejudice

A number of indicators of deprivation are contained in our data. To measure deprivation or privilege acquired from parents, there are questions on income, occupation, and education. These questions asked teenagers to report on their parents' status and, therefore, are prefaced by the assumption that these youngsters knew this information about their parents (some did not) and were willing to report it accurately. In spite of this limitation, though, they provide reasonable approximations of family socioeconomic standing. As a supplement to these measures, several indications of teenagers' own economic status are also available. A number of questions measure status within the school environment such as social standing, academic performance, and school satisfaction. And, finally, there are indicators of expected future status, both in terms of aspirations and actual expectations. We are interested in relating these to prejudice singly as well as in combination to determine their cumulative effect.

Family Socioeconomic Status

An important component of any teenager's social status is the socioeconomic standing he acquires from his parents. If he has been blessed with the proverbial silver spoon, he stands in a favored position to obtain a variety of the benefits available to youth. Family affluence may bestow on him material possessions—clothes, record albums, a car, spending money—sufficient to make him a much-sought-after companion among his classmates. Economic wherewithal also undoubtedly precludes his having to take a job to help his family meet expenses, freeing him to maintain his academic average and take part in sports, music, or other extracurricular activities. More importantly, he holds a tremendous advantage toward achieving a favored socioeconomic position of his own in the form of a good education, a prestigious job, and a comfortable income. In contrast, the youth from an economically deprived family may be forced to spend his hours at an after-school job away from the normal round of high school social and academic activities. Moreover, his chances for attaining future socioeconomic standing remain slim in comparison with his more well-to-do peers.

We would expect teenagers from deprived socioeconomic backgrounds to be more highly prejudiced, aside from other reasons, simply because of the values and beliefs communicated to them by their parents. One recent study, for example, has shown that adults occupying blue-collar, low-income economic strata display anti-Semitism at a 2-to-1 ratio over those in more privileged strata.[8] It would be remarkable, then, if children from economically deprived homes were not more exposed to prejudiced attitudes. Deprived youths also find themselves on the outskirts of intellectual activity within their school milieu. Having, perhaps, less opportunity to take part in academic activities and seeing such activities as less relevant for their future careers, they inadvertently miss the training in democratic, interpersonal values that may inhibit prejudiced beliefs.

To determine if socioeconomic deprivation is, in fact, associated with greater prejudice, a scale of socioeconomic status was constructed. Two items—father's income and prestige of father's occupation—were included in this scale. The scale, which gives equal weight to each of these items, varies from 0 to 6, where 0 represents the lowest socioeconomic level and 6 the highest. Further details of the construction of this scale are reserved for Appendix A.[9]

Table 21 presents separately for the three towns the relationship between this socioeconomic scale and anti-Semitism. In Table 21, and in all subsequent tables where anti-Semitism is the dependent variable, the convention that is followed is to consider teenagers who score 4 to 7 on the scale of anti-Semitism—that is, all those who do not outrightly reject such stereotypes—to be anti-Semitic and those scoring 1 to 3 not to be anti-Semitic.[10] The table reports the proportion of teenagers who are anti-Semitic by this criterion according to the level of their fathers' economic status.

The relationship between parents' socioeconomic status and teenage anti-Semitism is different, it turns out, for the three communities. In Commuter-

Table 21   ANTI-SEMITISM BY FATHERS' SOCIOECONOMIC STATUS
FOR WHITE NON-JEWISH ADOLESCENTS

Percent anti-Semitic for those whose fathers'
socioeconomic status was:

| | Low | | | | | High | | | |
	0	1	2	3	4	5	6	Gamma	Xs
Commutertown	81%	77%	68%	59%	57%	57%	41%	−0.316	0.001
	(74)	(66)	(244)	(59)	(129)	(30)	(49)		
Oceanville	43%	49%	57%	53%	52%	42%	32%	−0.055	NS
	(42)	(37)	(271)	(53)	(89)	(31)	(22)		
Central City	44%	45%	37%	40%	33%	*	*	−0.116	NS
	(283)	(135)	(592)	(60)	(45)	(9)	(8)		

* Too few cases for stable percentage.
NS—Not significant.

town, the more deprived the teenagers' socioeconomic backgrounds, the greater the likelihood they will be anti-Semitic. With each decline in fathers' socioeconomic status, the proportion of teenagers who are anti-Semitic increases from a low of 41 percent among the most privileged to a high of 81 percent among the most deprived. Thus, in Commutertown there is a consistent relationship between socioeconomic status and anti-Semitism. The relationship is also of moderate strength (gamma = −0.316). In the other two towns, however, there are neither moderate nor consistent relationships. The most that can be said is that there is a weak tendency for the most deprived to be more highly prejudiced than the least deprived. The notion of prejudice being rooted among the deprived more than among the privileged receives only limited support from these data. Still, the possible indirect and more subtle effects of socioeconomic deprivation on prejudice must not be discounted, for family status greatly influences many of the other criteria by which teenagers compare themselves to their peers.

Teenage Economic Status

In discussing the effects of family socioeconomic status on adolescents, we suggested that teenagers from economically disadvantaged homes may be more prejudiced because they are excluded from participating fully in the subculture of their peers due to personal economic difficulties, such as insufficient spending money or commitment of spare time to earning money to help meet the expenses of their families. Two questions included in our questionnaires make it possible to test this proposition. First, teenagers were asked to indicate whether they held a parttime job. Although such a job might be taken for any number of reasons, we hypothesized that, in general, holding a parttime job while in high school is a sign of economic deprivation. Second, respondents were asked whether they received an allowance from their parents. Here, we took *not* receiving an allowance as a sign of economic deprivation. These two items were combined to create an index of teenage economic status. One point was given for receiving an allowance, one for not having a parttime job. Thus, the scale ranges from 0, indicating low economic status, to 2, indicating high status.

As Table 22 indicates, economically deprived teeenagers exhibit a greater propensity toward prejudice than more privileged teenagers. In Commutertown, for example, 57 percent of the teenagers scoring 0 (low) on economic deprivation manifest anti-Semitism; among those scoring 1 (medium) the proportion rises to 69 percent; and among those scoring 2 (high) on economic deprivation, it increases again to 77 percent. Similar patterning occurs in Oceanville and Central City. Again, Commutertown is the only sample showing a relationship both consistent and of moderate statistical strength. In Central City the relationship is consistent but of only weak strength, and in Oceanville it is only partially consistent and neither statistically significant nor associated. It is evident that the indicators upon which we are forced to rely provide only a rough approximation of teenage economic status. From this evidence, we can claim only weak support for the idea that it is the deprived who are most prejudiced.

Table 22   ANTI-SEMITISM BY TEENAGE ECONOMIC STATUS FOR WHITE NON-JEWISH ADOLESCENTS

| | Percent anti-Semitic among teenagers whose economic status was: | | | | |
	High	Medium	Low	Gamma	Xs
Commutertown	57% (307)	69% (266)	77% (157)	0.296	0.001
Oceanville	52% (235)	50% (242)	60% (123)	0.069	NS
Central City	38% (591)	40% (497)	48% (221)	0.107	0.05

NS—Not significant.

Teenage Social Status

To the typical high school student, the kind of privilege or deprivation that perhaps counts more than anything else is the respect he holds among his classmates. Respect may, of course, accrue to teenagers in a variety of ways. One youngster may be well known in his community due to his athletic ability, another may be popular with the opposite sex, a third may be a highly admired scholar, and still another may be honored with positions in various clubs and organizations. Frequently the same teenagers rank highly on a number of these measures, constituting a highly favored "elite" in the eyes of their peers. Still, the presence of these different avenues of status must be recognized, making it difficult to determine precisely where a teenager stands in comparison with his peers.

Unfortunately our data do not permit us to develop exact calculations of teenage social status. Several attempts to elicit such information were included in the questionnaire but, upon hindsight, did not prove entirely satisfactory. One such attempt asked respondents simply whether they were part of the leading crowd in their school. This question did not prove particularly useful, however, since many respondents answered it to indicate what they would like to be rather than what they are. Another question asked about social club affiliations, but responses proved difficult to interpret since several dozen clubs were mentioned, most of them different in the three towns, and all undoubtedly varying in prestige.

The question finally selected as an indication of social status asked whether the youngster held any offices in his class. This measure provides a comparison between the few students who are sufficiently popular to obtain election to a class office and the majority of students who are not. It is fairly unambiguous and is comparable in all three towns.

Table 23 reports the relationship between prejudice and this measure of social status. Clearly the two are related. In all three towns teenagers holding class offices are consistently less likely to hold anti-Semitic beliefs than their relatively less favored classmates. Once again the hypothesis that deprivation and prejudice are associated is at least not disconfirmed, but

Table 23   ANTI-SEMITISM BY TEENAGE SOCIAL STATUS FOR WHITE NON-JEWISH ADOLESCENTS

| | Percent who are anti-Semitic for teenagers whose social status was: | | | |
	Class Officers	Non-Class Officers	Gamma	Xs
Commutertown	60% (58)	67% (639)	0.132	NS
Oceanville	47% (87)	54% (507)	0.134	NS
Central City	34% (289)	43% (998)	0.188	0.01

NS—Not significant.

neither is it strongly confirmed. As the gammas in the table reveal, the relationships are weak in all three towns and significant only in Central City.

School Performance

Teenagers judge themselves and are judged by their peers according to the status of their families, their economic wherewithal, and their success in competing socially with other youth of their age. As important as these measures of social standing are, however, they are typically overshadowed by academic performance. The teenager's standing among parents, teachers, and friends is importantly influenced by how well he does academically. His evaluation of himself is also likely to depend in some measure upon his grades. Furthermore, school performance plays a vital role in determining chances for future socioeconomic standing, especially in qualifying or disqualifying the teenager for further academic training and in providing motivation to pursue such training.

School performance is highly related to innate skills and to abilities and opportunities acquired from family socialization processes. To the extent that these influence prejudice, school performance should also be related. But there are additional reasons for expecting prejudice to be associated with school performance. Primary among these is that, in theory at least, students who perform more successfully in school develop more sophisticated cognitive skills, more refined understandings of human nature, greater awareness of their own attitudes, and better abilities to shape their own modes of thinking. In contrast to students who perform poorly, they are thus in a better position to reject prejudiced beliefs and to adopt more enlightened attitudes toward those different from themselves. These cognitive differences are the subject of further examination in Chapter 3; the consistent relationships that have been found between higher education and lower degrees of prejudice, however, suggest that such processes may be operative.[11]

Other reasons for expecting greater academic involvement and success to be associated with less prejudice include: less frustration and, therefore, less need for scapegoating; higher self-esteem and, thus, less need to project negative images onto others; greater inclusion in the informal social and cultural life of the school community creating more exposure to ideas, values, and personalities different from one's own; and more awareness of democratic processes, intergroup relations, and the complexities of modern society writ large. To be sure, some of these factors may not be important, at least not for every teenager, but they do suggest that academic privilege or deprivation is an important condition to investigate if the sources of prejudice are to be understood.

To test the relationship between school performance and prejudice, we shall focus on two indicators: amount of time spent on homework and average grades earned. Unfortunately, information on both of these is available only from self-reports elicited from students themselves. Especially for grade point averages, researchers have learned to go directly to school records for their information, but in the present case we were not able to do this. To some extent, though, homework time and grades provide a check on each other. For example, we would not expect many students with excellent grades to have studied but small amounts. Our analysis will proceed, therefore, by first examining the separate effects of homework time and grades on prejudice and then by examining their joint effect.

One would expect homework time to be negatively related to prejudice. Students with sufficient time and motivation to spend time studying are likely to reap more fully both the cognitive benefits offered by such activity and the approval of teachers and other authorities. According to deprivation theory, these students should have least cause to hold prejudiced beliefs. Students with less opportunity or motivation to spend time studying should demonstrate a greater amount of prejudice. Table 24 substantiates this relationship. As amount of time spent on homework per day increases from ½ hour or less to 1 to 1½ hours, we note a commensurate decrease in anti-Semitism scores, and as homework time increases even further to 2 hours or more per day, there is an additional decrease in anti-Semitism. This pattern of consistency holds true in all three of our communities. The relationships are statistically significant at a high level of confidence in each community as well. And, in comparison with the relationships thus far, they

Table 24   ANTI-SEMITISM BY TIME SPENT ON HOMEWORK
FOR WHITE NON-JEWISH ADOLESCENTS

	Percent anti-Semitic for those whose time spent on homework was:				
	2 hours per day or more	1 hour or 1½ hours	½ hour or less	Gamma	Xs
Commutertown	53% (216)	67% (343)	78% (191)	0.334	0.001
Oceanville	40% (169)	54% (326)	71% (117)	0.359	0.001
Central City	34% (364)	41% (671)	48% (294)	0.176	0.01

provide the strongest degree of confirmation for our hypothesis. In Oceanville the gamma is strong and in Commutertown moderate, although it is only weak in Central City.

These results, then, provide some confirmation for the notion that prejudice is rooted in deprivation. Students who haven't either the desire or the chance to spend time studying find themselves outsiders to the intellectual dialogue taking place within their high school environment. First of all, they are a minority; for example, only about one-fourth of the students in our three cities studied less than ½ hour a day. But of greater consequence, they are in a disadvantaged position in competing with other students for grades, awards, and admission to college. And, most importantly, they are likely to share less fully in the mental and cultural enlightenment offered by the educational process. This is part of the context in which prejudice is maintained and perpetuated.

Grade point average should also be expected to show a negative relationship with prejudice, and the data in Table 25 reveal this to be the case. In each town teenagers earning the highest grades are least likely to show anti-Semitic beliefs. Moreover, the relationship between grades and anti-Semitism is consistent. Each successive decrease in grades is associated with a corresponding increment in anti-Semitism scores.

Table 25   ANTI-SEMITISM BY GRADES FOR WHITE
NON-JEWISH ADOLESCENTS

	Percent who are anti-Semitic for those whose grade point average was:					
	A to B+	B	B− to C	C− to D	Gamma	Xs
Commutertown	50%	63%	69%	75%	0.279	0.001
	(137)	(160)	(221)	(231)		
Oceanville	38%	43%	56%	64%	0.302	0.001
	(104)	(122)	(169)	(216)		
Central City	28%	36%	46%	50%	0.260	0.001
	(281)	(306)	(397)	(341)		

Since grades and homework time are highly related and both indicate academic status, we wish to have a summary measure of them in combination for later use. Moreover, we have suggested previously that deprivation has an additive effect on prejudice such that disadvantage on two counts produces greater prejudice than disadvantage on only one. Thus, we wish to see if homework time and grades produce greater variation in prejudice than either separately.

To construct a summary measure of school performance, scores were first assigned to responses on homework time and grades. Homework time of ½ hour or less per day was given a score of 0; 1 to 1½ hours, a score of 1; and 2 hours or more, a score of 2. Grades of C or D were assigned a score of 0; between B and C, a score of 1; B, a score of 2; and better than B, a score of 3. These scores were then simply added, creating a scale ranging from 0 to 5, where 0 indicates low school performance and 5 represents high performance.

The relationship between this scale and prejudice is reported in Table 26. Teenagers scoring lowest are most highly prejudiced and each successive increase in school performance is associated with a decrease in prejudice. In all three communities the relationships are of at least moderate strength (gamma = 0.328, 0.362, and 0.244). Moreover, the effects of the two items comprising the scale are at least somewhat additive, for the scale produces greater variation in prejudice than was produced by either homework time or grades alone. In Central City, for example, the proportions anti-Semitic in this table range between 25 percent and 58 percent, whereas in Table 25 showing their relationship with grades alone, they varied only between 28 percent and 50 percent, and in Table 24 they varied with homework time between 34 percent and 48 percent. Similar patterning occurs in Oceanville and Central City.

Table 26   ANTI-SEMITISM BY SCHOOL PERFORMANCE FOR WHITE NON-JEWISH ADOLESCENTS

Percent who are anti-Semitic for those whose school performance was:

	High					Low		
	5	4	3	2	1	0	Gamma	Xs
Commutertown	39%	59%	61%	68%	76%	81%	0.328	0.001
	(67)	(109)	(148)	(168)	(162)	(90)		
Oceanville	32%	37%	44%	56%	68%	71%	0.362	0.001
	(47)	(79)	(134)	(146)	(143)	(62)		
Central City	25%	31%	39%	45%	47%	58%	0.244	0.001
	(137)	(220)	(257)	(319)	(271)	(120)		

School performance, then, is an important component of the social context of prejudice. That prejudice is related to this objective measure of school status suggests that it should also be related to subjective measures of status. To test this proposition, teenagers were classified according to the extent of their school satisfaction as determined by responses to the question: "How do you feel about school? Do you like it very much, some, not much, or don't you like it at all?" The relationship between this question and anti-Semitism is reported in Table 27. In each town we see that prejudice varies according to school satisfaction. Teenagers who are unhappy with school are consistently (with only one exception) more likely to be prejudiced than those who are satisfied. In Commutertown and Oceanville, the relationships are at moderate statistical strength. These results, then, broaden the grounds upon which we can claim prejudice and deprivation associated. Not only objective criteria of deprivation are useful for locating prejudice, subjective criteria show the same relationship.

Table 27   ANTI-SEMITISM BY SCHOOL SATISFACTION FOR WHITE NON-JEWISH ADOLESCENTS

| | Percent who are anti-Semitic for those who like school: | | | | | |
	Very Much	Some	Not Much	Not at All	Gamma	Xs
Commutertown	56% (202)	68% (412)	73% (100)	80% (39)	0.249	0.01
Oceanville	44% (180)	54% (317)	68% (82)	63% (32)	0.254	0.01
Central City	36% (606)	43% (622)	56% (71)	59% (29)	0.191	0.001

College Aspirations

The analysis thus far has led from status characteristics acquired from one's family to various standards by which teenagers are compared with their peers to a measure of subjective status. By each of these indications, prejudice has been found somewhat more prevalent among the deprived than among the privileged. We have suggested that these various forms of deprivation have a cumulative effect on prejudice, a prediction yet to be tested. We have also suggested that these and other signs of present status lead to certain aspirations and expectations regarding future status, which are also likely to be related to prejudice.

Aspirations for college training are almost universal among today's youth. In our three samples combined, only 14 percent of white non-Jewish youth indicate that they do not wish to attend college, with another six percent answering that they "don't care." The teenager who does not seek a college education defines himself, in effect, as an outsider to the usual pattern of maturation in modern society. Parents, teachers, and friends all have a tendency to expect the average youth to plan on college training or at least to want it. Their concern, and perhaps their pity or even disgust, is likely to be expressed toward the youth who fails to conform to these expectations. Moreover, the youth who does not aspire to a college education is likely to voluntarily exclude himself from many of the academic and cultural activities available to him since these are generally designed for purposes of college preparation, for which he has little interest and sees little need.

To some extent, college aspirations merely reflect the status characteristics we have already discussed—parents' economic well being, school performance, liking school—as well as other conditions, such as IQ, parental pressures, and peer influences. But to the extent that college aspirations define some teenagers as "insiders" and others as "outsiders" with respect to typical career expectations, they become independently relevant in our search for types of deprivation that one associates with prejudiced attitudes.

We expect college aspirations to be related to prejudice both because among other things they reflect other types of status already examined and because they indicate fuller inclusion in the regular round of social, academic, and cultural activities available in the high school community. Table 28 confirms this expectation. The relationships between college aspirations and prejudice are of moderate strength in all three towns, although not statistically significant in Oceanville. Students responding "yes" when asked, "If money were not a problem, and if your grades were good enough, would you like to go to college after you graduate from high school?" show the least propensity to be prejudiced. The proportions range from 62 percent in Commutertown and 51 percent in Oceanville to 38 percent in Central City, while the proportions for those answering "no" are 75, 62, and 51 percent, respectively. Also of interest is the finding that youngsters answering "don't care" score even higher on anti-Semitism than those answering "no." Although it is not entirely clear how to interpret this result,

Table 28   ANTI-SEMITISM BY COLLEGE ASPIRATIONS FOR
WHITE NON-JEWISH ADOLESCENTS

| | Percent who are anti-Semitic for those whose college aspirations were: | | | | |
	Like to Go	Not Like to Go	Don't Care	Gamma	Xs
Commutertown	62%	75%	88%	0.348	0.001
	(571)	(135)	(49)		
Oceanville	51%	62%	68%	0.239	NS
	(523)	(55)	(31)		
Central City	38%	51%	53%	0.261	0.001
	(1037)	(193)	(96)		

NS—Not significant.

one conclusion consistent with both the data and with the foregoing discussion is that those answering "no" may in effect be saying that they have thought about it and have decided that they really don't have the opportunity or abilities to make college a desirable option whereas those answering "don't care" are students who are genuinely apathetic to academic values and perhaps to the high school community more generally. Thus, the "don't cares" would be the ones who have truly placed themselves on the outskirts of the adolescent subculture.

College Expectations

Besides college aspirations, we are also interested in actual expectations concerning college attendance, since this affords an indication of future socioeconomic status. Parents' socioeconomic status has been seen affecting prejudice, as have social and academic performance relative to one's peers. Moreover, these measures of opportunity and ability are highly related to college plans; for example, the proportion of white non-Jewish teenagers from the highest socioeconomic level definitely planning to attend college is 83 percent, while it is 20 percent for those from the lowest socioeconomic level. Similarly, 84 percent of those highest on school performance, but only 10 percent of those lowest, plan to attend college. If it is found also that college plans are related to prejudice, we have then traced the complete cycle by which status and prejudice continue to be associated from one generation to the next. Parents deprived of society's economic and cultural benefits demonstrate prejudice; deprivation breeds deprivation, so that their children also tend to be excluded from equal shares in society's rewards; and the children, then, perpetuate further negative beliefs and attitudes.

Two measures are available for predicting which students will gain college educations and which will not. First, students were asked to indicate what program they are taking in high school. On this basis, we divided our sample into those who are taking a college preparatory program and those who are taking some other course (vocational, commercial, general, etc.). Table 29 compares the amount of anti-Semitism held by these two groups. As expected, students in college programs in all three towns show at least a moderate proclivity to hold such beliefs less often than those in other programs.

A second measure of college plans was obtained by asking students whether they expect to go to college. To make this as realistic an assessment as possible, respondents were asked first whether they would like to attend college (responses to this question were examined above), then they were

Table 29   ANTI-SEMITISM BY SCHOOL PROGRAM FOR
            WHITE NON-JEWISH ADOLESCENTS

Percent who are anti-Semitic for those whose
school programs were:

	College Preparatory	Other	Gamma	Xs
Commutertown	57% (360)	75% (353)	0.394	0.001
Oceanville	49% (437)	63% (168)	0.261	0.01
Central City	32% (574	48% (688)	0.314	0.001

confronted with the question: "Thinking realistically now, do you think that you will actually go to college?" This question reduced the 80 percent who indicated they would like to go to college to 41 percent who actually expect to go. As Table 30 reports, teenagers expecting to attend college are consistently the least likely to manifest prejudice, those not expecting to attend are most likely, and those who are not sure of their plans manifest intermediate proportions of prejudice.

Table 30   ANTI-SEMITISM BY COLLEGE EXPECTATIONS FOR
            WHITE NON-JEWISH ADOLESCENTS

Percent who are anti-Semitic for
those whose college expectations were:

	To Go	Don't Know	Not to Go	Gamma	Xs
Commutertown	53% (335)	72% (193)	80% (225)	0.430	0.001
Oceanville	47% (319)	57% (151)	64% (142)	0.249	0.01
Central City	34% (445)	42% (451)	48% (430)	0.197	0.001

To obtain a summary assessment of each teenager's likelihood of attending college, we divided our sample into three categories. Respondents stating that they are in a college program and expect to go to college were considered to have a "high" likelihood of attending college, students in a noncollege program and not expecting to go to college were given a "low" likelihood, and those giving any other combination of answers were scored "medium." The relationship between this college-expectation index and anti-Semitism is clearly shown in Table 31. The proportions manifesting anti-Semitism in Commutertown range consistently, albeit not strongly, from 52 percent for those with a high likelihood of attending college, to 70 percent for those classified as medium, and to 79 percent for those with low chances of going to college. Scores in Oceanville and Central City show similar patterns.

Table 31   ANTI-SEMITISM BY LIKELIHOOD OF ATTENDING COLLEGE FOR WHITE NON-JEWISH ADOLESCENTS

| | Percent who are anti-Semitic for those whose likelihood of attending college was: | | | | |
	High	Medium	Low	Gamma	Xs
Commutertown	52%	70%	79%	0.320	0.001
	(261)	(260)	(191)		
Oceanville	47%	54%	68%	0.211	0.001
	(300)	(197)	(108)		
Central City	32%	41%	49%	0.167	0.001
	(377)	(502)	(379)		

It is noteworthy that differences in prejudice should appear in a comparison of high school students who expect to attend college with those who do not. When adults with college educations are compared with those having high school educations only, somewhat greater differences in prejudice appear, but these differences are generally attributed to influences received while attending college. The present findings, however, demonstrate that a significant part of these differences exist even before some youths experience college.[12] In part these differences are undoubtedly due to greater abilities and opportunities associated with teenagers expecting to go to college. They may also derive in part from anticipatory socialization processes through which college-bound youths have already begun to acquire some of the values and ideas communicated in college. At any rate, it is evident that the large differences in prejudice associated with education and other measures of socioeconomic status among adults have already begun to develop before adolescents leave high school. Inequities in the larger society indeed influence prejudice even at this age.

A Summary Index of Deprivation

On the whole, the preceding analysis has confirmed the notion that we started out with: deprivation is the context in which prejudice occurs. Each form of deprivation tested showed fairly consistent relationships with anti-Semitic beliefs. However, these relationships, while significant statistically, have been generally weak. Differences in anti-Semitism between the most privileged and the most deprived on many of these measures have been only on the order of 20 percent to 25 percent. These findings add information about the sources of prejudice, but no single measure of deprivation that we have examined provides a very powerful predictor of prejudice. Throughout our analysis, however, we have suggested that these measures would be looked at, not only singly, but also in combination. One has merely to reflect upon one's own experience to recognize that a particular belief or action is but rarely the result of a single factor or condition. When a variety of conditions are combined, their examination often provides a powerful means of predicting resultant beliefs and actions. In the present case, the cumulative effect of the various forms of deprivation may have a more profound effect on prejudice than any single one of them.

To examine the cumulative effects of various types of deprivation on prejudice, it would be possible simply to lump all the measures investigated thus far into a single additive scale of deprivation. On logical grounds, however, it does not make sense to do so. All the variables analyzed in this chapter are indicators of deprivation, but on closer inspection it is clearly evident that at least two distinct types of deprivation are at issue. Some of the measures concern economic status—father's socioeconomic status and teenager's economic status—while most of the measures have to do with academic status, especially school performance, school satisfaction, and college plans. Our understanding of prejudice would be enhanced by knowing the separate and joint effects of these two forms of deprivation on anti-Semitism.

Summary measures of economic deprivation and academic deprivation were therefore constructed. Father's socioeconomic status and teenager's economic status were combined to form a summary index of economic

Table 32 ANTI-SEMITISM BY ECONOMIC DEPRIVATION FOR
WHITE NON-JEWISH ADOLESCENTS

| | Percent who are anti-Semitic for those whose economic deprivation scores were: | | | | | | | |
| | Low | | | | | High | | |
	0	1	2	3	4	5	Gamma	Xs
Commutertown	29%	53%	64%	66%	84%	89%	0.296	0.001
	(31)	(118)	(190)	(172)	(101)	(18)		
Oceanville	36%	49%	50%	51%	62%	*	0.148	NS
	(11)	(79)	(183)	(167)	(87)	(9)		
Central City	*	33%	37%	38%	46%	52%	0.139	0.05
	(5)	(58)	(373)	(389)	(246)	(42)		

* Too few cases for stable percentage.
NS—Not significant.

deprivation ranging from 0 to 5. Academic deprivation is measured by a scale ranging from 0 to 4 which combines school performance, school satisfaction, and college plans. Details of the construction of these two indexes are presented in Appendix A.[13]

Given the relatively weak relationships between the several individual indicators of economic deprivation and anti-Semitism reported on earlier, the summary measure would not be expected to be a powerful predictor of prejudice, and as can be seen from Table 32, it is not. Yet it is a better predictor than the individual indicators taken one by one. In each community, the relationships are linear and consistent: the greater the economic deprivation, the larger the proportion of anti-Semites. However, while moderate in strength in Commutertown, the relationships are weak in the other two communities and are not significant in Oceanville. Economic deprivation and anti-Semitism are clearly related but such deprivation accounts for only a small amount of the variation in prejudice.

The individual indicators of academic deprivation proved to be more highly associated with prejudice than the individual indicators of economic deprivation. And, as can be seen from Table 33, the summary measure of academic deprivation is more highly related to anti-Semitism than the summary measure of economic deprivation. The relationships are virtually consistent in all three communities, except for an unexplained aberration in Oceanville. Moreover, the gammas in all three communities are of at least moderate strength, being strong in Commutertown.

Separately examined, then, both economic deprivation and academic deprivation are revealed to be associated with anti-Semitism in smaller and larger degree. Pondering the possibilities of their joint effect before examining the data, three outcomes are conceivable because one of three distinct underlying processes may be at work.

Table 33   ANTI-SEMITISM BY ACADEMIC DEPRIVATION FOR WHITE NON-JEWISH ADOLESCENTS

Percent who are anti-Semitic for those whose score on the academic deprivation scale was:

| | Low | | | | High | | |
	0	1	2	3	4	Gamma	Xs
Commutertown	43% (93)	53% (135)	61% (144)	80% (145)	80% (183)	0.413	0.001
Oceanville	28% (215)	48% (240)	63% (277)	53% (255)	67% (263)	0.311	0.001
Central City	28% (105)	35% (116)	37% (138)	42% (112)	59% (132)	0.276	0.001

Deprivation of any kind may be a stimulus to prejudice with the effect being additive: the more deprivation, the greater the tendency to anti-Semitism. In the present instance, the operation of this process would be signaled statistically by the finding that economic and academic deprivation are independently related to anti-Semitism. Such a finding would call for further work to find out just what it is about deprivation, generally conceived, that produces anti-Semitism.

A second possibility is that while academic deprivation and anti-Semitism tend to go together, this is not because anything about academic deprivation causes anti-Semitism. Rather, it is because both academic deprivation and anti-Semitism are a product of economic deprivation. Statistically, this process would be represented if the result of considering the joint effect of the two forms of deprivation on anti-Semitism were to show economic deprivation and anti-Semitism to be related irrespective of level of academic performance. Academic deprivation, however, would show no relation to anti-Semitism within levels of economic privilege. Given such a result, subsequent work would be indicated to discover what it is about economic deprivation that causes anti-Semitism. Academic performance would no longer occupy the investigator's attention as a source of anti-Semitism.

The third possibility is that academic deprivation is the major source of prejudice, with economic status being a factor only because it influences academic performance. If this process is at work, academic deprivation will be found to be related to anti-Semitism irrespective of level of economic status but the opposite will not apply: economic status and anti-Semitism will not be related within levels of academic performance. The implications for further work given this third possibility would be to concentrate efforts on identifying the elements in academic performance making for anti-Semitism.

Schematically, these three processes may be depicted as follows:

(1) *Economic and academic deprivation are independent sources of anti-Semitism.*

(2) *Economic deprivation is a source of both academic deprivation and anti-Semitism.*

(3) *Economic deprivation is a source of academic deprivation which,
in turn, is a source of anti-Semitism.*

Economic deprivation ———▶ Academic deprivation ———▶ Prejudice

Looking now at the data in Table 34, it is possible to tell which of these
three models comes closest to describing reality.[14] If the first model is
correct, there should be a relation down each column *and* across each row.
If the second model is correct, there should be a relation down each column
(economic deprivation should continue to be related to anti-Semitism) but
no relation across each row (academic deprivation should not be related
to anti-Semitism). Finally, the third model is correct if there is no relation
down each column (economic deprivation is not related to anti-Semitism)
but a continued relation across each row (academic deprivation is related
to anti-Semitism.)

Table 34 reveals that the third model best fits the data. Academic depriva-

Table 34   ANTI-SEMITISM BY ACADEMIC AND ECONOMIC
DEPRIVATION FOR WHITE NON-JEWISH ADOLESCENTS

(All three communities combined)

Percent who are anti-Semitic for those whose
academic deprivation scores were:

And whose scores on economic deprivation were:		Low 0	1	2	3	High 4	Total	Gamma	Xs
Low	0	16% (19)	46% (11)	* (5)	* (6)	* (2)	32% (47)	0.403	NS
	1	32% (73)	46% (68)	64% (47)	56% (39)	50% (20)	47% (255)	0.285	0.01
	2	31% (146)	39% (163)	45% (179)	58% (107)	71% (111)	47% (746)	0.365	0.001
	3	29% (113)	47% (118)	44% (142)	48% (147)	63% (170)	47% (728)	0.276	0.001
	4	58% (31)	36% (58)	51% (91)	54% (100)	77% (132)	58% (434)	0.347	0.001
High	5	* (7)	* (6)	46% (11)	71% (21)	71% (24)	61% (69)	0.381	NS
Total		32% (413)	43% (491)	49% (559)	55% (512)	67% (578)	51% (2698)	0.322	0.001
Gamma		0.140	−0.017	−0.036	−0.001	0.131	0.126		
Xs		0.05	NS	NS	NS	NS	0.001		

* Too few cases for stable percentage.
NS—Not significant.

tion is related to prejudice either moderately or strongly at each level of economic status, but economic deprivation is by and large no longer related when academic status is controlled. The exception to this pattern is among teenagers lowest on academic deprivation. In their case economic status still produces some variations in prejudice. All in all, however, academic deprivation appears to be the major source of prejudice. Whatever effect economic status has on teenage prejudice seems to come about only because economic advantage influences academic standing which, in turn, affects prejudice.[15]

Academic Deprivation and the Other Indicators of Anti-Semitism

The preceding results provide general confirmation to the hypothesis that prejudice is associated with social disadvantage. In addition, it has been seen that, among different ways of being disadvantaged, academic deprivation seems to have the greatest impact on prejudice. The analysis thus far, however, has been limited to an investigation of anti-Semitic beliefs. The other indicators of anti-Semitism will now be reintroduced to determine if academic deprivation is also related to them. These other indicators available in our data are: general unfriendliness toward Jews, social distance toward high-status Jews, and social distance toward low-status Jews.

The relationship between academic deprivation and general unfriendliness toward Jews is presented in Table 35. At each level of academic deprivation, the percentage of students feeling hostility toward Jews is reported. As the table clearly demonstrates, the results are consistent with our previous findings for anti-Semitic beliefs. Teenagers lowest on deprivation are least likely to feel unfriendly toward Jews, those highest are most likely, and with each increase in deprivation in between, there is a corresponding increase in prejudice.

Table 35   HOSTILITY TO JEWS BY ACADEMIC DEPRIVATION FOR WHITE NON-JEWISH ADOLESCENTS

Percent scoring high on hostility toward Jews among those whose level of academic deprivation was:

| | Low | | | | High | | |
	0	1	2	3	4	Gamma	Xs
Commutertown	1% (95)	7% (138)	8% (146)	20% (149)	29% (180)	0.289	0.001
Oceanville	3% (105)	7% (116)	10% (138)	8% (113)	25% (132)	0.194	0.001
Central City	3% (217)	6% (245)	10% (283)	11% (260)	16% (268)	0.187	0.001

The social distance measures, it will be recalled, proved to be indicators of anti-Semitism *and* of class prejudice, and there was no unequivocal way to sort out the two. We suspected, however, given the response of Jewish teenagers to the two measures, that anti-Semitism was more a motivating factor in the expression of social distance to a high-status Jewish referent whereas class prejudice was being expressed when the referent was a Jewish teenager of low status. This suspicion gains some confirmation when the relationship of academic status to the two measures is examined.

As can be seen from the top half of Table 36, in all three communities academic deprivation is consistently related to feeling social distance from a high-status Jewish referent. The relationship is strong in Commutertown and moderate in Central City although weak in Oceanville.

Comparatively, the relationships between academic status and social distance to a low-status referent are much less consistent and much weaker (see the lower half of Table 36). What these results suggest is, first, confirmation of the relationship between academic status and anti-Semitism,

Table 36   SOCIAL DISTANCE BY ACADEMIC DEPRIVATION FOR
WHITE NON-JEWISH ADOLESCENTS

Percent scoring high on social distance toward
high-status Jews among those whose level of
academic deprivation was:

| | Low | | | | High | | |
	0	1	2	3	4	Gamma	Xs
Commutertown	3% (94)	7% (135)	6% (144)	19% (139)	23% (176)	0.387	0.001
Oceanville	2% (105)	7% (113)	11% (133)	8% (108)	16% (128)	0.165	NS
Central City	4% (217)	3% (242)	9% (278)	8% (256)	15% (265)	0.250	0.001

Percent scoring high on social distance toward
low-status Jews among those whose level of
academic deprivation was:

| | Low | | | | High | | |
	0	1	2	3	4		
Commutertown	13% (93)	16% (135)	19% (144)	19% (143)	33% (178)	0.125	0.05
Oceanville	17% (105)	23% (111)	20% (132)	19% (107)	28% (129)	0.076	NS
Central City	25% (218)	17% (241)	21% (278)	24% (257)	24% (269)	0.044	0.05

NS—Not significant.

and second, that academic privilege, while it arms teenagers against anti-Semitism, doesn't especially arm them against class prejudice. For present purposes, of course, the significant result is the confirmatory one.

Conclusions

We began this chapter with the expectation that teenage anti-Semitism would be found especially among youngsters who are relatively deprived of the rewards that teenage society and the adult milieu of which it is a part have to bestow. By and large, the analysis has confirmed this expectation, but has specified it somewhat by indicating that being deprived of academic rewards is more highly associated with prejudice than being deprived of the rewards of coming from an educated and well-to-do family. Economic status and level of prejudice are related only because economic status affects academic status, which, in turn, affects level of prejudice.

The tendency for prejudice to be socially located among the economically and especially the academically deprived was present in all three communities, even though the communities themselves vary considerably in the nature of their populations. Thus, it seems likely that the associations found between deprivation and prejudice in our sample would also hold in other areas. The relative strength of the relationships did vary from town to town, however, which perhaps warrants some explanation.

A simple count of the foregoing relationships in each town which were strong, moderate, and weak reveals that Commutertown had the highest number of strong or moderate relationships between anti-Semitism and deprivation, Oceanville the next highest number, and Central City the lowest. Although it cannot be said for sure why this pattern exists, it appears likely that it is associated with the relative proportion of Jewish teenagers in the three communities. Attitudes toward Jews, it seems reasonable to suppose, are made more salient in a community where Jews are present than where they are not. Thus, the Commutertown teenagers having thought more about the issue, their answers to the stereotype items are probably more reliable and less subject to superficiality, making for less random error in the statistical presentation of the relationships in that community than in Oceanville, where there are fewer Jews, and in Central City, where there are virtually none.

The question we must now address is why prejudice is especially located among the academically deprived. In this chapter, we offered some speculations about possible answers, but did not put any of the speculations to a test. Now that the link between academic deprivation and prejudice has been firmly established, it is appropriate to do so.

3 Causes of Adolescent Anti-Semitism

Despite the illumination cast in the preceding chapter on the relationship between deprivation, especially academic deprivation, and the incidence of anti-Semitism, crucial questions remain unanswered. What precise aspect of academic success makes for the relative absence of prejudice? In turn, what in relative academic failure stimulates a tendency toward anti-Semitism? This chapter is devoted to trying to find answers to these questions for the white non-Jewish youth in the three sample communities.

To our knowledge, no previous research has addressed itself to exploring precisely the significance of academic deprivation for prejudice. The literature is rich, however, in its suggestions as to why deprivation, more generally conceived, is a source of prejudice. Much of the theory is germane to the present inquiry and, fortunately, our data permit us to examine a number of alternative explanations that have been hotly contested by scholars of prejudice. While we shall not be able to resolve these debates wholly, the grounds for discussion can be advanced, especially with respect to extending the boundaries of our understanding of adolescent anti-Semitism.

From among the theories that have been advanced to explain the social location of prejudice, there are four which we are able to subject to test. These are that prejudice is a result (1) of anxiety produced by frustration, (2) of identification with prejudiced primary groups, (3) of socialization to unenlightened rather than enlightened values, and (4) of a lack of cognitive sophistication.

One of the earliest and most widely accepted theories of prejudice holds that hostility toward minority groups results from anxiety produced by frustration.[1] According to this view, repeated failures to get what one wants, whether it be economic rewards, social status, or other desires, result in anxiety, guilt feelings, and repressed wishes that build up like steam in a boiler until they must find some outlet. Hostility toward others results when more direct means of resolving such tension break down. Frustrations and guilt feelings in this case are not confronted directly but are projected onto others. Since minority groups are easily identified and frequently without power to defend themselves, they often become targets or scapegoats for such aggression. This theory suggests that among high school students those failing to compete successfully for grades, friends, admission to college, and other rewards may find themselves beset by anxiety and self-blame to the point where they seek excuses for their failures. Groups other than themselves, such as blacks and Jews, provide easy excuses and thus become likely candidates for jealousy and hatred.

The frustration–aggression theory of prejudice has been examined in innumerable studies, including the famous Authoritarian Personality research, with the result that such words as "frustration," "aggression," and "scapegoating" are now common household expressions.[2] Several serious weaknesses in the explanatory structure of frustration–aggression theory have made it subject to criticism and have created interest in alternative theoretical perspectives.[3]

One of these weaknesses is the failure of the theory to specify the conditions under which frustration is likely to generate hostility instead of direct attempts to overcome the frustrating obstacle. In many cases, frustration results merely in renewed efforts to triumph over hindering circumstances. In other cases, it seems to be internalized, absorbed, and diffused without the use of any safety-valve techniques, contrary to the steam-in-a-boiler analogy. Only in certain instances does frustration lead to aggressive acts against others. Yet, by itself, frustration–aggression theory offers little help in determining when such instances are likely to arise. A further weakness is the theory's inability to predict who will become the target of hostility when such acts do occur. No reasons are offered as to why aggressive attacks are frequently vented against minority groups except that these groups are typically conspicuous and hampered in their ability to ward off aggression.

Finally, the shortcoming that has perhaps proved most damaging to this perspective is its failure to acknowledge the ease with which prejudice is learned and made a natural part of one's cultural outlook. Critics have argued persuasively that prejudice is most often adopted merely because one has grown up in its presence, not because it had to be invented to dissipate some deep-seated psychological tension.[4]

These inadequacies have stimulated interest in alternative theories of prejudice, most of which emphasize the effects of cultural environment. One such approach suggests that prejudice is maintained primarily through interaction with other prejudiced persons.[5] Contrary to the frustration–aggression argument, this theory points out that people acquire most of their attitudes simply because they are exposed to them, not because they need these particular attitudes to cope with psychic problems. Thus, persons with prejudiced attitudes hold such notions simply because they learn them from their associates. Once acquired, prejudicial attitudes, to be sure, may function to relieve anxieties and tensions. But to concentrate only on psychological needs and their resolution, claim the proponents of this view, misses the social and cultural setting in which prejudice is learned.

When applied to teenagers, this theory suggests that adolescent prejudice is probably acquired primarily from parents, with the academically deprived showing a greater propensity for such attitudes because of home environments in which prejudice is prominent. This possibility has already been implied by our finding that the social strata which contain the most highly prejudiced adults also exhibit teenagers with high anti-Semitism scores. Unfortunately our data do not contain direct information about parents' attitudes, so our investigation of this socializing influence must rest upon argument by inference.[6]

Besides parents, peers have been thought to be an important source of teenage prejudice. Adolescents are known for their tendency to establish tight networks of social interaction and to surround their friendship patterns with strict codes of conduct governing fashion, bases of popularity, academic performance, and other behavior.[7] It seems reasonable, therefore, to expect peer pressures to also affect prejudice. Among adults, prejudice has been found to be significantly influenced by friendship patterns.[8] Among teenagers, it seems likely that friends will have an even greater influence, for research has shown that peer pressure plays a particularly important role in prejudice when attitudes are in a process of development and change, a condition especially characteristic of adolescents.[9] The reason that academically deprived teenagers are more prejudiced, then, may lie simply in the fact that they associate with peers who are more prejudiced, thereby reinforcing one another's negative views. We shall examine this proposition.

Whatever we find about the impact of teenagers' friendship patterns on prejudice, however, the question will remain as to why the incidence of anti-Semitism is greater in some cultural settings than in others. To learn that prejudiced people tend to congregate together and that unprejudiced people tend to do likewise is no explanation of why prejudice is present in the one instance and absent in the other. No previous research on adolescent prejudice affords a clue as to what the causal factors might be. Research on adult prejudice, however, has produced some additional hypotheses aside from frustration–aggression whose operation among teenagers we are able to test with the data at hand.

A primary notion emerging from studies examining the cultural setting of prejudice among adults is that the deprived are more prejudiced because they are less exposed to democratic values of equality, civil liberties, brotherhood, and respect for the rights of others.[10] There are at least two cultures in American society, claim the advocates of this viewpoint: an ideal culture based on sophisticated equalitarian values, and a common culture rooted in folk beliefs that are predemocratic and prescientific. The first is portrayed as being transmitted primarily through the educational institutions of our country; the other is pictured characteristically as being passed along verbally from parent to child and among friends in local communities isolated from centers of cultural advancement, especially in rural areas or in urban slums.

Although considerable efforts have been made to differentiate these two cultures, it seems to the authors that the precise factors that perpetuate or dissipate prejudice in either remain somewhat ambiguous. It has been frequently demonstrated that the deprived have less enlightened values, but it has not been shown convincingly that equalitarian values actually militate against prejudice.[11] On the surface, such values would seem to be distinctly contradictory to hatred and hostility. Yet a strong case has been made both theoretically and empirically that democratic values *per se* do not reduce prejudice and may, under certain conditions, actually increase it.

Gunnar Myrdal's *An American Dilemma* affords the most familiar statement of this argument, although it is derived from observations of black–white rather than Jewish–non-Jewish relations.[12] Myrdal argues that Americans perceive a discrepancy between the equalitarian values of the American creed and the actual deprived condition of black people. The discrepancy is resolved by white Americans, less by efforts to bring reality into conformity with the ideal than by a resort to prejudices that serve to rationalize the unequal treatment. Ironically, then, democratic ideals may actually occasion prejudice rather than preclude it. The pronouncement alone of enlightened values is not sufficient, in Myrdal's view, to generate conformity to them.

Simply assuming that enlightened values are the cure for prejudice also runs into the difficulty that individual value systems are characterized by a considerable degree of inconsistency and compartmentalization. Research has shown that it is quite possible for highly equalitarian and libertarian values to be held in abstraction along with bigoted and prejudicial attitudes at a more concrete level, with the contradictions going unrecognized.[13] Moreover, when subjects are confronted with the contradictions, they are prone either to deny them or to bring forth other values to justify their prejudice.

Nevertheless, not enough evidence exists to conclude that there is no potential for reducing prejudice through education to enlightened values. Certainly, we shall still want to examine the effect of such values on adolescent anti-Semitism to determine if early socialization can be used to reduce prejudice. Conversely, we shall want to determine if a lack of such values provides the reason why academic deprivation tends to be associated with prejudice.

Enlightened values, however, are not the only cultural trait that varies with privilege and deprivation. According to a considerable body of literature, privilege tends also to be associated with more cognitive sophistication and an accompanying ability to bring powers of reason to bear more effectively on interpreting one's world.[14] Characteristically, the less privileged are more prone to a simplistic world view, to accepting simple answers to complicated questions, to dividing life naively into the "good" and the "bad" or other simple either/or categories.

Being cognitively sophisticated is attributable in part undoubtedly to inherited abilities, but it is also nurtured in more socially privileged settings. Those of higher social status typically have more opportunity to pursue advanced education and more time to keep abreast of news and cultural affairs. Teenagers from privileged families benefit from the ideas of their parents and also have more opportunities available to reap the most from their school training. Youngsters from deprived families, in contrast, seem more likely to be encapsulated within the beliefs and outlooks of their own day-to-day associates. Relative to the more privileged, they tend neither to have the time nor the interest to expose themselves as deeply to the world of ideas and to abstract modes of thought. Society not only excludes them from more obvious rewards, such as money and prestige; it also deprives them more subtly of the advantages of knowledge and cognitively advanced tools for coping with their worlds.

Cognitive sophistication has been advanced as one reason for the relationship between social status and prejudice. A sophisticated world view, it has been argued, is likely to prove incompatible with prejudiced attitudes characterized by overgeneralization and oversimplification. Categorizing the world into "we" and "they" is as alien to sophisticated thought patterns as is the use of ethnic labels as explanations for behavior different from one's own. Rather than blaming the inferior position of minorities on ascribed attributes such as laziness or immorality, the social processes by which groups acquire differential status are likely to be sought. Indeed, there is convincing empirical basis for these assertions, as witnessed, for example, by Selznick and Steinberg's recent research in which cognitive sophistication loomed as the primary link between social status and anti-Semitism among adults.[15]

Cognitive sophistication should be distinguished from enlightened values, even though both may be nourished in the same settings. Unfortunately the distinction between the two has not always been clearly maintained. Whether education and other sources of exposure to advanced culture actually create altruistic and democratic values that directly counteract prejudice and promote positive actions toward minority groups, or whether a scientifically enlightened culture merely generates more sophisticated thought patterns so that any simplistic attitudes are viewed suspiciously, has not been established with clarity.

Along with the other possible interpretations of the relationship between deprivation and prejudice which we have discussed (frustration, peer-group effects, and enlightened values), we shall also be interested in cognitive sophistication and particularly in comparing its effects with those of enlightened values.

Frustration

The first of the four factors postulated as providing the link between academic privilege and anti-Semitism is frustration. To determine whether frustration does play this role, the results of three psychological scales, each of which is directly or indirectly an indicator of frustration, will be investigated. The first of these is the familiar "F scale" from the Authoritarian Personality studies.[16]

Authoritarianism

Although *The Authoritarian Personality* is one of the most widely known of social science monographs and has generated a plethora of subsequent studies and speculations (well over five hundred by the mid-sixties), to make clear its relevance to the present inquiry it is necessary to review briefly what the F scale purports to measure and what has been postulated about the bearing of scores on that scale to prejudice.[17]

Considerable controversy has developed about the meaning of a high score on the scale. Its architects left the matter somewhat ambiguous, and the ambiguity has been heightened by subsequent comment and use. The social psychologist Roger Brown has sought to distill what is common to extant interpretations of the meaning of the scale.[18] His conservative estimate is that a high score on the scale taps self-glorification, repressed resentment toward parents, status anxiety, a tendency to project guilt and inadequacy onto others, and a proneness to rigid ways of thinking.

Whatever agreement exists about these as the components of the "authoritarian personality," considerable disagreement remains about whether these factors cluster together because of some psychic impairment or because of cultural, social, or some other factors. The authors of the original research, however, postulated the source as a psychic impairment resulting from repressive and frustrating home training. Mainly from clinical studies, they deduced that persons with this type of personality typically are raised by parents who, anxious about their own social status, rear their children with strict authority and discipline.[19] The effect of this upbringing is to frustrate the children and to generate aggression. Because it cannot be directed against its legitimate target (the parents), this aggression is displaced onto less dangerous targets such as minority groups. Furthermore, the authoritarian grows up feeling ambivalence and resentment toward his parents. Combined with his early discipline, this ambivalence creates insecurity that is manifested in status anxiety, a tendency toward self-glorification, and rigid, defensive patterns of thought. As such persons move through life, these handicaps create further frustrations and anxieties that cannot be resolved successfully and consequently perpetuate needs to vent hatred and hostility onto others.

Although some of these propositions have been challenged by more recent research, we shall for present purposes utilize a high score on the F scale as an indicator of a frustrated psychological condition characterized by repressiveness and rigidity.[20] The hypotheses to be tested are these: (1) that a high score on the F scale will be associated with academic deprivation, either because deprivation produces insecurity and anxiety or because this type of personality hinders academic functioning, and (2) that as an indication of a frustrated, anxious psychological condition, a high score on the F scale will prove to be the explanation of why deprivation and prejudice are linked. In other words, while prejudice tends to be socially located among the deprived, it is the frustration and aggression that deprivation brings about which is the more immediate cause of prejudice.

Neither hypothesis receives support from the data. Looking first at the relationship between deprivation and F (see Table 37), we find in each of the three towns that the proportion of teenagers who score high on F is remarkably the same at each level of academic deprivation. Contrary to our expectations and to the results of studies of adults, less privileged teenagers are not more subject to authoritarian tendencies than are their more privileged counterparts. Moreover, F scores are not related to anti-Semitism (see Table 38). In all three communities, anti-Semitism scarcely varies between the more and the less authoritarian youngsters. Again, the finding is anomalous when compared to the usual high correlations found between authoritarianism and prejudice among adults.

Table 37   F SCORES BY ACADEMIC DEPRIVATION FOR WHITE NON-JEWISH ADOLESCENTS

Percent scoring high on F among those whose level of academic deprivation was:

	Low				High		
	0	1	2	3	4	Gamma	Xs
Commutertown	37% (82)	35% (112)	35% (116)	30% (114)	30% (136)	−0.026	NS
Oceanville	40% (94)	43% (94)	32% (113)	33% (95)	36% (111)	−0.080	0.05
Central City	31% (153)	24% (164)	20% (198)	26% (176)	24% (147)	−0.040	NS

NS—Not significant.

It is tempting to conclude from these findings that frustration is not an element in adolescent anti-Semitism and therefore that it does not explain why academic deprivation and anti-Semitism are linked. Such a conclusion must be accepted cautiously, however, for it is possible that the absence of relationships is a fault of the measure of F that we have employed.

The Christie reversed version of the F scale has enjoyed wide usage in social psychological research.[21] We adopted it because it was designed to eliminate possible response set effects of the original scale and also because it is widely regarded as a superior measure. What we failed to reckon with is that the scale was developed and standardized using adults as subjects and that its suitability for use with teenagers had not been demonstrated.

On hindsight, it seems quite possible that the items included in the scale are much too complicated for the average adolescent. Here, for example, are three of the ten statements comprising the scale.

If it weren't for the rebellious ideas of youth there would be less progress in the world.

One of the most important things children should learn is when to disobey authorities.

No normal decent person would ever think of hurting a close friend or relative.

Table 38   ANTI-SEMITISM SCORES BY F SCALE SCORES FOR WHITE NON-JEWISH ADOLESCENTS

Percent anti-Semitic among those whose F scale scores were:

	Low 0	1	2	3	4	5	6	7	8	9	High 10	Gamma	Xs
Commutertown	* (0)	* (3)	* (6)	57% (21)	70% (70)	64% (134)	70% (160)	69% (119)	60% (52)	71% (21)	* (1)	+0.042	NS
Oceanville	* (0)	* (1)	* (3)	55% (11)	52% (48)	59% (122)	49% (138)	58% (110)	50% (52)	50% (22)	* (2)	−0.006	NS
Central City	* (0)	* (0)	* (6)	29% (34)	41% (113)	39% (281)	45% (231)	39% (140)	31% (61)	30% (10)	* (1)	−0.002	NS

* Too few cases for stable percentage.
NS—Not significant.

Statements such as these, we suspect, are beyond the capabilities of many teenagers, and even the more sophisticated might have difficulty in expressing their views in terms of the relative agree–disagree responses that the measure calls for. We don't know this for sure, of course. Yet, it is obviously necessary that we entertain the possibility, for if there were a great amount of error and random fluctuation in responses because of misunderstanding and guessing, it could account for the striking differences between our results and the results of others.

The alternative possibility, of course, is that authoritarianism simply does not yet operate among persons of this age. It is plausible that anxiety, rigidity, and repressiveness do not build up until later when persons are confronted with adult responsibilities and pressures, or at least that they remain latent if already present. Some evidence exists for this interpretation since even the clearest items in the scale when analyzed separately show no consistent relationship with academic deprivation or anti-Semitism. Yet, to argue that authoritarianism does not operate among teenagers runs counter to the results of previous clinical studies suggesting that the trait is acquired in early childhood due to overly strict parental discipline. Only if it could be shown that these clinical cases were not typical of a broader cross section of youth or that such retrospective data are not reliable, both of which conditions are plausible, could these previous conclusions be reconciled with this interpretation of our findings. Unfortunately, this question as it pertains specifically to the F scale as a measure of frustration must be left open. We are able, however, to pursue the matter using other direct or indirect measures of frustration that were included in the research instruments administered to our adolescent subjects.

Self-acceptance

Our interest in self-acceptance is primarily that anxiety about one's abilities and self-blame for one's failures are, from one vantage point, indications of frustration that has not been resolved directly but has been repressed and, as a result, has produced anxiety and low self-confidence. From this perspective of frustration–aggression theory, such anxiety is one potential source of aggression and hatred displaced onto others.

In examining self-acceptance, however, we are again confronted by the problem of using a psychological scale designed in a different context and with different intentions in mind. A revision of the Gough self-acceptance scale, a measure tapping anxiety primarily with respect to interpersonal relations, was included in the research instrument. However, its use as designed was not as well suited for our purpose as the use instead of several of its component items.[22] Having examined the relationship between the entire scale and anti-Semitism and finding the two essentially unrelated, we decided to select those items that seemed most suggestive of low self-confidence and anxiety about one's personal capabilities and to create a new subscale of our own. By eliminating items that were more projective in nature and of less obvious relevance to self-acceptance, four items were finally chosen, two of which indicate high self-acceptance:

My daily life is full of things that keep me interested.
When I work on a committee, I like to take charge of things.

and two of which indicate low self-acceptance:

When I am in a group of people I usually do what the others want rather than make suggestions.

It is hard for me to act natural when I am with new people.

To create an index of self-acceptance, one point was assigned for agreement with each of the first two items and disagreement with each of the latter two, resulting in a scale ranging from 0 to 4. The scale is obviously not entirely appropriate to indicate anxiety, guilt, and frustration, but it does seem to capture an insecure psychological condition, particularly regarding interpersonal relationships.

The relationship between self-acceptance and deprivation is reported in Table 39. If anxiety in the form of low self-confidence is the factor relating deprivation and anti-Semitism, there should be, as a minimal condition, a relationship between self-acceptance and deprivation. This is what the data demonstrate. Among teenagers in the most privileged circumstances, this proportion declines with the most academically deprived demonstrating the least tendency to hold self-accepting attitudes. The patterning, while not completely consistent, is of moderate strength and is repeated in all three communities.

Table 39 SELF-ACCEPTANCE BY ACADEMIC DEPRIVATION
FOR WHITE NON-JEWISH ADOLESCENTS

Percent scoring high on self-acceptance among those whose level of academic deprivation was:

	Low 0	1	2	3	High 4	Gamma	Xs
Commutertown	54% (86)	40% (127)	41% (135)	28% (131)	29% (170)	−0.185	0.01
Oceanville	53% (102)	40% (110)	42% (131)	34% (110)	29% (121)	−0.238	0.001
Central City	54% (209)	34% (232)	35% (260)	30% (241)	22% (241)	−0.249	0.001

This finding encouraged us to examine the relationship between self-acceptance and anti-Semitism. Since both are related to academic deprivation, we would expect them to be related to one another. As Table 40 shows, however, this expectation is only weakly substantiated. Increasing self-acceptance produces very little change in anti-Semitism except for those scoring highest on self-acceptance. Only between scores of 3 and 4 do consistent differences in anti-Semitism occur, and these are quite small.

Table 40   ANTI-SEMITISM BY SELF-ACCEPTANCE FOR WHITE NON-JEWISH ADOLESCENTS

| | Percent anti-Semitic among those whose level of self-acceptance was: | | | | | | |
| | Low | | | | High | | |
	0	1	2	3	4	Gamma	Xs
Commutertown	73% (37)	66% (147)	70% (249)	61% (193)	56% (55)	−0.120	NS
Oceanville	50% (30)	55% (130)	54% (192)	56% (165)	45% (60)	−0.026	NS
Central City	44% (77)	46% (321)	41% (423)	39% (325)	26% (86)	−0.130	0.05

NS—Not signifiant.

Although the deprived suffer from less confident self-concepts, then, this condition does not seem to explain their greater proclivity for prejudice. This conclusion provides further grounds for our suspicion, derived from examining authoritarianism, that anxiety resulting from frustration is not the link between deprivation and anti-Semitism. Apparently teenagers find some way of coping with anxiety about their capabilities other than by projecting negative feelings onto Jews. Again, we must acknowledge that this result may be merely an artifact of the items available to us for testing frustration and anxiety. With this limitation in mind, we turn then to an examination of Rosenberg's self-esteem scale, which is perhaps our strongest measure of frustration-invoked anxiety.

Self-esteem

Rosenberg's scale of self-esteem was developed and tested among respondents similar in age to those in our sample and has been shown to be correlated with a wide variety of attitudes, values, and background characteristics.[23] The purpose of this scale, according to its author, is to measure the degree to which an individual respects himself and considers himself a worthy person, not better than others but not worse either. For our purposes, a low score on this scale is considered indicative of generalized anxiety regarding one's worth. There is ample support for this interpretation since low scores have been shown to be more characteristic of persons subject to depression, manifesting psychosomatic symptoms, feeling sensitive to criticism, and feeling psychically isolated. The scale has also been found correlated with a variety of background characteristics indicative of frustration; for example, low self-esteem is more likely among teenagers from broken homes, less likely among teenagers with sibling statuses giving them "unconditional acceptance" from their families (a condition exactly counter to the authoritarian home), and more likely among those from dissonant religious backgrounds.

To replicate Rosenberg's scale as nearly as possible, we combined the ten items measuring self-esteem into a scale ranging from 0 to 6, using Rosenberg's procedures.[24] As with our previous measures, we are interested to see if low self-esteem is the link between academic deprivation and prejudice. Consequently, the relationship between self-esteem and deprivation is first examined, then that between self-esteem and anti-Semitism.

Table 41 shows no relation between academic deprivation and self-esteem. The incidence of high esteem does not decline, as we had expected, with each increase in deprivation. Rather the relationship is erratic. That the most deprived in all three towns are less likely to possess high self-esteem than the most privileged is about the only confirmation which the data afford for the notion that deprivation produces anxiety about one's self-image.

When self-esteem and prejudice are examined (Table 42), anti-Semitism scores remain approximately the same at all levels of self-esteem. The gammas also reveal an absence of an association. Feelings of low self-worth do not seem to generate hatred that is manifested as anti-Semitism.

Table 41 SELF-ESTEEM BY ACADEMIC DEPRIVATION
FOR WHITE NON-JEWISH ADOLESCENTS

Percent who score high on self-esteem among those whose level of academic deprivation was:

| | Low | | | | High | | |
	0	1	2	3	4	Gamma	Xs
Commutertown	39% (87)	41% (115)	30% (120)	29% (113)	32% (136)	−0.096	NS
Oceanville	38% (93)	38% (93)	27% (117)	24% (91)	32% (109)	−0.095	NS
Central City	33% (159)	19% (167)	18% (188)	24% (178)	21% (144)	−0.029	0.05

NS—Not significant.

Table 42   ANTI-SEMITISM BY SELF-ESTEEM
FOR WHITE NON-JEWISH ADOLESCENTS

Percent anti-Semitic for those whose
score on self-esteem was:

	Low 0	1	2	3	4	5	High 6	Gamma	Xs
Commutertown	* (1)	64% (11)	65% (46)	71% (192)	60% (145)	64% (97)	65% (102)	−0.063	NS
Oceanville	* (5)	* (4)	52% (62)	52% (154)	47% (120)	60% (88)	59% (71)	+0.105	NS
Central City	* (1)	44% (18)	31% (110)	43% (387)	45% (168)	37% (121)	23% (75)	−0.053	0.01

* Too few cases for stable percentage.
NS—Not significant.

All three of our indicators of frustration-invoked anxiety (F, self-acceptance, self-esteem), then, fail to show any relationship with prejudice. Two of these scales, we have noted, seem somewhat unreliable for drawing valid inferences, but the third, Rosenberg's scale, seems sufficiently adequate. Apparently, frustration does not provide the reason why prejudice is disproportionately characteristic of the deprived. This conclusion is also supported by the fact that elsewhere in our analysis we have failed to find any traces of frustration operating to produce prejudice. If frustration were an important source of anti-Semitism among teenagers, it should have been revealed at two points in the analysis in the previous chapter. First, we should have discovered that wanting to go to college but not expecting to was a frustrating condition leading to high prejudice. Examining the joint effects of these two items on prejudice should have revealed a relationship like this:

		Want to go to college:	
		Yes	No
Expect to go	Yes	Low prejudice	Medium prejudice
to college:	No	High prejudice	Medium prejudiice

Instead, a relationship like this appeared:

		Want to go to college:	
		Yes	No
Expect to go	Yes	Low prejudice	Medium prejudice
to college:	No	Medium prejudice	High prejudice

Thus, we argued that both these items were merely indicators of academic deprivation whose effect on prejudice was additive. Similarly, if frustration were an important factor in generating prejudice, students spending a large amount of time on homework but receiving low grades should have been found especially prone to anti-Semitism. Again, this did not prove to be true. Rather the effect on prejudice of both homework time and grades was additive.

Nowhere in our analysis, then, has frustration been found to be a source of prejudice. The possibility that this is because the measures used to tap frustration were not sensitive enough cannot be ruled out entirely. Given the consistency of the findings using quite different measures and in all three communities, however, it is more likely that frustration is simply not an important source of prejudice among these teenagers. This is not to say that these youngsters are not subject to becoming frustrated; the evidence says they are. Apparently, however, they find ways to cope with it other than through aggressive feelings toward Jews.

It must be remembered that our data were collected during a period of relative national and local calm and quiet. As history has taught us, hostility and prejudice in their most virulent forms may erupt when there is reason for mass public frustration and anxiety. Thus, even if factors other than frustration account for the anti-Semitism found among these adolescents, the potential of frustration to be the source of severe prejudice in more serious situations should not be overlooked.

Primary Groups

A second proposition to be explored about the relationship between academic deprivation and prejudice is that it is a result of academically deprived youngsters being more likely to associate with peers who are prejudiced and thereby having their own prejudices nourished and reinforced.

We are in a relatively good position to test the several parts of this proposition because among the things asked of these teenagers were the names of their five closest friends in their class. Since all students in a class were included in the study, we know just how prejudiced these friends are. Consequently, we can check whether academically deprived youngsters are indeed more likely than the academically privileged to have anti-Semitic friends, and if so, whether prejudiced friendships are associated with being prejudiced oneself.

To test the first part of the proposition, we divided the teenagers in each of the three towns according to their scores on the index of academic deprivation and then computed the average level of anti-Semitism of their friends. The proportions of teenagers at each level of academic deprivation who had friends with average anti-Semitism scores of 4 or more are reported in Table 43.

Table 43   FRIENDS' ANTI-SEMITISM BY ACADEMIC DEPRIVATION FOR WHITE NON-JEWISH ADOLESCENTS

Percent of anti-Semitic friends for those whose level of academic deprivation was:

	Low				High		
	0	1	2	3	4	Gamma	Xs
Commutertown	39% (52)	32% (90)	43% (105)	54% (98)	55% (118)	0.234	0.01
Oceanville	34% (68)	31% (71)	39% (79)	41% (69)	51% (81)	0.186	NS
Central City	21% (152)	21% (173)	31% (191)	32% (179)	46% (169)	0.280	0.001

NS—Not significant.

While the relationships are not entirely consistent, they are in the expected direction and moderate in strength in two of the three communities. The academically deprived are indeed more prone to anti-Semitic friendships than are the academically privileged. Moreover, as can be seen in Table 44, having anti-Semitic friends is disposing to being anti-Semitic oneself. This is not true in Oceanville, but there is a moderate association in Commutertown and a weak association in Central City.

Table 44   ANTI-SEMITISM BY FRIENDS' ANTI-SEMITISM FOR WHITE NON-JEWISH ADOLESCENTS

Percent anti-Semitic for those whose friends' anti-Semitism scores average:

	Low					High			
	1	2	3	4	5	6	7	Gamma	Xs
Commutertown	58% (26)	60% (163)	59% (261)	73% (166)	89% (37)	64% (11)	* (2)	+0.223	0.01
Oceanville	47% (15)	52% (122)	53% (279)	50% (114)	52% (25)	* (8)	* (1)	−0.002	NS
Central City	36% (75)	36% (389)	39% (485)	47% (212)	52% (54)	60% (10)	* (0)	+0.142	0.05

* Too few cases for stable percentage.
NS—Not significant.

These results suggest that a part, albeit a small part, of the reason academic deprivation and prejudice are linked is that the former leads to friendship choices that sustain, if they do not produce, anti-Semitism. Statistically and substantively, however, we cannot be sure that this is the underlying process at work until the relationship between all three variables is examined simultaneously. Because the matter is somewhat complex, it seems wise to pause to consider the possible outcomes of the trivariate relation and what these outcomes would mean.

A first possibility is that the causal sequence of the three variables will be found to be sequential: academic deprivation leads to having anti-Semitic friends which, in turn, leads to one becoming anti-Semitic oneself. Given such an outcome, our search for an explanation of why academic deprivation and anti-Semitism are linked would be satisfied, at least in part.

A second possible outcome is that, for reasons still to be uncovered, academic deprivation leads simultaneously to teenagers being anti-Semitic themselves and to being prone to seek out anti-Semitic friends. The causal sequence in this instance would be:

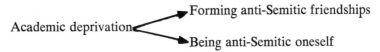

Academic deprivation → Forming anti-Semitic friendships
Academic deprivation → Being anti-Semitic oneself

Given this result, the relation between forming anti-Semitic friendships and anti-Semitism reported in Table 44 would be an artifact of academic deprivation being the source of both phenomena.

Still a third possibility is to find the underlying causal sequence to be:

Academic deprivation → Anti-Semitism
Forming anti-Semitic friendships → Anti-Semitism

which would signify that academic deprivation and forming anti-Semitic friendships both contribute independently to prejudice.[25]

To demonstrate the first of these processes, what would have to happen statistically when the joint effects of academic deprivation and friendship patterns on anti-Semitism are considered, is for a relationship between forming anti-Semitic friendships and being anti-Semitic oneself to remain and for the relationship between academic deprivation and anti-Semitism to disappear. If it should turn out that the relation between academic deprivation and anti-Semitism remains whereas the other relation disappears, the second outcome will have been achieved. The third possibility would be demonstrated if both academic deprivation and the friendship variable are found to be independently related to anti-Semitism.

Confronting the three possibilities with the evidence produces the results reported in Table 45 (to produce enough cases, the samples for the three communities have been combined).

By and large, the results reveal that the principal process at work is the third one, that academic deprivation and forming anti-Semitic friendships are independent factors. Looking first across the rows of the table, we see that a relationship between academic deprivation and anti-Semitism prevails however prejudiced the teenagers' friends are. The vertical columns of the table reveal that having friends who are anti-Semitic is disposing to being anti-Semitic oneself, whatever one's level of academic deprivation or privilege. In sum, the two variables are mostly related to anti-Semitism, independently of each other. This means also, however, that their effect is additive. Academically deprived youngsters are more anti-Semitic if they

Table 45   ANTI-SEMITISM BY ACADEMIC DEPRIVATION AND FRIENDS' ANTI-SEMITISM FOR WHITE NON-JEWISH ADOLESCENTS

Percent who are anti-Semitic for those whose academic deprivation scores were:

And whose friends' anti-Semitism scores were:	Low 0	1	2	3	High 4	Total	Gamma	Xs
Low 1	20% (20)	39% (28)	32% (22)	44% (16)	65% (23)	42% (116)	+0.377	0.05
2	34% (127)	38% (145)	44% (144)	48% (115)	64% (99)	45% (674)	+0.257	0.001
3	28% (177)	42% (209)	53% (223)	53% (188)	60% (185)	48% (1,025)	+0.283	0.001
4	33% (64)	53% (70)	49% (106)	63% (103)	72% (128)	57% (492)	+0.346	0.001
5	* (9)	57% (14)	74% (19)	.58% (24)	71% (41)	64% (116)	+0.220	NS
6	* (0)	* (2)	* (8)	* (8)	60% (10)	59% (29)	+0.243	NS
High 7	* (0)	* (0)	* (2)	* (1)	* (0)	* (4)	−01.000	NS
Total	32% (413)	43% (491)	49% (559)	55% (512)	67% (578)	51% (2,698)	+0.322	0.001
Gamma	0.004	0.157	0.147	0.183	0.101	0.162		
Xs	NS	NS	0.05	NS	NS	0.001		

* Too few cases for stable percentage.
NS—Not significant.

form anti-Semitic friendships than if they don't. Academically privileged youngsters exhibit less prejudice if their friends are unprejudiced than if they are prejudiced.

These results leave enigmatic why academic deprivation and the formation of anti-Semitic friendships go together as Table 43 demonstrates they tend slightly to do. Such friendships, according to Table 45, do not come about because academic deprivation is a cause of their being sought out. Why then do they occur? Although the data do not offer a definitive answer, they imply that academic deprivation leads one to seek friends of similar academic status and, by virtue of the association between academic deprivation and anti-Semitism, these academically deprived friends tend to be anti-Semitic. Thus, anti-Semitism itself does not seem to be the motive for forming friendships, although the prejudice is undoubtedly nourished and reinforced, and possibly even produced, in contexts where one's friends are anti-Semitic.

The results of this brief exploration of the influence of peer groups on prejudice formation and sustenance are neither new nor startling. Generally, they explain what other researchers have found, that social context makes a difference in prejudice maintenance and reduction. The results leave essentially unanswered the very questions which inspired the investigation. We are still in the dark as to what it is about academic performance that stimulates or inhibits prejudice. Let us now consider the thesis that the influencing factor is the presence or absence of enlightened values.

Enlightened Values

As defined, our study was also designed to pursue the idea that the prejudice of academically deprived youngsters is a result of their not having learned the enlightened values that mitigate prejudice. To this end, we asked a series of questions designed to elicit teenagers' views on a variety of civic, moral, and interpersonal values that both previous research and common sense suggested might have some influence on prejudice. To ensure that the teenagers' response would not be affected by the realization they were taking part in a study of prejudice, these value questions were asked early in the interviewing sessions before any items on prejudice had been introduced.

Civic Values

Belief in the virtues of democracy, in the importance of civil liberties, in the necessity of responsible and informed citizenship, and in the need for diverse opinions to be heard and taken account of in the political arena—these are civic values that undergird our society. Every child is exposed to them. Yet, because they are difficult concepts to teach and to learn, they are not universally understood, accepted, or valued in our society. And because they are lofty ideals not readily applied, they do not always find their way into practice even when they are understood.

Among adults, such civic ideals have been found to be more commonly held by the more privileged strata of the society: by those who have received advanced, nontechnical educations; by persons whose cultural horizons have been broadened by exposure to the arts, by reading, and through travel; by members of civic and other voluntary organizations; by community leaders, and so on.[26] Judging from the evidence on adults, it would seem likely that these values will also be more in evidence among privileged youth than the underprivileged. In terms of our measure of academic deprivation, it is the low scorers who should be found the most likely to acknowledge these values.

If this proves to be the case, having enlightened civic values could be one possible reason why privileged teenagers exhibit less tendency to be anti-Semitic. Holding strong beliefs in equality and democracy should convince even persons in their teens that derogatory attitudes toward other groups are wrong.

Three items are available for testing the relationship between enlightened civic values, academic deprivation, and anti-Semitism:

> People should be interested in doing things in their community; be useful citizens.
>
> People should support movements or groups that are working for equal rights for everyone.
>
> People should let everyone have his fair share in running business and politics in this country.

These statements were presented to only half of the teenagers in our samples. The other half, those answering the "teenage" rather than the "adult" form of the questionnaire, were asked instead about values pertaining to school life. Consequently, the results presented here are based on fewer cases than usual in this study, although the number is still sufficient for making generalizations.

Table 46 shows for each of the three communities the proportion of youngsters at each level of academic deprivation who agree with the three civic values cited. Of the nine relationships, only one is both consistent and of moderate strength, another is consistent but weak, and one is moderately strong although not entirely consistent. Two others show weak but inconsistent patterns, and the remainder show no association. The lack of consistency and the predominant weakness of the relationships make it unlikely that holding civic values such as these will prove to be a major reason for the lower level of prejudice of the privileged youngsters. Still, it seems warranted to examine the data to determine whether those who hold these values are less disposed to anti-Semitism.

Again the results, as Table 47 shows, are neither very strong nor entirely consistent. Indeed, in Central City, there is no relationship between the three civic-value items and anti-Semitism. In Commutertown and Ocean-

Table 46   ACCEPTANCE OF CIVIC VALUES BY ACADEMIC DEPRIVATION FOR WHITE NON-JEWISH ADOLESCENTS

Percent who agree with civic values quoted
among those whose academic deprivation score was:

	Low 0	1	2	3	High 4	Gamma	Xs
"People should be interested in doing things in their community; be useful citizens":							
Commutertown	38% (45)	40% (76)	33% (76)	36% (75)	25% (84)	−0.185	NS
Oceanville	52% (60)	44% (57)	42% (81)	40% (62)	31% (52)	−0.193	NS
Central City	52% (123)	52% (126)	48% (141)	44% (124)	40% (139)	−0.136	0.01
"People should support movements or groups that are working for equal rights for everyone":							
Commutertown	48% (44)	45% (76)	40% (77)	28% (75)	22% (84)	−0.224	0.05
Oceanville	27% (59)	30% (57)	37% (81)	23% (60)	28% (51)	−0.067	NS
Central City	36% (122)	39% (126)	35% (141)	36% (124)	27% (141)	−0.048	0.05
"People should let everyone have their fair share in running business and politics in this country":							
Commutertown	23% (43)	39% (75)	23% (77)	19% (75)	21% (82)	−0.119	NS
Oceanville	22% (60)	21% (57)	24% (81)	21% (61)	24% (50)	−0.077	NS
Central City	33% (123)	31% (126)	28% (142)	26% (123)	25% (140)	−0.074	NS

NS—Not significant.

ville, however, weak and somewhat consistent relations do prevail. Believing in any one of these civic values does reduce the incidence of anti-Semitism slightly.

Given the questioning procedure that obliged us to work with only half the usual number of cases, it is not possible to pursue this analysis further. On the basis of the limited evidence developed, however, the possibility needs at least to be entertained that socialization to democratic values can

Table 47   ANTI-SEMITISM BY ACCEPTANCE OF CIVIC VALUES FOR WHITE NON-JEWISH ADOLESCENTS

| | Percent who are anti-Semitic for those whose response to the item quoted was: | | | | |
	Shouldn't or Don't Care	Should	Strongly Should	Gamma	Xs
	"People should be interested in the community":				
Commutertown	70% (43)	66% (205)	57% (125)	−0.185	NS
Oceanville	52% (25)	56% (159)	46% (129)	−0.154	NS
Central City	60% (42)	37% (316)	44% (322)	+0.028	0.02
	"People should support groups working for equal rights":				
Commutertown	74% (90)	59% (150)	60% (133)	−0.170	0.05
Oceanville	58% (86)	53% (132)	44% (93)	−0.176	NS
Central City	41% (161)	43% (285)	41% (235)	−0.001	NS
	"People should let everyone have their fair share":				
Commutertown	71% (119)	63% (153)	58% (98)	−0.172	NS
Oceanville	59% (116)	47% (127)	47% (68)	−0.166	NS
Central City	43% (164)	41% (320)	42% (195)	−0.006	NS

NS—Not significant.

have a salutary effect in combating prejudice. We shall withhold final judgment until our examination of the enlightened-values thesis is completed.

Moral Values

In examining the culture of deprived groups to discover the roots of their prejudice and bigotry, investigators have singled out moralistic values as an important factor.[27] Extremist groups, for example, have been shown to have a characteristic tendency to reduce complex political processes to a struggle between "the good" and "the bad" in which the good triumph only through persistent loyalty to moralistic values, identified variously as patriotism, sexual purity, hard work, and loyalty to a religious creed. Intermingled with these moral virtues is a strong element of individualism in which strength of character and good intentions are seen as the primary forces shaping social life. Reducing life and moral values to such simplistic notions leads easily to stereotyping minority groups and others different from oneself as immoral, treacherous, lazy, debauched, irreligious—in general, as the antithesis of all good moral virtues.

In our sample of teenagers we have seen a strong tendency to stereotype Jews as immoral, lazy, and unscrupulous. Consequently, we might expect that teenagers holding to conventional moral virtues would be even more prejudiced than their less moralistic classmates. However, this is not the reality we observe. The relationships between anti-Semitism and the five items that have been regarded as conventional moral values as reported in Table 48 show virtually no tendency for the more highly moral to be more anti-Semitic. Neither is moralism more characteristic of the deprived (Table 49). In practically all cases, it is instead the privileged who are more likely to believe in conventional morality.

These findings are inconsistent with previous conclusions in which moralism has been found more highly characteristic of deprived, bigoted groups. Yet careful consideration suggests that high moral values, such as working hard, being religious, or following the rules, in themselves contain nothing suggestive of prejudice. It is only when these values are used by extremists as slogans for carving society into the virtuous and the sinful that they become conducive to prejudice. Among the teenagers in our sample, such extremism does not seem to be a problem. As with civic values, there is perhaps some slight tendency for those who reject moral values to be more prone to anti-Semitism. Again, however, the relations are neither strong enough nor consistent enough to suggest that anti-Semitism can be combated effectively simply by doing a better job of inculcating moral values.

Table 48   ANTI-SEMITISM BY ACCEPTANCE OF MORAL VALUES
FOR WHITE NON-JEWISH ADOLESCENTS

| | Percent who are anti-Semitic for those whose level of acceptance of moral values on the items quoted was: | | | | |
	Low	Medium	High	Gamma	Xs
	"Should be religious":				
Commutertown	62% (257)	68% (243)	68% (244)	+0.093	NS
Oceanville	61% (179)	51% (233)	49% (197)	−0.154	0.05
Central City	41% (376)	40% (550)	41% (392)	−0.002	NS
	"Should be honest":				
Commutertown	59% (22)	70% (209)	64% (519)	−0.105	NS
Oceanville	75% (16)	54% (126)	53% (469)	−0.088	NS
Central City	80% (20)	41% (268)	40% (1,033)	−0.090	0.01
	"Should follow rules":				
Commutertown	76% (98)	66% (363)	62% (286)	−0.151	0.05
Oceanville	65% (82)	54% (288)	49% (239)	−0.158	0.05
Central City	54% (111)	40% (560)	39% (642)	−0.110	0.01
	"Should be moral":				
Commutertown	69% (216)	63% (322)	65% (197)	−0.065	NS
Oceanville	55% (137)	56% (267)	50% (206)	−0.076	NS
Central City	47% (305)	39% (624)	39% (389)	−0.094	NS
	"Should be hard-working":				
Commutertown	73% (95)	65% (379)	63% (270)	−0.109	NS
Oceanville	61% (75)	55% (289)	49% (247)	−0.149	NS
Central City	52% (102)	39% (592)	40% (623)	−0.051	NS

NS—Not significant.

Table 49   ACCEPTANCE OF MORAL VALUES BY ACADEMIC
DEPRIVATION FOR WHITE NON-JEWISH ADOLESCENTS

Percent accepting the moral values quoted whose
level of academic deprivation was:

	Low 0	1	2	3	High 4	Gamma	Xs
"Should be religious":							
Commutertown	33% (96)	34% (137)	34% (146)	36% (149)	28% (183)	−0.054	NS
Oceanville	43% (107)	34% (115)	33% (137)	27% (114)	27% (132)	−0.149	NS
Central City	33% (221)	38% (241)	26% (282)	33% (261)	23% (271)	−0.145	0.001
"Should be honest":							
Commutertown	83% (96)	78% (138)	70% (147)	72% (151)	55% (187)	−0.225	0.001
Oceanville	88% (107)	81% (115)	79% (138)	72% (114)	67% (133)	−0.198	0.01
Central City	84% (221)	84% (244)	77% (282)	82% (260)	67% (274)	−0.145	0.001
"Should follow rules":							
Commutertown	46% (96)	45% (137)	42% (147)	34% (150)	27% (184)	−0.236	0.001
Oceanville	55% (107)	44% (115)	38% (136)	38% (113)	29% (133)	−0.245	0.001
Central City	56% (220)	51% (243)	52% (280)	52% (259)	34% (268)	−0.170	0.001
"Should be moral":							
Commutertown	42% (96)	33% (137)	21% (146)	24% (148)	23% (181)	−0.186	0.05
Oceanville	43% (106)	38% (116)	36% (138)	28% (111)	26% (133)	−0.225	0.05
Central City	42% (221)	34% (245)	27% (281)	28% (258)	18% (269)	−0.235	0.001
"Should be hard-working":							
Commutertown	51% (96)	44% (138)	33% (147)	36% (150)	25% (183)	−0.259	0.001
Oceanville	58% (107)	47% (116)	36% (138)	32% (113)	33% (133)	−0.255	0.001
Central City	56% (221)	52% (245)	46% (281)	54% (259)	31% (270)	−0.193	0.001

NS—Not significant.

Interpersonal Values

Much emphasis has been placed by previous investigators of prejudice on macroscopic social and political implications.[28] Consequently, it has been assumed that belief in democratic values and awareness of complex political processes, as opposed to simplistic and moralistic views of society, would lead to a greater tolerance of minority groups and a reduction of prejudice. Thus far, our data have given only little support for these assumptions, as applied to teenagers, but prejudice also includes a less macroscopic, interpersonal side. Especially among young people, the value of friendliness and respect in face-to-face interaction may be more important than political and

Table 50 ACCEPTANCE OF INTERPERSONAL VALUES BY ACADEMIC DEPRIVATION FOR WHITE NON-JEWISH ADOLESCENTS

Percent accepting interpersonal values quoted whose level of academic deprivation was:

	Low 0	1	2	3	High 4	Gamma	Xs
"Should respect others":							
Commutertown	77% (96)	66% (137)	63% (147)	54% (151)	46% (187)	−0.238	0.01
Oceanville	65% (107)	68% (116)	61% (138)	62% (114)	61% (133)	−0.051	NS
Central City	63% (221)	64% (245)	60% (282)	62% (260)	47% (272)	−0.137	0.001
"Should not be conceited":							
Commutertown	76% (96)	78% (138)	67% (147)	62% (151)	51% (187)	−0.181	0.01
Oceanville	84% (107)	70% (116)	72% (138)	69% (113)	71% (133)	−0.065	0.05
Central City	71% (221)	72% (246)	68% (282)	69% (260)	59% (271)	−0.089	0.001
"Should not be self-centered":							
Commutertown	60% (96)	64% (138)	59% (146)	49% (149)	60% (183)	−0.069	NS
Oceanville	70% (107)	66% (116)	63% (137)	57% (114)	55% (133)	−0.144	NS
Central City	66% (221)	68% (245)	61% (281)	59% (258)	48% (273)	−0.168	0.001

NS—Not significant.

moral values in generating openness to others and in preventing or reducing prejudiced attitudes.

Given our failure to find civic and moral values to be highly related to academic privilege, we were hesitant to predict such a relationship between privilege and interpersonal values. Still, if the two were found to be related, it would seem that this would be the direction that the relation would take. Although existing studies do not provide evidence on the matter, it would seem that teenagers who have been exposed to greater advantages in their socialization, both at home and at school, should have received more careful training in the codes of interpersonal contact than those who have been deprived of such advantages. Moreover, they may have had to compete less

Table 51   ANTI-SEMITISM BY INTERPERSONAL VALUE ITEMS FOR WHITE NON-JEWISH ADOLESCENTS

| | Percent who are anti-Semitic for those whose level of acceptance of interpersonal values on the item quoted was: | | | | |
	Shouldn't or don't care	Should	Strongly Should	Gamma	Xs
	"Should respect others":				
Commutertown	75% (47)	73% (262)	60% (441)	−0.266	0.01
Oceanville	54% (28)	58% (197)	51% (387)	−0.116	NS
Central City	62% (71)	41% (472)	39% (780)	−0.131	0.001
	"Should not be conceited":				
Commutertown	78% (41)	70% (226)	63% (484)	−0.181	0.05
Oceanville	74% (27)	54% (138)	52% (446)	−0.119	NS
Central City	52% (63)	46% (369)	38% (890)	−0.178	0.01
	"Should not be self-centered":				
Commutertown	72% (79)	69% (238)	62% (428)	−0.163	NS
Oceanville	72% (53)	52% (182)	51% (376)	−0.139	0.02
Central City	60% (108)	45% (424)	36% (790)	−0.251	0.001

NS—Not significant.

intensively with others for their rewards and thus have developed more altruistic attitudes. Whatever the reason, our data do provide some support for the notion that interpersonal values are more strongly held by the privileged (see Table 50). Of the nine relationships examined, five are at least weakly in the right direction, although not entirely consistent.

These findings suggest that one element in the greater anti-Semitism of the academically deprived may be their lesser commitment to interpersonal values. For this to be plausible, however, it must be demonstrated that strong interpersonal values are associated with less prejudice. Table 51 indicates that this is indeed the case.

On all three items and in all three towns, teenagers rejecting interpersonal values show the highest anti-Semitism scores while those strongly accepting such values show the lowest. The differences are not so great as might be expected, however. Only a few points separate the scores of the different categories and the gammas range from -0.116 only up to -0.266. Since each of the three interpersonal values produces some consistent effects on prejudice, they might be expected to have more powerful consequences in combination. As Table 52 demonstrates, this is the case. When the three items are combined to form a scale ranging from 0 to 6, more noteworthy effects on prejudice are revealed.[29] Teenagers holding all three interpersonal values strongly are lowest on prejudice and, with minor exceptions, there is an increase in anti-Semitism with each decrease in interpersonal values. The relationship is still only moderate (it is weak in Oceanville), yet it suggests that interpersonal values may, indeed, be one reason why the privileged are less prejudiced than the less privileged.

To determine if interpersonal values constitute a link between academic

Table 52   ANTI-SEMITISM BY INTERPERSONAL VALUES FOR
WHITE NON-JEWISH ADOLESCENTS

Percent who are anti-Semitic for those whose
score on the interpersonal values scale was:

Xs	Low	0	1	2	3	4	High 5	6		Gamma
Commutertown	*	86%	73%	79%	66%	65%	58%		-0.218	0.01
	(6)	(14)	(40)	(105)	(157)	(159)	(263)			
Oceanville	*	*	70%	54%	59%	51%	49%		-0.139	NS
	(6)	(8)	(23)	(57)	(118)	(154)	(244)			
Central City	80%	60%	51%	46%	47%	39%	34%		-0.203	0.001
	(10)	(15)	(61)	(180)	(264)	(284)	(501)			

* Too few cases for stable percentage.
NS—Not significant.

deprivation and prejudice, it is necessary to examine all three of these variables simultaneously. If the relationship between deprivation and prejudice partly disappears when interpersonal values are controlled, we can infer that variations in interpersonal values are a reason why deprivation is associated with prejudice. Table 53 presents the results of our test. (All three towns are presented together here, since separate tables would reduce the number of cases in each cell too greatly for confidence.) Generally speaking, the data do not confirm the expectations. Even though interpersonal values are related to both deprivation and anti-Semitism, there is no indication that they provide the reason why anti-Semitism is rooted in deprivation. This lack of relationship is revealed by reading across the table, comparing the anti-Semitism scores in the columns with those in the row

Table 53 ANTI-SEMITISM BY ACADEMIC DEPRIVATION AND INTERPERSONAL VALUES FOR WHITE NON-JEWISH ADOLESCENTS

| And whose score on the interpersonal-values scale was: | Percent who are anti-Semitic for those whose level of academic deprivation was: | | | | | | | |
	Low 0	1	2	3	High 4	Total	Gamma	Xs
Low 0	* (1)	* (1)	* (2)	* (4)	82% (11)	68% (22)	+0.571	NS
1	* (3)	* (3)	* (3)	71% (14)	82% (11)	70% (37)	+0.444	NS
2	40% (10)	47% (15)	56% (16)	58% (26)	72% (47)	61% (124)	+0.334	NS
3	35% (37)	40% (43)	55% (66)	53% (75)	77% (96)	58% (342)	+0.406	0.001
4	27% (73)	48% (100)	59% (127)	72% (89)	64% (123)	56% (539)	+0.338	0.001
5	31% (94)	45% (118)	52% (126)	55% (115)	63% (112)	49% (597)	+0.273	0.001
High 6	33% (194)	40% (207)	39% (215)	46% (183)	62% (167)	44% (1,008)	+0.241	0.001
Total	32% (413)	43% (491)	49% (559)	55% (512)	67% (578)	51% (2,698)	+0.322	0.001
Gamma	+0.044	−0.076	−0.254	−0.185	−0.177	−0.191		
Xs	NS	NS	0.01	0.01	0.10	0.001		

* Too few cases for stable percentage.
NS—Not significant.

labeled "Total" at the bottom. If interpersonal values were the link between deprivation and anti-Semitism, the five percentages in each row should be approximately the same, or at least not as diverse as those in the "Total" row. For example, all teenagers scoring 3 on interpersonal values should have approximately the same likelihood of being anti-Semitic regardless of their levels of academic deprivation. This, however, is not what Table 53 indicates. Instead, deprivation produces as much variation in prejudice when interpersonal values are controlled as when they are not. The proportions manifesting anti-Semitism for the five levels of deprivation among those scoring highest (6) on interpersonal values, for example, are 33, 40, 39, 46, and 62 percent. These scores are approximately the same as those for all students ("Total") regardless of interpersonal values scores, namely 32, 43, 49, 55, and 67 percent. This is also true for students receiving other scores on the interpersonal values scale. This table indicates, then, that although the deprived are less likely to hold high interpersonal values, this does not explain why they are more anti-Semitic.

The question remains: Do interpersonal values have any *independent* effects on prejudice or was the relationship seen earlier merely an artifact produced because those scoring high in interpersonal values are also more privileged? This question is answered by reading down each column in the table. If interpersonal values are related to prejudice only because they are related to deprivation, then anti-Semitism scores in each column should be approximately the same regardless of levels of interpersonal values.

Reading down the columns, it is evident that at each level of academic deprivation, there is still some relation between interpersonal values and anti-Semitism. However, the relationships are smaller (except in column 2) than the relation in the "Total" column. This tells us that while having interpersonal values exerts some independent reducing influence on anti-Semitism, its influence is less than might be surmised by looking only at the two-variable relation between interpersonal values and prejudice. In other words, part of the power of interpersonal values to predict prejudice comes from their being associated with academic privilege. Although interpersonal values show some independent effect upon prejudice, it is not the case, to repeat, that less acceptance of interpersonal values provides the reason the academically deprived are more anti-Semitic.

While the task of interpreting the relation between academic deprivation and anti-Semitism remains, our exploration of the association between enlightened values and prejudice has borne fruit. Our study, as no single study, is capable of offering a definitive answer. The message which comes through with clarity and consistency is that the failure to internalize enlightened values is not a major source of teenage anti-Semitism. The promulgation of enlightened values as a means to combat this form of prejudice is unlikely to be harmful and may perhaps do some slight good. Judging from the evidence we have developed, however, it does not afford the leverage to make serious inroads into the problem.

Cognitive Sophistication

The final proposition we wish to test is that the academically deprived are more susceptible and the academically privileged less prone to anti-Semitism because of differences in their levels of cognitive sophistication.

Prejudice is an inherently complex phenomenon. Highly developed powers of reasoning are required to recognize it, to judge it for what it is, and to reject it. Awareness of stereotyping and sensitivity to its dangers are called for. Awareness of the sometimes subtle distinction between relative and absolute differences is required as is an avoidance of the pitfall of automatically assigning to particular members of a group traits or characteristics which characterize the group as a whole only to a degree. An understanding of the cultural, historical, and social forces at work that make for group differences is also demanded as well as being knowledgeable and sophisticated enough to separate true differences from false ones.

Having the cognitive capacity to do all these things does not necessarily guarantee freedom from prejudice. Circumstances can be imagined, for example, where peer group pressure might be a more powerful stimulant to prejudice than reason and restraint against prejudice. Nevertheless, a cognitively sophisticated understanding of prejudice would appear a necessary, if not a sufficient, condition for its prevention.

Cognitive sophistication, however, is not something that one is simply born with or without. Whatever innate capacity is present, it must be nourished, a process which occurs to a large extent within the schools. In the present context, it seems reasonable to expect that the academically privileged will have developed cognitive sophistication better than the academically deprived. If so, an absence of cognitive sophistication could be the factor linking academic deprivation and anti-Semitism for which we have been searching.

Our data afford no direct means to test this possibility. No test of reasoning power was included in the data collection instruments simply because we had not anticipated needing it when the study was designed. Fortunately, however, three indirect indications of cognitive sophistication are present in the questionnaire items and they provide a basis for exploration, if not for thorough test.

The first of these indications is how much interest and involvement these adolescents exhibit in intellectual pursuits. Presumably the more intellectually alive and alert a youngster, the broader his vision will be, the better he will be able to understand his world, and, in the present context, the more capable he will be of recognizing prejudice for what it is and be armed to avoid becoming prejudiced.

The questionnaires afforded five indications of teenagers' intellectual interests and activities: liking science, liking poetry, valuing the ability to think clearly, reading books for pleasure, and perceiving teachers as people whose ideas about things matter. We judged teenagers' intellectual commitment to be the greater, the more of these things they like or do. Assigning one point for each of these items answered affirmatively, a scale of intellectual commitment was created ranging from 0 (low) to 5 (high).

A second indirect measure of cognitive sophistication included in the research instruments was Gough's flexibility scale.[30] This scale measures one's willingness or unwillingness to entertain new and complicated ideas and to risk uncertainty and ambiguity in the pursuit of such ideas. Included in the scale are such items as "For most questions there is just one right answer once a person is able to get all the facts" and "I often wish people would be more definite about things." The scale ranges from 0 (low flexibility) to 3 (high flexibility).[31]

The third set of items that we propose to use to indicate relative cognitive sophistication concern interpretations of human nature. Four such items were included in the questionnaires.[32] They are:

Most people are honest chiefly through fear of getting caught.
Most people inwardly dislike putting themselves out to help other people.
Most people make friends because friends are likely to be useful to them.
I commonly wonder what hidden reason another person may have for doing something nice for me.

Taken at face value, acceptance of these items appears to afford more a measure of cynicism about human nature than of a lack of cognitive sophistication. We decided to use them as a back-up indicator of cognitive sophistication because we assumed that a reasoning person would find them too simplistic to accept even if he were skeptical about human nature. Also, agreement with these items is associated with scoring low on the index of intellectual pursuits and the flexibility scale. To combine these items into a scale, one point is assigned for agreement with each, creating a scale running from 0 (low cynicism) to 4 (high cynicism).

Table 54 reports the relations between these three measures of cognitive sophistication and academic deprivation. In all three towns, a strong and highly consistent relation is shown between academic deprivation and intellectual values. Likewise, with increasing deprivation teenagers are moderately and consistently more prone to a simplistic view of human nature. Flexibility shows less consistent and less significant relations, although in Commutertown the relation is of moderate strength. Our expectation, then, that academic privilege and cognitive sophistication would go together is on the whole confirmed.

But not only are these measures of cognitive sophistication associated with academic deprivation and privilege, they are also associated with anti-Semitism—strongly in Commutertown, and moderately in Oceanville and

Table 54 COGNITIVE SOPHISTICATION ITEMS BY ACADEMIC DEPRIVATION FOR WHITE NON-JEWISH ADOLESCENTS

Percent who score high on scales of cognitive sophistication whose academic deprivation score was:

| | Low | | | | High | | |
	0	1	2	3	4	Gamma	Xs
Intellectual values							
Commutertown	57% (90)	48% (134)	31% (134)	25% (135)	11% (169)	−0.432	0.001
Oceanville	66% (104)	40% (114)	27% (129)	21% (110)	19% (126)	−0.438	0.001
Central City	57% (213)	52% (235)	28% (267)	29% (247)	12% (249)	−0.397	0.001
Gough flexibility scale:							
Commutertown	42% (84)	40% (118)	32% (124)	21% (122)	25% (136)	−0.211	0.01
Oceanville	32% (91)	18% (104)	21% (126)	25% (102)	16% (116)	−0.148	NS
Central City	24% (203)	18% (223)	18% (242)	18% (230)	18% (222)	−0.094	NS
Cynicism about human nature:							
Commutertown	28% (83)	38% (126)	43% (133)	63% (130)	67% (159)	+0.276	0.001
Oceanville	32% (102)	36% (111)	48% (129)	56% (110)	61% (122)	+0.249	0.001
Central City	54% (205)	62% (228)	70% (259)	75% (240)	85% (240)	+0.239	0.001

NS—Not significant.

Central City (see Table 55). The greater the interest in intellectual pursuits of teenagers, the more their cognitive flexibility, and the less simplistic their views about human nature, the less their anti-Semitism. The relationships for Central City are slightly erratic for those scoring lowest on the scale of intellectual interests. With this one exception, however, each increment in sophistication in all subtables consistently produces a reduction in anti-Semitism.

Table 55   ANTI-SEMITISM BY THREE MEASURES OF COGNITIVE SOPHISTICATION FOR WHITE NON-JEWISH ADOLESCENTS

Percent who are anti-Semitic for those whose interest in intellectual pursuits was:

| | Low | | | | | High | | |
	0	1	2	3	4	5	Gamma	Xs
Commutertown	88%	84%	72%	65%	54%	45%	−0.369	0.001
	(24)	(91)	(185)	(182)	(144)	(69)		
Oceanville	93%	72%	56%	51%	49%	37%	−0.266	0.001
	(14)	(58)	(158)	(160)	(134)	(63)		
Central City	31%	49%	51%	41%	32%	31%	−0.200	0.001
	(29)	(116)	(286)	(391)	(306)	(126)		
Gough flexibility scale:								
Commutertown	82%	80%	70%	48%			−0.427	0.001
	(11)	(109)	(311)	(183)				
Oceanville	69%	63%	55%	43%			−0.240	0.02
	(13)	(101)	(311)	(118)				
Central City	65%	45%	41%	34%			−0.142	0.02
	(17)	(285)	(641)	(219)				
Cynicism about human nature:								
Commutertown	48%	57%	74%	80%	82%		+0.396	0.001
	(138)	(185)	(168)	(108)	(66)			
Oceanville	31%	51%	59%	69%	74%		+0.387	0.001
	(125)	(182)	(126)	(94)	(49)			
Central City	26%	30%	40%	50%	53%		+0.273	0.001
	(130)	(227)	(357)	(304)	(197)			

Still to be explored, however, is the underlying process at work. Is the causal nexus from academic deprivation to a lack of cognitive sophistication to anti-Semitism? Is the relation between cognitive sophistication and anti-Semitism a result of both having their source in academic deprivation? Or do academic deprivation and cognitive sophistication influence anti-Semitism independently of one another?

Table 56 ANTI-SEMITISM BY COGNITIVE SOPHISTICATION
(COMPOSITE MEASURE) FOR WHITE NON-JEWISH ADOLESCENTS

Percent who are anti-Semitic for those whose
level of cognitive sophistication was:

	Low 0	1	2	3	4	5	6	7	8	9	10	High 11	Gamma	Xs
Commutertown	* (0)	* (4)	86% (14)	85% (46)	80% (55)	84% (80)	78% (113)	61% (85)	49% (73)	40% (70)	29% (24)	* (9)	−0.505	0.001
Oceanville	* (1)	* (8)	75% (12)	69% (29)	70% (57)	67% (79)	61% (77)	45% (96)	43% (76)	39% (66)	23% (22)	* (2)	−0.367	0.001
Central City	* (0)	* (9)	59% (39)	56% (102)	57% (181)	42% (184)	42% (206)	32% (173)	29% (118)	22% (68)	19% (21)	0% (10)	−0.312	0.001

* Too few cases for stable percentage.

To find out, the joint influence of academic deprivation and cognitive sophistication on anti-Semitism must now be examined. Because three measures of cognitive sophistication have been used, a single summary measure must first be developed. This measure is created by simply adding the scales used thus far (the intellectual-values scale is first collapsed to a four-point scale to give each scale more equal value, and the cynicism scale is reversed), resulting in a twelve-point index. Table 56, reporting the relationship between this scale and anti-Semitism, shows that our three indicators of cognitive sophistication have a powerful effect upon prejudice when combined. In Central City, the effect is only moderate, but in the other two communities it is strong, producing proportions in Commutertown ranging consistently from 29 percent anti-Semitic among those most sophisticated to 86 percent among the least cognitively sophisticated and in Oceanville from 23 percent to 75 percent, with gammas respectively of -0.505 and -0.367.

The simultaneous effect of academic deprivation and cognitive sophistication on anti-Semitism is reported in Table 57. What we find essentially is a mutual muting effect. That is to say, the power of cognitive sophistication to predict anti-Semitism is dampened when academic deprivation is taken into account. In turn, the relationship between academic deprivation and anti-Semitism is weakened when cognitive sophistication is controlled for.

The dampening effect of academic deprivation can be seen by reading down the columns of Table 57. Note the greater strength and consistency of the relation between a lack of cognitive sophistication and anti-Semitism in the "Total" column than in the columns controlling for academic deprivation. Reading now across the rows of the table, note that the association between academic deprivation and anti-Semitism is greater and more consistent when cultural sophistication is not controlled (see "Total" row) than when it is controlled (other rows).

The meaning of this unanticipated result is that our measures of cognitive sophistication and academic deprivation are overlapping and thus tapping the same phenomenon. In other words, our measure of cognitive sophistication, rather than being a distinct variable which is a product of academic privilege as we had expected, turns out to be essentially another way of measuring the same thing that our scale of academic privilege measures. To be academically deprived, then, is in effect to be "cognitively unsophisticated."[33]

All in all, these results afford strong support for a theory of adolescent prejudice that conceives it as rooted in inadequate cognitive capability. Not only does the theory gain support from different measures of cognitive sophistication but by its being confirmed consistently in three samples. Indeed, given the differences in the social composition of the three samples, the consistency of the results suggests that they may be generalizable to all adolescent populations.[34]

Impressive as the results are, however, a note of caution must be sounded

Table 57   ANTI-SEMITISM BY ACADEMIC DEPRIVATION AND COGNITIVE SOPHISTICATION FOR WHITE NON-JEWISH ADOLESCENTS

	Percent who are anti-Semitic for those whose academic deprivation scores were:							
And whose scores on cognitive sophistication were:	Low 0	1	2	3	High 4	Total	Gamma	Xs
0	* (0)	* (0)	* (0)	* (1)	* (1)	* (2)	. . .	. . .
1	* (0)	* (0)	* (2)	* (8)	91% (11)	71% (21)	+0.714	NS
2	* (2)	* (4)	* (5)	71% (14)	72% (32)	68% (65)	−0.015	NS
3	46% (11)	61% (18)	59% (34)	64% (44)	75% (64)	66% (177)	+0.257	NS
4	53% (15)	57% (28)	62% (71)	68% (68)	66% (93)	64% (293)	+0.101	NS
5	47% (36)	43% (53)	52% (82)	60% (75)	70% (76)	57% (343)	+0.259	0.05
6	44% (52)	57% (83)	58% (84)	51% (87)	68% (68)	56% (396)	+0.129	NS
7	29% (72)	35% (84)	44% (78)	57% (60)	61% (49)	43% (354)	+0.330	0.001
8	27% (59)	36% (73)	41% (54)	34% (47)	78% (27)	39% (267)	+0.289	0.001
9	28% (71)	39% (56)	32% (37)	38% (21)	39% (13)	34% (204)	+0.108	NS
10	7% (28)	46% (13)	31% (13)	* (8)	* (4)	24% (67)	+0.431	0.05
11	* (8)	* (8)	* (2)	* (2)	* (1)	10% (21)	+0.684	0.001
Total	32% (413)	43% (491)	49% (559)	55% (512)	67% (578)	51% (2698)	+0.332	0.001
Gamma	−0.340	−0.225	−0.216	−0.261	−0.137	−0.317		
Xs	0.01	0.01	0.05	0.01	NS	0.001		

* Too few cases for stable percentage.
NS—Not significant.

about concluding too much from them. What we have failed to do and are incapable of doing with the data at hand is to validate thoroughly the measures we have used to indicate teenagers' relative cognitive capabilities. As noted earlier, no direct means to test reasoning powers were included in the data collection instruments. The indirect measures we employed correlate with themselves, and in addition, they seem to meet the criterion of face validity. Still, without a validating criterion more directly and closely related to the phenomenon purported to be measured, it is not possible to be absolutely sure. Although unlikely, it is possible that our measures are not really tapping cognitive ability at all. Under the circumstances, it seems prudent to withhold unqualified proclamation of the significance of these results until they are confirmed in new research using more direct measures of cognitive reasoning.

A further note of caution which the skeptic is also likely to demand is that the present analysis may have proved, not that the more cognitively sophisticated are less prejudiced, but simply that they were canny enough to figure out the purpose of the questionnaire and give the "right" answers to make themselves appear unprejudiced. The proponents of this conclusion would argue that the sophisticated are as deeply prejudiced as anyone else but cleverer at covering their tracks. This is certainly a possibility and one which merits research to conceptualize, measure, and, hopefully, combat such subtle forms of prejudice. But we also argue that if cognitive sophistication does, indeed, militate against more overt expressions of prejudice, then this is in itself something laudable rather than something to be decried. If the cognitively sophisticated have a desire not to *appear* prejudiced, it seems more likely than unlikely that they will also have a desire not to *be* prejudiced. To be sure, cognitive sophistication may simply drive prejudice underground, but if it leads people to repudiate prejudice in public, it may also create dissonance against acting prejudiced in more covert ways. In the end, this is a matter which should be tested by actual efforts to combat prejudice, however, rather than being left to speculation.

Summary and Conclusions

To find, as we did in Chapter 2, that prejudice tends to be socially located among less privileged teenagers was scarcely a startling result. Most students of prejudice have made similar findings while working with different populations from ours.

Consensus about the relative social location of prejudice, however, has been accompanied by considerable disagreement in interpreting why that condition should apply. The present chapter has been devoted to trying to sort out the disagreement.

Our explorations have led us to consider several theories purporting to explain the social location of prejudice, all of which had received some support in earlier studies of adults. Testing these theories with data on adolescents has produced mixed results.

We found no support for the frustration–aggression theory of prejudice. We acknowledge that in one and possibly two instances this might be the fault of our measures rather than the theory. In the end, however, the failure to establish any relationships by approaching the question from four different vantage points led to an ultimate judgment against the theory. These teenagers experience frustration to be sure, but we could find nothing to suggest that they cope with it through hostility toward Jews.

That prejudice breeds prejudice, or at least is nourished and sustained by it, received support from the data. Teenagers whose close friends are anti-Semitic show a tendency, although not an overwhelming one, to be anti-Semitic themselves. This could be a result of prejudiced teenagers seeking each other out. More likely, we concluded, it comes about because academically deprived youngsters seek out their own kind and their own kind, like themselves, tend also to be prejudiced. While the effect of associating with prejudiced others is to exacerbate one's own prejudices, such association was not found to be the underlying reason why prejudice tends to be located among the less privileged.

The theory that the cause of prejudice in the academically deprived lies in their failure to be socialized to enlightened values also proved fruitless or almost so. Although the academically privileged are somewhat more prone to acknowledge democratic values, we found only slight evidence that such values are an independent stimulus to abandoning prejudice or to never taking it on. We concluded, therefore, that there is little likelihood that much progress toward the goal of prejudice reduction can be achieved through education to democratic ideals alone.

By far the most powerful result of the analysis was the strong, albeit indirect, confirmation afforded the cognitive theory of prejudice. The idea that prejudice is rooted in a failure cognitively to recognize and understand it, and therefore to be armed to combat it, has been effectively argued and demonstrated to have power in accounting for the anti-Semitism of adults. Our results show that cognitive inadequacy is also an important ingredient in adolescent prejudice.

These results have practical significance for efforts to combat prejudice. Before commenting on them, however, there are still unanswered questions to be addressed about the nature and sources of adolescent prejudice. Is it produced in the same fashion among black as among white teenagers? Why is it greater in communities having a Jewish presence? Are the dynamics of racial prejudice the same or different from anti-Semitism? The latter two questions are taken up in the succeeding two chapters. The question of prejudice formation in blacks, since it involves essentially a replication of Chapters 2 and 3 for black rather than white adolescents, is reserved for Appendix B.

Before proceeding, there is one loose end to be taken up—to see if the same results are achieved if we substitute other measures of anti-Semitism for the scale of anti-Semitic belief. We shall not report the details on the null findings since they correspond with the null findings using the belief measure. That is to say, frustration-aggression and enlightened-value theories gain no more support using the social-distance measures or the measure of hostility toward Jews than they did using the index of anti-Semitism.

Comparatively, how anti-Semitic a teenager's friends are is more strongly associated with the index of anti-Semitism than with the other measures of prejudice. As can be seen in Table 58, there is some tendency for hostility and social distance to increase, the greater the level of anti-Semitism of friends. However, the gammas are very small and they are significant only for hostility and for social distance to a high-status Jew.

It is also the case that a lack of cognitive sophistication is more strongly

Table 58   SOCIAL DISTANCE AND HOSTILITY TO JEWS BY EXTENT OF FRIENDS' ANTI-SEMITISM FOR WHITE NON-JEWISH ADOLESCENTS

(All three communities combined)

| | Low | | | | | High | | | |
Level of friends' anti-Semitism	1	2	3	4	5	6	7	Gamma	Xs
Hostility to Jews: Percent unfriendly to quite unfriendly	36% (117)	34% (684)	35% (1,036)	38% (491)	51% (120)	45% (29)	* (4)	0.081	0.01
Percent socially distant toward high-status Jews	15% (117)	19% (676)	19% (1,020)	24% (477)	34% (115)	37% (27)	* (4)	0.094	0.01
Percent socially distant toward low-status Jews	34% (117)	41% (675)	38% (1,020)	41% (476)	41% (117)	41% (29)	* (4)	0.037	NS

* Too few cases for stable percentage.
NS—Not significant.

Table 59 HOSTILITY AND SOCIAL DISTANCE TO JEWS BY COGNITIVE SOPHISTICATION FOR WHITE NON-JEWISH ADOLESCENTS

(All three communities combined)

Level of cognitive sophistication:

	Low 0	1	2	3	4	5	6	7	8	9	10	High 11	Gamma	Xs
Hostility to Jews: Percent unfriendly to quite unfriendly	* (1)	52% (21)	50% (66)	51% (177)	45% (294)	43% (344)	38% (396)	29% (353)	24% (270)	28% (208)	25% (68)	19% (21)	−0.246	0.001
Percent socially distant toward high-status Jews	* (1)	35% (20)	31% (64)	35% (174)	32% (291)	26% (342)	21% (394)	14% (348)	10% (270)	9% (201)	7% (68)	0% (21)	−0.323	0.001
Percent socially distant toward low-status Jews	* (1)	50% (20)	57% (65)	56% (173)	52% (292)	45% (338)	42% (395)	35% (350)	28% (268)	25% (201)	21% (67)	24% (21)	−0.238	0.001

* Too few cases for stable percentage.

associated with anti-Semitism as measured by the index of anti-Semitic belief than as measured by hostility or social distance (see Table 59). Unlike the relationships between these other measures of prejudice and the levels of prejudice of friends, however, the associations with cognitive sophistication are all quite consistent, moderate to strong in strength, and in all cases significant, thus confirming that the earlier findings are not an artifact of the measure used. In sum, among the range of factors tested, a failure of cognitive functioning emerges from our analysis as the most important source of anti-Semitism.

4 The Effects of a Jewish Presence

This study, it will be recalled, was especially designed to allow the exploration of the effects of a Jewish presence on anti-Semitism. Other things being equal, are the character and incidence of anti-Semitism the same or different when Jews are or are not present in a context? Does the size of the presence make a difference? And, if there are effects, how exactly are they produced and what is implied thereby for the control of anti-Semitism?

Thus far the analysis has touched lightly and intermittently on these questions. Attending to them systematically was postponed so as to address first the more general questions about the sources of anti-Semitism. Having gone as far with that task as the data allow, the effects of Jewish presence may now be confronted.

In designing the study, we anticipated being able to demonstrate that the main effect of a Jewish presence is to reduce anti-Semitism. Previous studies have shown consistently that the incidence of anti-Semitism is less among non-Jews who are in contact with Jews than among non-Jews who are not.[1] We saw no reason to expect a different result in our own inquiry.

Like most other students of prejudice, we had also come to assume that there is no factual basis for prejudice; the victims of prejudice are not among its progenitors. From this premise, it followed that the opportunity for non-Jews to meet and to get to know Jewish youngsters could have no other effect than to demonstrate how ridiculous anti-Semitism is. Stating it this way makes us out more naive perhaps than we actually were. Nevertheless, it is evident that such wishful thinking has been an element in much research on prejudice, as witnessed by the relative absence of research to determine precisely what the effects of presence might be.

The data at hand allow an examination of the matter from several perspectives. We can ask, as previous studies have done, about the effects on anti-Semitism of the nature and extent of actual interpersonal contact between Jewish and non-Jewish adolescents. We can also examine the effects

103

of context on anti-Semitism; that is, the effects of the existence or absence and of the size of a Jewish presence in a community, leaving aside the extent of actual social interaction. We shall take up the two questions in sequence, beginning with the contextual one.

Contextual Effects

Earlier it was found, contrary to expectations, that the incidence of attitudinal anti-Semitism is greatest in the community with the largest Jewish presence (Commutertown) and least in the town with a negligible Jewish presence (Central City). The proportion of anti-Semites among white non-Jewish teenagers was 66 percent in Commutertown, 53 percent in Oceanville, and 41 percent in Central City.

These differences, while they are sizable and statistically significant, allow no easy conclusion to be drawn. They may be attributable to the varying sizes of the Jewish presence in the three communities. Or they may result from other ways in which the three communities differ from one another. For example, there may be many more non-Jewish teenagers in Commutertown and Oceanville than in Central City with the traits found earlier generally to foster anti-Semitism. If this is the case, it could be that these "other factors" rather than the presence or absence of Jews account for the community differences in anti-Semitism.

Nonexperimental data such as ours provide no basis for deciding unequivocally between the two alternatives, and there is no practical way to conduct an experiment. Even if it were possible, it would be artificial to create three communities matched in every way except for the number of Jews in their populations. Longitudinal data from the three sample communities on the development of non-Jewish attitudes toward Jews from earliest childhood would probably provide a more adequate basis for drawing inferences than does the information at hand. But such data are not available and not readily collected. Under the circumstances, the best we can do is to infer, using the information available, just what may be going on to account for the differences in anti-Semitism in the three towns.

The burden of the evidence, as we interpret it, is that the Jewish presence in Commutertown and Oceanville is the source, in large part, of the greater incidence of anti-Semitism in these two communities than in Central City. We draw this conclusion because we can muster no sound support for the thesis that there are other factors distinguishing the three communities which would account for the differences in anti-Semitism. Moreover, upon examination, there appear to be perfectly logical, though invalid, reasons why a Jewish presence of the kind that exists in Commutertown and Oceanville may be instrumental in nourishing prejudice.

The "other factors" thesis, to be true, would require the greater incidence in Commutertown and Oceanville than in Central City of one or a combination of factors, other than a Jewish presence, that produce anti-Semitism. Many of the factors which we have found thus far to be associated with anti-Semitism, however, are more in evidence in Central City than in the other two communities. On such measures of deprivation, for example, as income, average education, and distribution of incomes, Central City is less privileged than either Commutertown or Oceanville. Moreover, non-Jewish teenagers in Central City are slightly less likely to do well in school, to like school, or to aspire to college than their counterparts in the other two towns. On measures of cognitive sophistication, youngsters in the three towns show on the average about the same amount of flexibility of mind and interest in intellectual pursuits. Central City teenagers, however, tend to be more simplistic in their views of human nature. Judging only from the relative incidence in the three communities of factors found earlier to be predisposing to anti-Semitism, teenagers in Central City ought to have the highest anti-Semitism scores, not the lowest as they do.

More significantly, when differences in predisposing characteristics are taken into account, anti-Semitism scores continue to be higher in Commutertown and Oceanville than in Central City. Tabulations in Chapters 2 and 3, made there to explore other sources of anti-Semitism, can now be re-examined to study community effects on anti-Semitism. Table 30 from Chapter 2 is reproduced here as Table 60 to demonstrate how the re-examination may be pursued.

Originally, this table was constructed to test the proposition that anti-Semitism would be related to the likelihood of teenagers going to college: the greater the likelihood, the less the anti-Semitism. The proposition, it will be recalled, was confirmed in all three communities, as a reminding glance across the rows of the table reveals. Reading now down the columns

Table 60   ANTI-SEMITISM BY COLLEGE EXPECTATIONS FOR WHITE NON-JEWISH ADOLESCENTS

	To Go	Don't Know	Not to Go	Gamma	Xs
Commutertown	53% (335)	72% (193)	80% (225)	0.430	0.001
Oceanville	47% (319)	57% (151)	64% (142)	0.249	0.01
Central City	34% (445)	42% (451)	48% (430)	0.197	0.001

Percent who are anti-Semitic for those whose college expectations were:

of the table, which we did not purposefully do before, we see the effect of community on anti-Semitism with level of college potential controlled. In all columns—that is, in three out of a possible three comparisons—Central City teenagers are the least likely and Commutertown teenagers are the most likely to be anti-Semitic. Judging from this table, whatever it may be that is producing community differences, it is not the teenagers' college potential.

By making the same kind of comparisons using all the other tables in Chapters 2 and 3 in which results were presented separately by community, we can find out whether community continues to make a difference when the other factors explored in our earlier search for the sources of anti-Semitism are taken into account. Out of 129 comparisons which can be made through such a re-examination, Central City scores as least prone to anti-Semitism in 124 of them; that is, in 96 percent of the comparisons. As between Commutertown and Oceanville, anti-Semitism scores are higher in Commutertown in 125 out of 129 comparisons, suggesting that when there are a significant number of Jewish teenagers in a school setting, it still makes a difference how many there are. With more, there is a higher incidence of anti-Semitism.

This evidence does not deny the "other factors" thesis unequivocally, of course. It is possible that the three communities are distinguished in other ways which, had they been taken into account, would show the relation between size of a Jewish presence and anti-Semitism to be spurious.

We have not been able to find such an alternative explanation, however, and thus we are obliged to consider seriously that the gross effect of a Jewish presence may indeed be to generate rather than to reduce anti-Semitism, at least as it is measured by our index of anti-Semitism.

This is an unexpected finding of our study, wholly unanticipated in the original design. Consequently, in trying to account for it, there is no pre-specified theory to test. The explanation which emerges from piecing together a number of clues in the data is that where there is a Jewish presence, Jewish success is a major source of anti-Semitism. Tendencies toward clannishness also seem to be a characteristic of a Jewish presence that is responded to negatively, although clannishness is less significant probably than success in stimulating anti-Semitism.

Success as a Source of Anti-Semitism

The facts are that Jewish youngsters are on the average a lot more successful in academic life than their non-Jewish counterparts. This is true in Commutertown where over half the students are Jewish and in Oceanville where a quarter are, and it is even true of the 13 Jewish students in the Central City sample. As can be seen in Table 61, Jewish teenagers get better grades, spend more time working on studies, and are more active in school affairs. They are also more often enrolled in college programs and more likely by far to plan to go to college. Moreover, the parents of Jewish teenagers are on the average more affluent, better educated, and, judging from their greater concern to have their children go to college, more anxious for their children's success.

Our study did not include any self-conscious effort to learn whether non-Jewish students are aware of the greater average success of Jewish youngsters nor did we try directly to determine what response Jewish success induces. Fortunately, however, a number of items in the anti-Semitism battery touch on these matters, and it is possible to construct a reasonable portrait, albeit an incomplete one, of non-Jewish attitudes.

The prevailing imagery of the Jewish teenager, it will be recalled, is that he or she is above average both with respect to intellectuality and academic drive. A substantial majority in all three communities—83 percent in Commutertown, 82 percent in Oceanville, and 75 percent in Central City—agree that Jewish teenagers are quite intelligent and well informed. Almost as many—79 percent in Commutertown, 79 percent in Oceanville, and 67 percent in Central City—conceive of Jewish students as getting good grades; very few—17 percent in Commutertown, 15 percent in Oceanville, and 22 percent in Central City—think of Jews as giving up easily on hard problems, never seeming to try hard in school. On these items, the size of a Jewish presence in a community makes some difference in response; Jewish intellectuality and ambition are slightly more likely to be accepted in Commutertown and Oceanville than in Central City, but in all three communities the prevalent view is that Jewish teenagers are intelligent and ambitious.

But differences between the three communities in the response to Jewish success are substantially greater than in awareness of it. Five items in the anti-Semitism battery bear on how the performance and success of Jewish youngsters are responded to. These items have to do with whether or not Jewish teenagers are thought to be conceited ("Jews think they are better than others"), powerful ("Jews have too much say about what goes on in school"), sly ("Jews try to get ahead by 'buttering up' the teachers"), vain ("Jews are loud and 'show-offy'"), and bossy ("Jews force their beliefs and wishes on other students").

To hold such views, it seems to us, is to believe that Jewish youngsters have achieved their relative success through deceit and that they maintain it with arrogance and conceit. As Table 62 shows, the views are most widely held in Commutertown where acceptance ranges from 52 percent to

Table 61 SELECTED BACKGROUND CHARACTERISTICS OF
JEWISH AND WHITE NON-JEWISH ADOLESCENTS

	Jewish Teenagers	White Non-Jewish Teenagers	Difference	Xs
Percent with grade average of B or better:				
Commutertown	66% (840)	40% (776)	26	0.001
Oceanville	57% (281)	37% (617)	20	0.001
Central City	54% (13)	44% (1,364)	10	0.001
Percent who spend 1½ hours or more per day on homework:				
Commutertown	69% (842)	48% (779)	21	0.001
Oceanville	58% (282)	53% (618)	5	0.05
Central City	62% (13)	48% (1,369)	14	NS
Percent who are active in school affairs:				
Commutertown	20% (800)	9% (723)	11	0.001
Oceanville	17% (275)	15% (599)	2	NS
Central City	39% (13)	22% (1,326)	17	0.05
Percent who are enrolled in a college program:				
Commutertown	90% (809)	51% (739)	39	0.001
Oceanville	95% (283)	72% (610)	23	0.001
Central City	58% (12)	45% (1,301)	13	0.001
Percent who plan to go to college:				
Commutertown	89% (840)	45% (782)	44	0.001
Oceanville	82% (283)	52% (618)	30	0.001
Central City	62% (13)	34% (1,365)	28	NS

	Jewish Teenagers	White Non-Jewish Teenagers	Difference	Xs
Percent whose fathers earn a high income:				
Commutertown	80% (794)	32% (676)	48	0.001
Oceanville	59% (272)	27% (550)	32	0.001
Central City	55% (11)	6% (1,171)	49	0.001
Percent whose fathers attended at least *some* college:				
Commutertown	77% (828)	36% (750)	41	0.001
Oceanville	60% (281)	40% (607)	20	0.001
Central City	50% (12)	16% (1,337)	34	0.001
Percent whose mothers attended at least *some* college:				
Commutertown	63% (803)	25% (756)	38	0.001
Oceanville	40% (281)	28% (606)	12	0.001
Central City	39% (13)	10% (1,352)	29	0.001
Percent whose parents want teenager to attend college:				
Commutertown	99% (836)	81% (760)	18	0.001
Oceanville	99% (283)	84% (607)	15	0.001
Central City	83% (12)	69% (1,348)	14	NS

NS—Not significant.

70 percent. There is somewhat less acceptance in Oceanville: here the range is from 48 percent to 61 percent. And, in Central City, the range is considerably lower—from 26 percent to 35 percent. Judging from the results for Central City, it doesn't require a substantial Jewish presence for ill feelings about Jewish success to be expressed. Where substantial numbers of Jewish students are present, however, direct exposure to their success appears to exacerbate ill feelings markedly.

To some extent, this response probably has nothing to do with Jewish success. An imagery of the Jew as being too powerful, conceited, and sly is part of the grab bag of anti-Jewish stereotypes that those inclined toward anti-Semitism are prone to accept. This kind of cultural anti-Semitism tends to be immune to facts and can be expected to manifest itself even in settings where the Jewish population is notably less well-to-do than their non-Jewish counterparts. In the present data, part of the response is undoubtedly understandable in these terms, especially in Central City where there are not enough Jews for an anti-Semitic imagery to have an existential base.

Conceiving of anti-Semitism as solely cultural, however, affords no explantation of the considerably greater response to Jewish success where there is greater exposure to it. Where it is experienced directly, Jewish success is apparently a direct and powerful stimulus to anti-Semitism. Why?

Among those in the Jewish community and outside it who have been sensitive to the possibility that Jewish success may be a source of anti-Semitism, the common view has been that if success has this effect, it is because of envy and jealousy on the part of non-Jews. An essentially psychological explanation of prejudice, along the lines discussed earlier in Chapter 3, is adopted. Successful Jews in one's environment afford a ready scapegoat for those frustrated and struggling to contend with their own failures.

Table 62   ACCEPTANCE OF NEGATIVE STEREOTYPES OF JEWISH SUCCESS AMONG WHITE NON-JEWISH ADOLESCENTS

	Commutertown	Oceanville	Central City
Percent accepting stereotype that Jewish teenagers:			
Think they are better than others	70%	62%	35%
Have too much say about what goes on in school	70%	55%	26%
Try to get ahead by buttering up teachers	58%	60%	31%
Are loud and show-offy	66%	58%	33%
Force their beliefs and wishes on other students	52%	48%	34%
N =	(388)	(300)	(667)

Such an interpretation harbors the aforementioned element of wishful thinking to which victims and students of prejudice have been prone. The assumption is made implicitly that there can be no truth in the stereotype and the possibility that there might be is not seriously considered. This failure does not mean that the interpretation is necessarily wrong. Even if there were truth in the stereotype, the psychological mechanisms could still be at work in the way ascribed. The evidence has simply not existed, however, to say for sure whether or not they are. Our own evidence does not sustain such an interpretation, it will be recalled; none of the psychological measures examined were found to be associated with anti-Semitism in a significant way.

The alternative explanation is that the negative imagery is true, not absolutely, of course, but relatively. Perhaps successful Jewish teenagers tend, in fact, to be bossy, conceited, and sly, just as so many in Commutertown and Oceanville think them to be. The negative response, therefore, is not to an illusion but to a "fact."

There is no hard evidence in the data to support this explanation; no direct effort was made to test the "truth" content of these stereotypes. On the assumption that widespread acceptance of the negative stereotypes on the part of Jewish youth would constitute *prima facie* evidence of their truth, however, we did examine the responses of Jewish teenagers to the anti-Semitism battery. As can be seen in Table 63, Jewish youth reject the negative attributions, although it may be of some significance that the negative items that gain any support at all are those which bear on Jewish success. In Commutertown, for example, four of the five items interpreting Jewish success invidiously—Jews are conceited, powerful, sly, vain, and bossy—get as much as 20 percent agreement. In Oceanville, these items get less support but again they get more support than other negative items. This can hardly be taken as proof that there is "truth" in the stereotypes. On the other hand, it doesn't settle the matter by proving them false either.

Reflecting further on the alternatives, it seems unlikely that so many Commutertown and Oceanville teenagers are wholly fantasizing the negative attributions out of psychological need. It is conceivable, of course, that they are and that we failed to tap the crucial factor in any of our psychological measures. More likely, we suspect, there is some truth in these youngsters' perceptions but, because of prejudice, they are wrong in how they interpret what they see. Successful Jewish youngsters probably do exhibit these negative traits to a degree, not because they are Jewish but because they are successful. That is to say, successful teenagers, whatever their religion, may be prone to traits that are here attributed to these youngsters' being Jewish.

Young people can be conceited without having any grounds except their own ego needs to be so, and certainly there are other sources of conceit than academic success. In school settings, however, where academic achievement is so highly valued, the probabilities are that the conceited will be found especially among the academically successful. Similarly, someone without leadership qualities may try to throw his weight around and thereby earn for himself the epithet "bossy." Generally speaking, however, being or appearing to be bossy is more often a characteristic of leaders in a social group than of followers. And, of course, leadership and being successful

Table 63   ACCEPTANCE OF ANTI-SEMITIC STEREOTYPES
BY JEWISH YOUTH

Percent who accept the stereotype that Jews are:

	Commutertown	%	Oceanville	%
Majority stereotypes accepted by 50% or more:	Intelligent	91	Intelligent	95
	School Spirit	83	School spirit	84
	Ambitious	74	Ambitious	77
	Athletic	70	Athletic	68
			Religious	58
Stereotype held by a substantial minority (accepted by from 25% to 49%)	Religious	49		
Minority stereotypes accepted by less than 25%	*Bossy	24	*Bossy	21
	*Sly	23	*Selfish	16
	*Powerful	23	*Conceited	14
	*Conceited	21	Different	14
	Different	17	*Sly	13
	*Selfish	17	*Powerful	12
	*Gaudy	16	*Pushy	8
	*Vain	12	*Gaudy	8
	*Unfriendly	12	*Immoral	7
	*Pushy	10	*Vain	6
	*Immoral	9	*Sloppy	5
	*Troublemakers	4	*Unfriendly	4
	*Sloppy	3	*Untrustworthy	4
	*Untrustworthy	2	*Quitters	2
	*Quitters	1	*Troublemakers	1
Mean proportion accepting outrightly negative stereotypes		13%		9%
N=	(437)		(146)	

* Stereotypes judged to be outrightly negative.

academically also tend to go together. The image of "buttering up" teachers also seems likely to be associated with the successful more than with the unsuccessful. The less successful in school probably have the greater need to "butter up" teachers but the more successful are likely to be the ones who give the impression of doing so, simply because they are more likely to seek teachers out. Power, too, goes with success and for those without both thinking that the successful are "too" powerful has, for them, a basis in fact.

The insidiousness of prejudice as well as the importance of knowledge and well developed reasoning powers to overcome it are especially revealed here. In a school setting where the more successful students tend to be Presbyterian or Episcopalian (as the more academically successful youngsters in Central City tend to be, incidentally), it would never occur to anyone to attribute tendencies toward conceit, vanity, or slyness on such students' part to their religion. There simply isn't that kind of anti-Episcopalianism or anti-Presbyterianism in the culture to cause an observer to falsely identify these traits as having their roots in religion.

Where a successful Jewish youngster exhibits these traits, however, even the unprejudiced observer must contend with the ready explanation afforded by the prevailing cultural anti-Semitism. It requires extraordinary sophistication not to fall victim to its appeal. A profound understanding of the nature of prejudice is required. One must be discerning enough to recognize the true source of the disliked traits. Some knowledge about the historical and social forces making for group differences is called for as well. For those without such sophistication, the barriers to falling prey to prejudice and, in this instance, feeling quite vindicated in doing so are simply not there.

Or so it would seem on the grounds of logic and common sense. To judge scientifically the correctness of these observations and their generalizability to other settings in which especially successful Jews are present will require other research than ours. If confirmed and found more widely applicable, it is evident that they would present new and especially difficult problems to the cause of prejudice reduction, but perhaps also new and exciting opportunities. We shall comment later on the possible implications.

Clannishness as a Source of Anti-Semitism

Anti-Semitism appears also to be nourished in settings where Jews are present by the tendency on their part to want to associate with other Jews and of Jewish parents to want their children to date, perforce to marry, Jews. Tendencies toward clannishness are not unique to Jews. All teenagers

in our samples manifest the inclination in one way or another. Yet clannishness, at least when it is perceived among others rather than in one's
own group, tends to be viewed, not favorably, but with distaste. And when
the clannishness is practiced by Jews, prejudice aggravates this negative
response.

Exploration of clannishness as a possible additional source of anti-
Semitism was stimulated by the finding, shown in Table 64, that in Commutertown and Oceanville anti-Semitism scores are greater the higher the
teenagers' grade in school, while the opposite pattern prevails in Central
City. The results for Commutertown and Oceanville took us by surprise.
Based on what had been learned about academic performance, cognitive
sophistication, and prejudice, we had expected a decline in anti-Semitism
with greater schooling in all three communities. More schooling, we thought,
ought to produce greater academic privilege and cognitive sophistication,
and consequently, less anti-Semitism, not more. Why, then, the discrepant
findings in Commutertown and Oceanville?

Part of the reason, we surmised, might be that the discrepancy between
Jewish and non-Jewish success grows with greater schooling. We found no
such tendency in Oceanville. Relatively, Jewish and non-Jewish teenagers
there differ from each other on the several indicators of success as much in
the 8th grade as they do in the 12th (Table 65). In Commutertown, the
discrepancy in status between Jewish and non-Jewish youngsters is greater
in most comparisons at the 12th than at the 8th grade. The largest discrepancies, however, tend to occur at the 10th rather than the 12th grade.
Thus, there is no evidence in Oceanville and inconsistent evidence in Commutertown that Jewish success is the source of the increase in anti-Semitism
with greater schooling in these communities.

It seemed also possible that the greater anti-Semitism is a result of
Jewish success becoming more visible and salient as teenagers approach
college age. In particular, older students more than younger ones might be

Table 64   ANTI-SEMITISM BY GRADE IN SCHOOL
FOR WHITE NON-JEWISH ADOLESCENTS

| | Percent who are anti-Semitic for those whose grade in school is: | | | | |
	8th	10th	12th	Gamma	Xs
Commutertown	53% (253)	71% (303)	74% (199)	+0.309	0.001
Oceanville	46% (202)	55% (239)	60% (171)	+0.190	0.02
Central City	44% (468)	44% (475)	33% (388)	−0.141	0.01

expected to be more aware of the large discrepancy between the proportions of Jewish and non-Jewish adolescents expecting to go to college. Unfortunately, the data do not allow us to establish whether or not such increased visibility occurs. Consequently, the surmise that increased awareness of Jewish success is an element in the greater incidence of anti-Semitism among older Commutertown and Oceanville teenagers must remain a speculation.

We were led to consider clannishness as a possible additional explanatory variable simply because it occurred to us that one of the things that happens to teenagers as they progress from the 8th grade to the 12th is that more and more of them enter the age of dating. Indeed, dating starts early. In the three communities, an average of 50 percent of white non-Jewish youngsters are dating by the 8th grade. By the 10th grade, the proportion has increased to 76 percent and by the 12th grade to 90 percent. Among Jewish teenagers, 44 percent are dating by the 8th grade, 80 percent by the 10th grade, and 96 percent by the 12th grade.

The advent of dating and the prospects of marriage that accompany it could trigger and make operative, especially among teenagers' parents, latent or subdued tendencies toward clannishness. Where it wasn't paid much mind before, now it matters if one's son or daughter begins to go around with someone who is of a different ethnic background, race, or religion. Concern of the latter kind, we anticipated, would grow disproportionately more in Commutertown and Oceanville than in Central City because of the Jewish presence in these communities.

If so, the greater anti-Semitism of older teenagers in Commutertown and Oceanville could be the product of growing clannish tendencies, produced out of discussion in non-Jewish homes as to why Jewish friendships and dates ought to be avoided. It could be also contributed to, of course, by an increase in clannishness among Jewish parents and their children that is responded to negatively by non-Jews.

Looking first to see whether non-Jewish teenagers and their parents become more clannish as the age of dating unfolds, we find that they do (see Table 66). The proportion of teenagers reporting parental concern that their friends and dates be of the same religion increases from the 8th to the 10th to the 12th grade in all three communities. The trend is more marked for dates than for friends. It is also more marked the larger the Jewish presence. Note, for example, that in Commutertown there is a 21 percentage point increase between the 8th and the 12th grades in the proportion of teenagers saying that their parents want them to date someone of their own religion. In Oceanville, the increase is 17 percentage points; in Central City, 12 percentage points.

Teenagers in all communities are less likely to report themselves to be

Table 65   RELATIVE STATUS OF JEWISH AND WHITE NON-JEWISH
ADOLESCENTS BY GRADE IN SCHOOL

	Commutertown			Oceanville		
	J*	N-J†	Difference	J*	N-J†	Difference
Percent with grade average of B or better:						
8th grade	66% (331)	44% (267)	22	73% (58)	46% (205)	27
10th grade	68% (296)	37% (306)	31	49% (134)	28% (240)	21
12th grade	64% (213)	39% (203)	25	61% (89)	38% (172)	23
Percent who spend 1½ hours or more per day on homework:						
8th grade	60% (332)	47% (266)	13	53% (59)	50% (205)	3
10th grade	77% (297)	50% (309)	27	66% (133)	59% (241)	7
12th grade	70% (213)	48% (204)	22	50% (90)	48% (172)	2
Percent who are active in school affairs:						
8th grade	19% (318)	7% (251)	12	21% (58)	23% (201)	−2
10th grade	17% (279)	10% (282)	7	19% (127)	11% (230)	8
12th grade	26% (203)	7% (190)	19	13% (90)	10% (168)	3
Percent who are enrolled in a college program:						
8th grade	85% (301)	54% (229)	31	97% (59)	74% (200)	23
10th grade	93% (295)	51% (309)	42	93% (134)	72% (240)	21
12th grade	91% (213)	46% (201)	45	96% (90)	71% (170)	25
Percent who plan to go to college:						
8th grade	88% (333)	49% (270)	39	81% (59)	54% (205)	27
10th grade	85% (204)	39% (309)	46	75% (134)	47% (241)	28
12th grade	95% (213)	49% (203)	46	92% (90)	58% (172)	34

	Commutertown			Oceanville		
	J*	N-J†	Difference	J*	N-J†	Difference
Percent whose fathers earn a high income:						
8th grade	82% (318)	37% (229)	45	63% (59)	21% (185)	42
10th grade	75% (277)	23% (260)	52	56% (127)	27% (215)	29
12th grade	83% (199)	40% (187)	43	60% (86)	34% (150)	26
Percent whose fathers attended at least *some* college:						
8th grade	77% (325)	39% (256)	28	70% (59)	35% (203)	35
10th grade	79% (292)	31% (292)	48	55% (132)	42% (236)	13
12th grade	74% (211)	39% (202)	35	60% (90)	45% (168)	15
Percent whose mothers attended at least *some* college:						
8th grade	67% (326)	27% (261)	40	30% (59)	31% (203)	−1
10th grade	60% (292)	22% (295)	38	40% (132)	23% (233)	17
12th grade	62% (212)	29% (200)	33	39% (90)	32% (170)	7
Percent whose parents want teenager to attend college:						
8th grade	98% (333)	83% (265)	15	100% (59)	87% (200)	13
10th grade	98% (292)	78% (296)	20	99% (134)	83% (237)	16
12th grade	100% (211)	80% (199)	20	97% (90)	82% (170)	15

* Jewish teenagers.
† Non-Jewish teenagers.

concerned about the religion of friends and dates than they are to say their parents care. Nevertheless, even among teenagers, the tendency to express concern increases with greater schooling. In turn, once again, the increase is greater the larger the Jewish presence.

Teenagers who express clannishness themselves (or who report having clannish parents) are more likely to be anti-Semitic than those without such proclivities. This is true in all three communities although, as Table 67 reveals, clannishness and anti-Semitism are more strongly related in the towns having a Jewish presence than in Central City.

It is *not*, however, because older, white non-Jewish teenagers in Commutertown and Oceanville are more clannish than their younger counter-

Table 66   CLANNISHNESS ITEMS BY GRADE IN SCHOOL FOR WHITE NON-JEWISH ADOLESCENTS

| | Percent of teenagers who want their friends to be of their religion: | | | | |
	8th Grade	10th Grade	12th Grade	Gamma	Xs
Commutertown	21% (262)	23% (301)	22% (200)	+0.023	NS
Oceanville	19% (204)	18% (239)	25% (170)	+0.102	NS
Central City	27% (476)	19% (481)	21% (394)	−0.120	0.01
	Percent of teenagers who say their parents want their friends to be of their religion:				
Commutertown	23% (267)	28% (304)	43% (203)	+0.298	0.001
Oceanville	26% (204)	30% (241)	38% (170)	+0.186	0.05
Central City	27% (480)	29% (484)	31% (392)	+0.060	NS
	Percent of teenagers who want their dates to be of their religion:				
Commutertown	42% (255)	46% (305)	52% (197)	+0.129	NS
Oceanville	40% (201)	45% (241)	48% (172)	+0.103	NS
Central City	41% (473)	37% (486)	45% (394)	+0.042	NS
	Percent of teenagers who say their parents want their dates to be of their religion:				
Commutertown	48% (259)	58% (298)	69% (198)	+0.268	0.001
Oceanville	50% (203)	52% (240)	67% (168)	+0.215	0.001
Central City	43% (466)	42% (483)	55% (391)	+0.158	0.001

NS—Not significant.

Table 67   ANTI-SEMITISM BY CLANNISHNESS FOR WHITE
NON-JEWISH ADOLESCENTS

| | Percent who are anti-Semitic in: | | |
	Commutertown	Oceanville	Central City
Want their dates to be the same religion:			
Yes	75% (340)	61% (269)	44% (541)
No	58% (394)	47% (340)	39% (774)
Gamma	+0.367	+0.275	+0.110
Xs	0.001	0.001	0.05
Parents want their dates to be the same religion:			
Yes	73% (425)	57% (334)	41% (605)
No	56% (307)	48% (271)	40% (702)
Gamma	+0.342	+0.170	−0.011
Xs	0.001	0.05	NS
Want their friends to be the same religion:			
Yes	79% (163)	68% (123)	49% (292)
No	63% (575)	50% (484)	38% (1,020)
Gamma	+0.381	+0.357	+0.214
Xs	0.001	0.001	0.01
Parents want their friends to be the same religion:			
Yes	73% (232)	62% (186)	50% (380)
No	62% (517)	49% (423)	37% (938)
Gamma	+0.244	+0.258	+0.255
Xs	0.01	0.01	0.001

NS—Not significant.

Table 68 ANTI-SEMITISM BY GRADE IN SCHOOL BY CLANNISHNESS FOR WHITE NON-JEWISH ADOLESCENTS

Percent who are anti-Semitic:

	Commutertown					Oceanville					Central City				
	8th Grade	10th Grade	12th Grade	Gamma	Xs	8th Grade	10th Grade	12th Grade	Gamma	Xs	8th Grade	10th Grade	12th Grade	Gamma	Xs
Want dates to be same religion:															
Yes	65% (101)	78% (139)	80% (100)	+0.244	0.05	61% (79)	58% (108)	65% (82)	+0.053	NS	50% (190)	45% (177)	37% (174)	−0.178	0.05
No	44% (140)	64% (160)	68% (94)	+0.326	0.001	35% (120)	52% (131)	56% (89)	+0.281	0.01	40% (267)	44% (296)	30% (211)	−0.112	0.01
Gamma	+0.407	+0.336	+0.304			+0.484	+0.129	+0.275			+0.206	+0.021	+0.144		
Xs	0.01	0.01	0.05			0.001	NS	NS			0.05	NS	NS		
Parents want dates to be same religion:															
Yes	64% (120)	75% (170)	77% (135)	+0.198	0.05	56% (99)	54% (123)	61% (112)	+0.071	NS	49% (193)	41% (200)	34% (212)	−0.202	0.01
No	42% (125)	66% (122)	67% (60)	+0.357	0.001	36% (101)	55% (115)	58% (55)	+0.308	0.01	39% (260)	46% (271)	33% (171)	−0.054	0.02
Gamma	+0.417	+0.216	+0.253			+0.386	−0.006	+0.052			+0.191	+0.114	+0.027		
Xs	0.001	NS	NS			0.01	NS	NS			0.05	NS	NS		

Teenagers want friends to be same religion:

Yes	73% (52)	79% (68)	86% (43)	+0.246 NS		67% (39)	67% (42)	69% (42)	+0.037 NS		59% (125)	46% (87)	36% (80)	−0.311 0.01
No	47% (194)	70% (228)	72% (153)	+0.344 0.001		41% (162)	52% (195)	57% (127)	+0.215 0.02		39% (334)	43% (381)	32% (305)	−0.079 0.05
Gamma	+0.501	+0.242	+0.414			+0.488	+0.301	+0.245			+0.395	+0.065	+0.084	
Xs	0.001	NS	0.05			0.001	NS	NS			0.05	NS	NS	

Parents want friends to be same religion:

Yes	63% (59)	77% (86)	77% (87)	+0.207 NS		59% (51)	60% (70)	68% (65)	+0.127 NS		60% (125)	50% (137)	39% (118)	−0.271 0.01
No	49% (192)	69% (213)	71% (112)	+0.324 0.001		41% (150)	53% (169)	56% (104)	+0.192 0.05		38% (339)	41% (334)	31% (265)	−0.083 0.05
Gamma	+0.264	+0.183	+0.145			+0.339	+0.148	+0.249			+0.424	+0.173	+0.176	
Xs	NS	NS	NS			0.01	NS	NS			0.001	NS	NS	

NS—Not significant.

parts that they are more prone to anti-Semitism. Whether judged by the preferences of teenagers or their parents for friends or for dates, clannishness makes less of a difference to the incidence of anti-Semitism at the 12th grade than it does at the 8th grade. Note in Table 68, for example, that in Commutertown the proportion of 8th graders who are anti-Semitic is 65 percent if they want their dates to be of the same religion and 44 percent if they don't care, a difference of 21 percentage points. Among 12th graders, there is more anti-Semitism among both the clannish and non-clannish subgroups. However, the two are here separated by 12 percentage points in the proportion anti-Semitic. This tendency for clannishness and anti-Semitism to be more strongly related at the 8th grade than at the 12th is true

Table 69   CLANNISHNESS ITEMS BY GRADE IN SCHOOL FOR JEWISH ADOLESCENTS

	8th Grade	10th Grade	12th Grade	Gamma	Difference*	Xs
Percent of teenagers who want their dates to be of their religion:						
Commutertown	66% (319)	67% (289)	70% (211)	0.059	+4	NS
Oceanville	61% (59)	66% (131)	80% (90)	0.285	+19	0.05
Percentage of teenagers who say their parents want their dates to be of their religion:						
Commutertown	74% (313)	82% (287)	88% (209)	0.294	+14	0.001
Oceanville	75% (56)	90% (130)	89% (89)	0.277	+14	0.02
Percent of teenagers who want their friends to be of their religion:						
Commutertown	28% (322)	34% (291)	33% (212)	0.082	+5	NS
Oceanville	15% (59)	32% (132)	42% (89)	0.355	+27	0.01
Percent of teenagers who say their parents want their friends to be of their religion:						
Commutertown	39% (326)	52% (290)	65% (211)	0.336	+26	0.001
Oceanville	42% (59)	64% (132)	67% (88)	0.276	+25	0.01

* 8th to 12th grade.
NS—Not significant.

in all communities, but in Central City anti-Semitism declines with more schooling whether youngsters are clannish or not. In Commutertown and Oceanville it increases.

If increasing clannishness on the part of non-Jewish youngsters does not account for the increase in anti-Semitism with more schooling in Commutertown and Oceanville, what does?

Jewish youngsters are not free of clannish tendencies. Indeed, as we have already learned from findings presented in Chapter 1, they are more inclined, at least in Commutertown, to within-group friendships than are non-Jewish teenagers. Jewish clannishness, like non-Jewish clannishness, is also more in evidence among older than among younger teenagers (Table 69). The further along they are in school, the greater the tendency for Jewish youngsters to want their friends and dates to be Jews. These proclivities are more than shared by these teenagers' parents.[2]

What limited evidence we have suggests that non-Jewish teenagers are aware of these tendencies and respond negatively to them. The frequency with which it is accepted that "Jewish teenagers are likely to be selfish; concerned only for their own group" and "Jews are unfriendly; do not mix with others; go around only with their own group" is not only greater in Commutertown and Oceanville than in Central City, but the frequency

Table 70   CLANNISHNESS STEREOTYPE ITEMS BY GRADE IN SCHOOL FOR WHITE NON-JEWISH ADOLESCENTS

	8th Grade	10th Grade	12th Grade	Difference*	Xs
Jews are selfish:					
Commutertown	50% (119)	66% (154)	62% (102)	12	NS
Oceanville	36% (100)	57% (110)	74% (85)	38	0.001
Central City	36%	29%	29%	−7	NS
Jews are unfriendly:					
Commutertown	38% (118)	59% (155)	48% (102)	10	0.01
Oceanville	26% (100)	40% (111)	55% (85)	29	0.01
Central City	30% (230)	25% (250)	18% (164)	−12	0.02

* 8th to 12th grade.
NS—Not significant.

increases with more schooling in the first two communities while decreasing in the last. Note, for example, that between the 8th and the 12th grades in Commutertown, there is an increase of 12 percentage points in acceptance of the first item and an increase of 10 points in acceptance of the second. In Oceanville, the equivalent figures are 38 and 29 percentage points, and in Central City −7 and −12 percentage points.

That the increasing tendency for Jewish teenagers to acknowledge clannishness is paralleled by an increasing non-Jewish negative response to Jewish clannishness will not satisfy the research purist nor does it satisfy ourselves that a causal connection has been established. In the absence of contrary data and taking into account that hostility declines with greater schooling in Central City, the most reasonable inference to be drawn from our data is that the connection is causal.

Other studies, however, will have the task of confirmation or disconfirmation. There are elements perhaps of psychological need in this response to Jewish clannishness. And for those with such needs, the amount and negative quality of such clannishness is likely to be exaggerated. Yet it would be a mistake to overlook the existential base in which the response is rooted. While it was possible only to infer that successful Jews were prone to the negative traits attributed to them, by their own admission and by their own behavior Jewish youngsters acknowledge clannish dispositions. Thus, Jewish clannishness is not an invention of hostile non-Jews; it exists and, with a larger Jewish presence, awareness by non-Jews of its existence increases.

This raises a fundamental question about how non-Jewish perception of Jewish clannishness is to be evaluated. In previous studies and in our own analysis so far, it has been adjudged an indicator of prejudice. Now, obviously, that judgment is called into question. If a perception is correct, what become of the grounds for calling it prejudiced?

As with the response to Jewish success, it depends essentially on how the perception is understood and explained. Clannishness is not exclusively a Jewish trait nor a trait of all Jews. And insofar as Jews are disposed to be clannish, there are historical forces, most notably the persecution of Jews, that account for the strong sense of community. Understood in these terms, it would seem unwarranted to attribute prejudice to a perception of clannishness. Such an attribution does appear to be called for, however, where the explanation is racist, where clannishness is conceived as a fundamental and universal character defect of Jews. Understood this way, a singularly negative response to clannishness is produced, whereas a neutral or positive affect would more likely be the consequence of the other understanding.

Given these alternative ways to understand clannishness, it is not altogether clear what it means for a teenager to agree with the two items we have used as indicators of clannishness—"Jews are unfriendly; do not mix with others; go around with their own group" and "Jews are likely to be selfish; concerned only for their own group." The items are not worded to sort out perception from evaluation and neither of them gets at explanation. The inclusion in both items of a negative evaluation probably justifies judging an agree response as negative. Moreover, in the construction of our index of anti-Semitism, it was found that those items tended to be accepted with much greater frequency by teenagers holding more clearly invidious images of Jews than by those rejecting such images. Still, in retrospect, our measurement of prejudice in this instance and generally would have been stronger had we had the foresight to differentiate perception from evaluation and made provision for getting at explanations as well.[3]

More generally, these results make dubious the strategy, followed in most past efforts to combat prejudice, of ignoring the possible "truth" content in negative stereotypes. Finding ways to explain to non-Jewish teenagers why Jews have a strong sense of community and a deep concern to maintain it would appear to be a preferable strategy to the prevailing one of allowing youngsters to draw their own conclusions, especially when so many of them are ill equipped by their knowledge and understanding of prejudice to do so. More, however, about implications later.

The Effects of Contact

Having discovered that anti-Semitism is nourished in contexts where Jews are present, it may appear paradoxical that we now turn to examine the effect of contact, but it cannot be assumed that where there is a Jewish presence, all non-Jews will be in equal contact with it. Consequently, it is relevant to ask what the effects of differential contact are.

It behooves us at the outset to acknowledge that our capability to answer this question is highly circumscribed by our having only cross-sectional data. Clearly any thoroughgoing study of the effect of contact on prejudice would require longitudinal data over an extended period of time and, presumably, beginning early in the life cycle. Such a study would be enormously complex and very costly, if at all practical. Yet, if the intricate interconnections between contact and prejudice are to be established firmly, a longitudinal study is the route we should be obliged to take.

Given our present data, the modest contribution we can make to the subject is to inquire into the relationship between the incidence of anti-Semitism and having friends who are Jewish. Teenagers were asked, it will be recalled, to name their five closest friends in their class at school. Since all teenagers enrolled in a class were included in our study, we were able to make an independent check to determine how many of the friends named are Jewish.

Of the total of 2,404 friendships reported by non-Jewish Commutertown teenagers, 22.5 percent were with Jews. In Oceanville, 15.5 percent out of 2,163 reported friendships were with Jews. Taking into account that there are proportionately twice as many Jewish teenagers in Commutertown as in Oceanville, interreligious friendships are relatively more frequent in the context with the smaller proportion of Jews. Indeed, Oceanville teenagers are about as likely to have one Jewish friend (36.2 percent did) as Commutertown teenagers (41.5 percent). As we saw in Chapter 1, interreligious friendships happen less frequently than would be expected by chance. Still, they happen frequently enough so that we can ask what may be implied by such friendships for the incidence of anti-Semitism.

By and large, as expected and as Table 71 shows, the greater the contact, the less the anti-Semitism. In Commutertown, the proportion of anti-Semitic teenagers ranges from 76 percent among those with no Jewish friends to 20 percent for those with five Jewish friends. In Oceanville, the range is from 60 percent for those with no Jewish friends to 25 percent for those with four Jewish friends; no students in Oceanville had five Jewish friends. In Central City, as is to be expected, very few—less than 1 percent—non-Jewish adolescents report having Jewish friendships. Still, even in that virtually non-Jewish context, having Jewish friends makes a difference in anti-Semitism. Of the teenagers with no Jewish friends 41 percent are anti-Semitic as compared to 31 percent for those with one friend, and 0 percent for those with two. Note that the contextual effects continue

Table 71   ANTI-SEMITISM BY NUMBER OF JEWISH FRIENDS AMONG WHITE NON-JEWISH ADOLESCENTS

| | Percent who are anti-Semitic for those whose Jewish friendships number: | | | | | | | |
	None	One	Two	Three	Four	Five	Gamma	Xs
Commutertown	76%	59%	49%	41%	39%	*	−0.447	0.001
	(441)	(158)	(82)	(51)	(18)	(5)		
Oceanville	60%	46%	35%	29%	*	*	−0.357	0.001
	(388)	(134)	(72)	(14)	(4)	(0)		
Central City	41%	31%	*	*	*	*	−0.276	NS
	(1,296)	(32)	(3)	(0)	(0)	(0)		

* Too few cases for stable percentage.
NS—Not significant.

Table 72 NUMBER OF JEWISH FRIENDS BY ACADEMIC DEPRIVATION/CULTURAL UNSOPHISTICATION FOR WHITE NON-JEWISH ADOLESCENTS

And whose friends number:	Percent whose score on academic deprivation/cultural unsophistication scale was:								Gamma	Xs
	0	1	2	3	4	5	6	7		
Commutertown										
0	43%	30%	39%	54%	65%	77%	94%	*	0.481	0.001
1–5	57	70	61	46	35	23	6	*		
N =	(56)	(84)	(93)	(90)	(97)	(77)	(46)	(2)		
Oceanville										
0	40%	51%	68%	59%	71%	77%	85%	*	0.363	0.001
1–5	60	49	32	41	29	23	15	*		
N =	(75)	(75)	(85)	(90)	(93)	(57)	(40)	(7)		

* Too few cases for stable percentage.

to hold; taking number of Jewish friends into account, the incidence of anti-Semitism is greater the larger the size of the Jewish presence.

Which comes first? Does the relative absence of prejudice lead to the formation of Jewish friendships? Are such friendships the source of the relative absence of prejudice? Or is the relation an artifact of some other factor—sophistication, for example, which determines both how many Jewish friends one has as well as how relatively prejudiced one is?

Academically privileged youngsters and culturally sophisticated ones, it turns out, are indeed more likely than their opposite numbers to form Jewish friendships. As reported in Table 72, only 6 percent who score high (6) on a combined scale of academic deprivation and cultural unsophistication have at least one Jewish friend as compared to 57 percent of those scoring at the lowest end of the scale. In Oceanville, the equivalent figures are 15 and 60 percent.[4]

It is not the case, however, that the association between the number of Jewish friends and the incidence of anti-Semitism is accounted for by level of privilege and sophistication. As can be seen by reading down the columns of Table 73 (which combines the results for Commutertown and Ocean-ville), teenagers having a Jewish friend are in all comparisons less anti-Semitic than those without such a friend. Privilege/sophistication also continues to have an independent relation to anti-Semitism (read across the rows of Table 73), meaning, in effect, that the causal chain is not from privilege/sophistication to having a Jewish friend to being unprejudiced.

It can be assumed from these results that the process at work is one in which friendship with Jews and attitudes toward them affect each other independently; friends generate friendliness and friendliness produces friends. Does one make Jewish friends first and develop favorable attitudes as a result, or vice versa? With our cross-sectional data, we cannot say which comes first, but we suspect that the beginning point is different for different people and that, once one thing happens, the effect is probably reciprocal thereafter.

The findings on contact make somewhat enigmatic the earlier results on context. If having Jewish friends is associated with the absence of prejudice, then, it would seem, there ought to be less rather than more prejudice in contexts where there are opportunities for such friendships. Given the vastly greater chance to form Jewish friendships in Commutertown, for example, teenagers there ought to show a lot less anti-Semitism than adolescents in Central City.

The fact that they do just the opposite is undoubtedly because not all forms of contact between Jews and non-Jews generate friendship. Our data, unfortunately, afford no bases for exploring qualities of contact other than friendship.

Table 73   ANTI-SEMITISM BY COMBINED MEASURE OF ACADEMIC AND CULTURAL DEPRIVATION BY HAVING A JEWISH FRIEND FOR WHITE NON-JEWISH ADOLESCENTS

(Results for Commutertown and Oceanville combined)

Percent anti-Semitic among those whose score on the combined measure of academic and cultural deprivation was:

	0	1	2	3	4	5	6	7	Gamma	Xs
Have no Jewish friends:	35% (52)	48% (63)	66% (94)	65% (100)	76% (128)	84% (102)	75% (77)	* (9)	0.387	0.001
Have one or more Jewish friends:	22% (77)	47% (95)	46% (82)	56% (78)	67% (61)	68% (31)	* (9)	* (0)	0.384	0.001

* Too few cases for stable percentage.

Summary and Conclusions

Our inquiry into the effects of context and contact on prejudices has produced mixed results. In settings where Jews are present and where opportunities for interreligious friendship are taken up, the net effect is a reduction in the incidence of anti-Semitism. At the same time, however, the gross amount of anti-Semitism is greater where there is a Jewish presence than in a community where there is not. Moreover, the larger the Jewish presence the greater the anti-Semitism.

We must be cautious about generalizing these contextual effects. The communities studied cannot be considered to represent other communities with varying proportions of Jews in their populations, nor is it justifiable to conclude that what applies to adolescents will also apply to adults. Still, if for no other reason but that they break new ground in the study of prejudice, these results about contextual effects must be judged the most innovative produced by our inquiry so far.

For reasons associated probably with the liberal bias of investigators, the possibility that the victims may be a source of prejudice has rarely been examined. Generally, it has been taken for granted that negative stereotypes constitute misperceptions or misrepresentations of reality. The possible truth content of stereotypes has either been overlooked or denied; the latter more often because of the absence of supporting evidence than of the presence of counter evidence.

Our own predelictions, we must confess, were in the same direction. As we have indicated, our firm expectation was that the contextual effect would be just the opposite from what we have found. It was only because we could find no other explanation of the unanticipated positive association between anti-Semitism and the size of a Jewish presence that we were led to consider the truth content of the stereotypes judged to be anti-Semitic.

Our exploration was limited since we were obliged to work with the evidence available rather than to begin inquiry afresh. Fortunately, however, Jewish adolescents were included among those from whom data were collected and it was possible, therefore, to check on at least some of the attributions made by non-Jews about them. We were in an especially good position to confirm the positive stereotypes of Jewish intellectuality and success. It was also evident that Jewish adolescents were relatively more disposed than non-Jews to associate with their own group and to express a preference for so doing.

We had no direct evidence that Jewish youngsters were especially disposed to be conceited, too powerful, sly, vain, and bossy, five attributions made about them by a majority of non-Jewish youth in the two communities having a Jewish presence. We were led to surmise some truth in these stereotypes partly because as many as a quarter of Jewish youth acknowledged some of them and also because such traits tend to be associated with being successful, and in the two communities, Jewish youngsters were on the average more successful on a variety of counts than their non-Jewish counterparts.

What truth we found in the stereotypes was relative rather than absolute. That is to say, it was not that all Jewish youngsters manifested a particular trait but only that they were more prone to do so than the non-Jews in the sample. This being the case, it is obviously prejudice when a Jewish teenager is responded to on the basis of a stereotype associated relatively with Jewish youth in general. However, considerable sophistication about the nature of prejudice is required for a teenager to avoid it when he or she subscribes to negative stereotypes. Even greater sophistication is required, we discovered, to produce sensitivity to what it means for a group to be relatively like what a stereotype attributes it to be.

As our analysis proceeded, it became increasingly clear that, not only what traits are attributed to an outgroup, but also how the ingroup understands these traits to have come about, counts in the formation, and presumably in the undoing, of prejudice. Indeed, we came to believe that how the presence of a stereotype is explained is, if anything, more important than the fact that it is believed. This was most markedly in evidence with respect to those stereotypes that conceive of Jewish teenagers as having been deceitful in achieving academic success and conceited and bossy in their maintenance of it.

As just indicated, we cannot say for sure how much Jewish youngsters in Commutertown and Oceanville manifest these traits, but insofar as they do, the response is determined not so much by the behavior as by how the behavior is explained. Attributing the behavior to a deficiency in the character of Jews leads to anti-Semitism if it hasn't existed before or to nourishing it if it has. Ascribing the traits as concomitants of success rather than of Jewishness is not only a sign of great sophistication on a teenager's part but also an indication of his or her capacity to deal with and to transcend being prejudiced. By and large, the evidence suggests that most teenagers are not that sophisticated and, because of the anti-Semitism prevalent in the culture, they fall ready prey to an explanation that feeds anti-Semitism rather than starves it.

Similarly, the response to clannishness on the part of Jewish teenagers also appears to be determined mostly by how the clannishness is understood. In and of itself, clannishness is probably not as negatively evaluated as conceit, bossiness, or arrogance. When Jews are clannish, however, it is more negatively evaluated where it is conceived as an inherently Jewish character trait than where it is understood to be a natural outcome of persecution by non-Jews. To come to the latter understanding, however, requires not only sophistication but obviously also a knowledge of history. Most teenagers, judging from the negative response to attributions of Jewish clannishness, have neither the necessary sophistication nor historical knowledge.

These results on the significance of a Jewish presence for anti-Semitism underscore our earlier findings of the importance of cognitive sophistication in prejudice reduction. They also make evident the importance of considering the truth content of stereotypes in future research on prejudice. The most significant contribution of our findings, we believe, lies in their identification of what may be labeled "explanatory modes" as a central element in prejudice formation, maintenance, and reduction. The evidence at hand is not sufficient to make an unequivocal case but it seems to make common sense as well as most sense of the data to conceive of prejudice, at least its cognitive element, as rooted not in how a group is perceived but in how perceptions are explained.[5]

From this perspective, anti-Semitism is constituted, not by the perceptions one harbors about Jews, but by a "racist" mode of explaining what one perceives. To be sure, the anti-Semite's perceptions are more likely to be negative than those held by the unprejudiced person. What distinguishes the two, however, is that the anti-Semite will interpret whatever he perceives invidiously, whether it be negative, neutral, or positive; indeed, whether it be true or false. In contrast, the unprejudiced person, even when he or she makes attributions that would have to be judged negative and true from an objective standpoint, has the capacity to recognize either the cultural, historical, and social conditions underlying them or that Jewishness has nothing to do with the attributes.

It is because such capacities have not been developed, we believe, that so many young people fall prey to anti-Semitism. What the possibilities are for more effectively bringing young people to such levels of understanding and how they may be pursued are questions we shall take up in the last chapter of this book.

5 Adolescent Racial Prejudice

Adolescent prejudice is not limited to anti-Semitism, of course, which raises the question of how much of what has been learned about adolescent anti-Semitism is applicable to other forms of adolescent prejudice. This question was explored in our inquiry through a parallel examination of the nature and sources of racial prejudice among the adolescents in our three samples.

The Incidence of Racial Prejudice

Racial prejudice, like anti-Semitism, has components of belief, feeling, and behavior, and these were measured in equivalent ways for the two forms of prejudice. Consequently, it is possible to compare what white non-Jewish teenagers believe Jews and blacks to be like, to see how much social distance separates the respective groups, and also, as we have already done in Chapter 1, to compare the extent of interreligious as against interracial contact.

Racial Stereotypes

In a fashion equivalent to that used to assess their perceptions of Jews, teenagers were presented with the same battery of stereotypes, this time, however, purported to be descriptive of blacks. They were then asked to report the extent of their agreement with each stereotype, half of the sample being told to do so having a black teenager in mind and the other matched half being instructed to answer with reference to blacks in general. Just as with Jewish stereotypes, there were minor differences in response depending upon the referent. For purposes of brevity, we shall here consider the response only of that half of the sample who answered with black teenagers as the referent.[1]

As can be seen in Table 74, white non-Jewish teenagers show a marked proclivity to accept rather than to reject negative attributions about their black peers. Of 14 stereotypes worded in an outrightly negative way, 10 are accepted by a majority in Commutertown, 7 in Oceanville, and 10 in Central City. Immorality, troublemaking, gaudiness, and vanity are the charges most frequently leveled against black teenagers. The only negative stereotypes receiving negligible support (if acceptance from 20 percent to 22 percent can be so classified) are that blacks are sly and too powerful.

Table 74   ACCEPTANCE OF STEREOTYPES OF BLACK TEENAGERS BY WHITE NON-JEWISH ADOLESCENTS

	Commutertown	%	Oceanville	%	Central City	%
Majority stereotypes (accepted by 50% or more)	Athletic	90	Athletic	93	Athletic	89
	*Troublemaker	84	*Troublemaker	79	*Troublemaker	79
	*Gaudy	78	*Gaudy	75	*Vain	74
	*Immoral	75	*Immoral	68	*Immoral	71
	*Vain	71	*Sloppy	62	*Gaudy	71
	*Untrustworthy	63	*Vain	60	*Pushy	69
	*Bossy	62	Different	56	*Sloppy	64
	Different	61	School spirit	55	*Bossy	61
	*Sloppy	59	*Quitter	54	*Conceited	61
	*Selfish	58	*Untrustworthy	50	Different	61
	*Quitter	56			*Selfish	58
	*Pushy	54			*Quitter	58
	*Conceited	52			*Untrustworthy	57
Stereotypes held by a substantial minority (accepted by from 25% to 49%)	*Unfriendly	48	*Bossy	48	School spirit	49
	School spirit	43	*Pushy	44	*Unfriendly	49
	Religious	35	*Unfriendly	42	Intelligent	37
			*Selfish	40	*Powerful	36
			Religious	39	Religious	34
			*Conceited	37	*Sly	32
			Intelligent	33	Ambitious	26
Minority stereotypes (accepted by less than 25%)	Intelligent	24	Ambitious	20		
	*Powerful	22	*Sly	15		
	*Sly	20	*Powerful	9		
	Ambitious	14				
Mean proportion accepting outrightly negative stereotypes		56%		49%		64%
N =		(388)		(301)		(667)

*Stereotypes judged to be outrightly negative.

This strong tendency to accept negative attributions is combined with an almost equal inclination to reject positive ascriptions. A majority in all three communities acknowledge black athletic prowess, but otherwise, positive ascriptions are rejected about as frequently as negative ones are accepted. Judging from the mean proportion accepting negative stereotypes, the incidence of racial prejudice is greatest in Central City (64 percent), least in Oceanville (49 percent), with Commutertown falling in between (56 percent). These community differences are not attributable, however, to the size of the minority presence, as we found community differences in anti-Semitism to be. The proportion of black teenagers in the total student body is roughly the same in the three communities—14.7 percent in Commutertown, 13.6 percent in Oceanville, and 15.4 percent in Central City.

Judging once again from the mean proportion accepting outrightly negative stereotypes, white non-Jewish teenagers in all three communities are comparatively more prone to negative stereotyping of black than of Jewish teenagers. In Commutertown, 13 percentage points separate the average proportion of teenagers accepting negative stereotypes about blacks and Jews; in Oceanville the figure is 12 percentage points. The Central City figure of 38 percentage points is the result of Central City teenagers exhibiting the most racial prejudice but the least anti-Semitism. Such gross comparisons, however, mask substantial differences in the acceptance of particular stereotypes.

To portray the differences, what we have done in Table 75 is to locate each stereotype on a grid to show simultaneously the degree to which it is ascribed to black and Jewish teenagers. Thus, for example, being athletic is ascribed to blacks by 91 percent of white non-Jewish teenagers; 27 percent make the same ascription of Jews. Or, to take an example where the differences are not so great, blacks are judged unfriendly by 48 percent of non-Jewish whites, Jews by 51 percent.

The bulk of the stereotypes, it can be seen, fall in the upper-left and lower-right quadrants of the table, indicating that items accepted by the majority as applying to blacks are accepted by a minority as applying to Jews, and vice versa. More specifically, labels such as troublemakers, sloppy, and quitters are applied to blacks by more than half of the respondents but to Jews by fewer than one-fourth. In contrast, stereotypes such as sly and ambitious are much more likely to be attached to Jews than to blacks.

Table 75 uses data from Commutertown only. However, the same tendency for racial stereotyping to be distinct from anti-Semitic stereotyping is also in evidence in the other two communities. Whether this means that the conditions giving rise to the two forms of prejudice are also distinct we shall examine later.

Social Distance

The questions used to judge teenagers' willingness to associate with Jewish peers were asked in a parallel way to assess their openness to association with black peers. Teenagers were asked both how they would feel about interacting with "a student in the college preparatory program who is

Table 75 ASCRIPTION OF STEREOTYPES TO JEWISH AND BLACK TEENAGERS BY WHITE NON-JEWISH ADOLESCENTS
(Commutertown only)

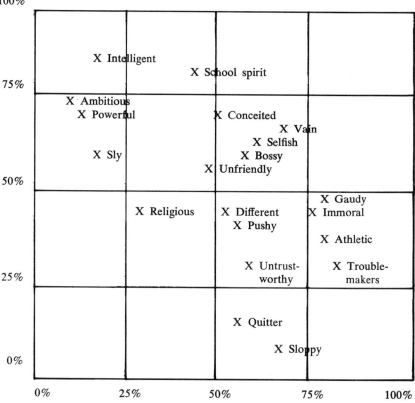

Percentage ascribing stereotypes to Jewish teenagers

Percentage ascribing stereotypes to black teenagers

black and is getting B's" and with "a student in the vocational program who is black and is getting failing grades."

Judging from teenagers' willingness to associate with a high-status black, the considerable negative stereotyping we have just witnessed is not translated for many into a reticence to engage in interaction. As is indicated by Table 76, the only form of interaction rejected by a majority, and even this by only a bare majority, is having a successful black peer date one's sibling. To be sure, a sizable minority (approximately a third) are unwilling to countenance even such activities as working on the same committee, belonging to the same social club, and having a black teenager home to dinner. However, all the other less intimate forms of contact are acceptable to all but a few white teenagers.

Table 76 SOCIAL DISTANCE TO A HIGH-STATUS BLACK TEENAGER AMONG WHITE NON-JEWISH ADOLESCENTS

Percent unwilling to have successful black student:	Commutertown %	Rank Order	Oceanville %	Rank Order	Central City %	Rank Order
Date sibling	56.2	1	55.3	1	63.0	1
On same committee	32.9	2	40.8	2	39.5	4
Home to dinner	32.2	3	28.9	5	42.3	3
As close friend	31.2	4	31.9	4	38.7	5
Member of same club	29.9	5	33.3	3	42.9	2
As speaking acquaintance	17.7	6	11.3	8.5	27.8	6
To lunch	11.3	7	11.6	7	19.6	8
Sit next to in class	10.9	8	12.9	6	15.0	9
At party	10.4	9	11.3	8.5	22.5	7
N =	(388)		(300)		(667)	
Mean =	25.9		26.4		34.6	

This lack of correspondence between stereotyping and proclaimed willingness to associate turns out to be a function of the high status of the referent. When teenagers are asked about associating with an unsuccessful black, the majority are unwilling to engage in most forms of interaction (see Table 77). The only exceptions are sitting next to a black peer in class and having a black as a speaking acquaintance. Three out of four, in fact, are unwilling to have a low-status black teenager as a close friend or even as a dinner guest. And nine in ten are unwilling to have a low-status black teenager date his or her sibling.

These results identify a significant element of class prejudice in racial

Table 77   SOCIAL DISTANCE TO A LOW-STATUS BLACK TEENAGER
AMONG WHITE NON-JEWISH ADOLESCENTS

Percent unwilling to have unsuccessful black student:	Commutertown %	Rank Order	Oceanville %	Rank Order	Central City %	Rank Order
Date sibling	93.1	1	96.2	1	97.7	1
Home to dinner	74.9	2	82.8	2	88.5	2
As close friend	73.0	3	74.7	3	82.5	3
Member of same club	60.5	4	73.5	4	72.9	4
At party	58.6	5	70.9	5	71.1	5
To lunch	49.5	6	50.3	7	66.8	6
On same committee	45.7	7	52.4	6	58.6	7
As speaking acquaintance	29.5	8	29.6	8	48.0	8
Sit next to in class	24.3	9	27.2	9	33.4	9
N =	(388)		(300)		(667)	
Mean =	56.6		62.0		68.8	

social distance just as the earlier results demonstrated the importance of class prejudice in teenagers' expressions of social distance toward Jews. Racial distance is not entirely a matter of class prejudice, of course, as is indicated by teenagers being less willing to cross racial lines and interact with a black teenager than religious lines to interact with a Jewish peer when both are of equally high or low status. However, demonstrating the power of class prejudice, considerably more non-Jewish white teenagers would be agreeable to interacting with an upper-status black than to associating with a lower-status Jewish teenager, even to the extent of having them date their siblings. This can be seen in Table 78, which uses the data from Commutertown to make the demonstration.

Unfortunately, it is not possible to sort out what is uniquely racial in racial social distance from what is class-based. The presence of both elements, however, makes it probable that, as the social status of blacks improves, some reduction in gross prejudice is to be expected.

Social distance was also tapped, it will be recalled, through responses to the single question, "Suppose you had just met someone and all you knew about him was that he is Jewish (black)—how would you feel about him?" This question elicited little outright hostility when it was asked about Jews and it elicits little more, indeed even less in Commutertown, when asked about blacks. As can be seen in Table 79, the proportion who would feel unfriendly or quite unfriendly is 11 percent in Commutertown, 12 percent in Oceanville, and 22 percent in Central City. The equivalent figures for

Table 78   SOCIAL DISTANCE TO HIGH-STATUS BLACK AND
LOW-STATUS JEWISH TEENAGERS AMONG
WHITE NON-JEWISH ADOLESCENTS

(Commutertown only)

Social distance to:

Percent unwilling to have:	High-Status Black Teenager	Low-Status Jewish Teenager
Date with sibling	56.2%	73.6%
On same committee	32.9%	50.0%
Home to dinner	32.2%	52.1%
As close friend	31.2%	56.8%
Member of same club	29.9%	49.7%
As speaking acquaintance	17.7%	27.5%
To lunch	11.3%	27.5%
Sit beside in class	10.9%	26.4%
At party	10.4%	22.8%
N =	(388)	(388)

Jews were 16 percent in Commutertown, 10 percent in Oceanville, and 9 percent in Central City. The modal response is to say one would feel friendly on first meeting with a black and indeed, in all three communities, the majority say their feelings would be friendly or quite friendly.

Table 79   HOSTILITY TO BLACKS AMONG
WHITE NON-JEWISH ADOLESCENTS

Feelings toward black teenagers:	Commutertown	Oceanville	Central City
Quite friendly	23%	18%	16%
Friendly	34	41	40
Nothing either way	32	28	23
Unfriendly	9	7	11
Quite unfriendly	2	5	11
N =	(383)	(299)	(655)

Interracial Friendships

The verbal expression of friendliness is not carried over into behavior. Heterophily scores (which, it will be recalled from Chapter 1, range from +1 for maximum acceptance of an outgroup to −1 for maximum rejection) of white non-Jewish teenagers with respect to black teenagers are strongly negative in all three communities: −0.85 in Commutertown,

−0.92 in Oceanville, and −0.89 in Central City. Racial barriers to friend-ship formation are especially more in evidence than religious ones. In the two towns—Commutertown and Oceanville—in which there is a Jewish presence, there are considerably more Jewish–non-Jewish than black–white friendships.

In sum, while it cannot be concluded for sure since other measures might have produced different results, the net impression conveyed by the several indications of racial prejudice we have examined is that it is more virulent in these three communities than anti-Semitism. These differences are tempered, however, by signs that there is a larger class factor in racial prej-udice than in anti-Semitism. Hostility toward Jews is more purely religious than hostility toward blacks is purely racial.

An Index of Racial Prejudice

To examine the sources of racial prejudice and to permit a comparison of these sources with those producing anti-Semitism, a summary measure of racial prejudice is needed. As with anti-Semitism, given the contamination of the social-distance items by status considerations and given the absence of intergroup friendships that makes impossible a measure based on extent of contact, the most useful measure of racial prejudice appears to be one based upon racially prejudiced beliefs. Using the same stereotype items for the measure of racial prejudice as were used to indicate anti-Semitism is also an advantage in facilitating comparison between anti-Semitism and racial prejudice. Whether or not this use is warranted, however, given the differences already observed in anti-Semitic as against racial stereotyping, merits examination.

Eight items were combined to produce the summary index of anti-Semitism used in Chapter 2. These, according to their abbreviated labels, were: selfish, unfriendly, gaudy, conceited, pushy, immoral, vain, and troublemakers. To determine whether or not these same eight items, when asked regarding blacks, could be combined to form a scale of racial prej-udice, a factor analysis was conducted upon the entire list of twenty avail-able stereotype items.[2] The results of this analysis show that the same eight items included in the anti-Semitism index, when asked with respect to blacks, have sufficiently high factor loadings to warrant their use in the construction of a summary measure of racial or anti-black prejudice. It will be recalled that the further advantage of these particular items is that they are worded identically or almost identically on the teenage and adult forms of the questionnaire so as to warrant combining the forms for analysis.

There is one disadvantage in using all these items as indicators of racial prejudice, however. At least two of the items—"Black teenagers are frequently in trouble with school authorities and the police" and "Black teenagers often dress in a loud and flashy way"—may contain, although it cannot be said for sure, a sufficient grain of truth to make them suspect as signs of hostility. Agreement with these items could come from teenagers who are not prejudiced against blacks, but who are sufficiently knowledgeable to recognize that there is some objective basis for these descriptions.

If this were the case, though, these items should not load highly on the same factor as the other six more unambiguously negative items. The fact that they do load highly indicates that they are more a sign of prejudice than of a sophisticated assessment of racial differences. Consequently, given the additional advantage of having comparable scales of racial prejudice and anti-Semitism, the two items have been retained in the measure.

Combining these eight items in the same fashion as we did for anti-Semitism produces a summary scale of racial prejudice which ranges from 1 (low) to 7 (high). (Further details regarding the construction of the scale may be obtained by referring to Chapter 2 since the same procedures were followed as in the construction of the anti-Semitism measure.) The proportions exhibiting either clear racial prejudice, or at least an unwillingness to reject it (scores of 4 through 7) on the basis of this scale, are 82 percent for teenagers in Commutertown, 73 percent in Oceanville, and 84 percent in Central City. On equivalent criteria, it will be recalled, 66 percent were found to be anti-Semitic in Commutertown, 53 percent in Oceanville, and 41 percent in Central City. Thus, in all three communities, racial prejudice is more prevalent than anti-Semitism.

The relationship between this measure of racial prejudice and other measures at our disposal is presented in Table 80. Responses to each of these other measures—social distance to a high-status black, social distance to a low-status black, and feelings of hostility on first meeting a black—are predicted strongly by scores on the summary measure of racially prejudiced belief. With this additional guarantee of the validity of the scale, then, we shall embark upon an exploration of the social location of racial prejudice, relying primarily upon this measure and introducing the other measures only at important junctures along the way.

The Social Location of Racial Prejudice

The first question we shall want to address is whether racial prejudice is socially located among the same or different categories of teenagers as anti-Semitism. The analytic path to be followed, consequently, will parallel that taken in Chapter 2 where the social location of anti-Semitism was investigated. However, to avoid burdening the text with a proliferation of statistical tables, the results will be reported using primarily the summary measures developed in the analysis of anti-Semitism. The results using unsummarized measures will be reported only where they reveal findings either different from or in elaboration of those obtained using the summary measures.

One preliminary clue that suggests the social location of racial prejudice is likely to be the same as rather than different from that of anti-Semitism is the high correlation between the two forms of prejudice. In each of the three communities (see Table 81), teenagers scoring lowest on anti-Semitism have the lowest racial prejudice scores and there is a steady upward progression of such scores with each increase in anti-Semitism. The respective gammas for Commutertown, Oceanville, and Central City are 0.526, 0.474, and 0.526.

Table 80   RACIAL PREJUDICE BY SOCIAL DISTANCE TO A HIGH-STATUS AND TO A LOW-STATUS BLACK AND BY HOSTILITY TO BLACKS AMONG WHITE NON-JEWISH ADOLESCENTS

Percent prejudiced among teenagers where social distance to a high-status black was:

| | Low | | | | High | | |
	0	1	2	3	4	Gamma	Xs
Commutertown	69% (198)	76% (142)	86% (162)	93% (145)	94% (71)	0.475	0.001
Oceanville	57% (101)	60% (98)	75% (153)	85% (164)	91% (69)	0.446	0.001
Central City	62% (172)	77% (242)	87% (323)	90% (321)	96% (266)	0.507	0.001

Percent prejudiced among teenagers where social distance to a low-status black was:

Commutertown	61% (142)	74% (120)	83% (134)	89% (184)	97% (134)	0.549	0.001
Oceanville	56% (68)	57% (70)	70% (114)	83% (189)	86% (140)	0.403	0.001
Central City	61% (129)	78% (170)	79% (232)	88% (345)	94% (446)	0.483	0.001

Percent prejudiced among teenagers where hostility to blacks was:

Commutertown	69% (157)	80% (275)	87% (210)	95% (60)	100% (31)	0.426	0.001
Oceanville	47% (96)	71% (253)	83% (176)	93% (44)	91% (33)	0.511	0.001
Central City	66% (194)	81% (525)	92% (322)	95% (140)	97% (145)	0.545	0.001

Table 81 RACIAL PREJUDICE BY ANTI-SEMITISM
AMONG WHITE NON-JEWISH ADOLESCENTS

Percent racially prejudiced for those
whose anti-Semitism score was:

| | Low | | | | | | High | | |
	1	2	3	4	5	6	7	Gamma	Xs
Commutertown	28%	64%	83%	86%	92%	90%	96%	0.526	0.001
	(47)	(77)	(132)	(189)	(178)	(98)	(25)		
Oceanville	32%	53%	73%	84%	86%	82%	100%	0.474	0.001
	(44)	(90)	(150)	(139)	(113)	(60)	(10)		
Central City	62%	75%	87%	92%	97%	96%	93%	0.526	0.001
	(126)	(311)	(345)	(285)	(174)	(67)	(15)		

It is also likely, given these correlations, that aside from being similar in social location, the two forms of prejudice will also be found to prevail especially among the cognitively unsophisticated. To determine the extent of the correspondence, if it exists as predicted, attention is given first to determining whether racial prejudice, like anti-Semitism, is especially to be found among teenagers experiencing varying forms of relative deprivation.

The direction of all the relationships is that the deprived are relatively more likely to be racially prejudiced than the privileged. However, the relationships are consistently weaker for racial prejudice than they were for anti-Semitism. The summary measure of economic deprivation and racial prejudice, while virtually consistent in all three communities, is of moderate strength (gamma = 0.284) only in Commutertown. In Oceanville the gamma (0.100) barely meets our criterion for a weak relationship and in

Table 82 RACIAL PREJUDICE BY ECONOMIC DEPRIVATION
AMONG WHITE NON-JEWISH ADOLESCENTS

Percent racially prejudiced among those
whose score on the economic deprivation
scale was:

| | Low | | | | | High | | |
	0	1	2	3	4	5	Gamma	Xs
Commutertown	61%	75%	80%	84%	88%	100%	0.284	0.01
	(31)	(118)	(193)	(171)	(100)	(18)		
Oceanville	64%	67%	73%	73%	79%	*	0.100	NS
	(11)	(78)	(183)	(165)	(87)	(9)		
Central City	*	86%	84%	84%	86%	87%	0.042	NS
	(6)	(58)	(375)	(395)	(245)	(45)		

* Too few cases for stable percentage.
NS—Not significant.

Central City it is so small (0.042) as to indicate no association at all. (See Table 82.)

Academic deprivation is also less strongly related to racial prejudice than to anti-Semitism. In Commutertown and Oceanville the gammas are moderate in strength, being respectively 0.207 and 0.232, but in Central City a gamma of 0.057 suggests no relationship between academic deprivation and racial prejudice.

Table 83   RACIAL PREJUDICE BY ACADEMIC DEPRIVATION AMONG WHITE NON-JEWISH ADOLESCENTS

	\multicolumn{5}{c	}{Percent racially prejudiced for those whose score on the academic deprivation scale was:}		
	Low				High		
	0	1	2	3	4	Gamma	Xs
Commutertown	73% (93)	78% (136)	83% (144)	91% (143)	84% (178)	0.207	0.01
Oceanville	62% (105)	71% (116)	74% (137)	77% (111)	82% (130)	0.232	0.01
Central City	80% (217)	85% (242)	86% (279)	84% (257)	85% (265)	0.057	NS

NS—Not significant.

That these indicators of deprivation have a smaller association with racial prejudice than with anti-Semitism is, in part, a statistical artifact of the considerably greater incidence of racial prejudice in the three communities. This means that there is simply less possibility for variation in racial prejudice than in anti-Semitism and, consequently, less potential for relationships to be strong. It is also likely that the greater element of class prejudice in racial prejudice than in anti-Semitism has the effect of generating more racial prejudice than anti-Semitism among privileged youngsters.

Whatever the processes at work, it is evident that racial prejudice is not as distinctively located among more deprived teenagers as is anti-Semitism. Still, it cannot be gainsaid that both forms of prejudice tend to be socially located more among the deprived than among the privileged.

The Sources of Racial Prejudice

As we did for anti-Semitism, we propose to pursue an explanation for the social location of racial prejudice by exploring the propositions that it is a result (1) of anxiety produced by frustration, (2) of identification with prejudiced primary groups, (3) of socialization to unenlightened rather than enlightened values, and (4) of a lack of cognitive sophistication. The same scales and variables will be used as were used in examining anti-Semitism, and to heighten comparison the analysis will be conducted in a parallel way. To keep to a minimum what must necessarily be some repetitiousness, results will be reported combining the samples for all three communities except where there are noteworthy community differences in relationships.

Frustration

None of the three tests made supported frustration–aggression theory as an explanation for anti-Semitism. Making the same tests for racial prejudice produces just about equal results. For all three communities combined, the gammas using the F scale, our shortened version of Gough's self-acceptance scale, and Rosenberg's scale of self-esteem are respectively -0.029, -0.057, and -0.016, all insignificant and well below our criterion for even a weak relationship. Moreover, as can be seen, none of the relationships are consistent or significant (see Table 84).

Table 84   RACIAL PREJUDICE BY FRUSTRATION MEASURES
AMONG WHITE NON-JEWISH ADOLESCENTS
(All three communities combined)

Percent racially prejudiced among those whose score on the F scale was:

| Low | | | | | | | | | | High | | |
0	1	2	3	4	5	6	7	8	9	10	Gamma	Xs
*	*	80%	82%	82%	83%	81%	84%	77%	79%	*	−0.029	NS
(0)	(4)	(15)	(66)	(230)	(536)	(531)	(370)	(163)	(53)	(4)		

Percent racially prejudiced among those whose score on the self-acceptance scale was:

| Low | | | High | | |
0	1	2	3	4	
79%	84%	82%	81%	77%	−0.057 NS
(145)	(599)	(863)	(683)	(202)	

Percent racially prejudiced among those whose score on the self-esteem scale was:

| Low | | | | | High | | |
0	1	2	3	4	5	6	
*	94%	80%	82%	82%	83%	79%	−0.016 NS
(7)	(34)	(216)	(725)	(432)	(306)	(249)	

* Too few cases for stable percentage.
NS—Not significant.

Once again, the absence of relationships may be due to the inappropriateness of using on teenage samples measures standardized for adults. Without a new study we have no way of establishing whether this is the case. Based on available data, however, the proposition that racial prejudice results from hostility generated by frustration must be counted as unproved for both forms of adolescent prejudice.

Primary Groups

The investigation of anti-Semitism showed that the academically deprived are somewhat more likely than the academically privileged to have anti-Semitic friends and that those with anti-Semitic friends are somewhat more likely to be anti-Semitic themselves. While we could not be sure of the exact process at work, we concluded that the deprived probably do not seek out prejudiced friends, which then cause them to become prejudiced themselves. It seems more likely that deprived youngsters either seek out other deprived teenagers as friends and these friends merely happen to be anti-Semitic as well, or that deprivation causes one to be anti-Semitic, which, in turn, leads one to pick out anti-Semitic friends.

The same processes do not appear to be at work with respect to adolescent racial prejudice. As can be seen in Table 85, the academically privileged are as likely to have racially prejudiced friends as the academically deprived. (Indeed, a surprising aspect of Table 85 is the extremely high proportion of these teenagers' friends who score as racially prejudiced by our criterion.) Moreover, there is no relationship (gamma +0.068) between teenagers' racial prejudice and the incidence of racial prejudice among their friends (Table 86).

Whether or not the absence of a relationship is due to the class element in racial prejudice dampening the effect of variables that were found to dis-

Table 85   FRIENDS' RACIAL PREJUDICE BY ACADEMIC DEPRIVATION FOR WHITE NON-JEWISH ADOLESCENTS
(All three communities combined)

Percent of teenagers whose friends are racially prejudiced for teenagers whose academic deprivation score was:

Low				High		
0	1	2	3	4	Gamma	Xs
91%	88%	91%	88%	91%	−0.004	NS
(409)	(476)	(531)	(467)	(498)		

NS—Not significant.

Table 86   RACIAL PREJUDICE BY FRIENDS' RACIAL PREJUDICE
FOR WHITE NON-JEWISH ADOLESCENTS
(All three communities combined)

Percent racially prejudiced among those whose
friends' level of racial prejudice was:

Low						High		
1	2	3	4	5	6	7	Gamma	Xs
88%	73%	80%	80%	82%	83%	83%	0.068	NS
(8)	(60)	(449)	(1,075)	(707)	(132)	(23)		

NS—Not significant.

criminate on anti-Semitism cannot be established with the data at hand. It is evident, however, that peer group friendships exercise an influence on the one form of prejudice, albeit indirect, but not the other.

Enlightened Values

Adherence to enlightened values was not found to be a significant factor in precluding adolescent anti-Semitism. Of the three kinds of values examined—civic, moral, and interpersonal—no relationships were found between adherence to civic and moral values and the incidence of anti-Semitism. A significant but weak relationship was found between subscribing to interpersonal values and being free of anti-Semitism.

The results for racial prejudice are in some respects parallel to and in others different from those for anti-Semitism. The differences manifest themselves mostly with reference to civic values. It makes a difference to the incidence of racial prejudice whether such values as people should "support movements or groups that are working for equal rights for everyone" and "let everyone have his fair share in running business and politics in this country" are subscribed to, whereas adherence to such values had no bearing on the incidence of anti-Semitism. As can be seen in Table 87, the relationships between responses to these two questions and racial prejudice are moderate in strength and are as strong or stronger than other relationships we have encountered in our investigation of teenage racial prejudice. The discriminating power of these items derives apparently from their reference to the theme of equality. The third civic value item, "People should be interested in doing things in their community and be useful citizens," does not espouse this theme and, as can be seen, responses to it are unrelated to the incidence of teenage prejudice.

Subscription to moral values has only a weak relationship to racial prejudice, and on most of the indicators used to tap moral values there is no relation at all to prejudice. Here the results for racial prejudice and anti-Semitism are about equivalent. They also correspond with respect to inter-personal values. Teenager subscription to such values is weakly related to their level of racial prejudice (gammas range from −0.123 to −0.198).

To explore further the relationship between adherence to equalitarian values and level of prejudice, an additive scale was constructed combining the responses to the "equal rights" and "fair share" items. As can be seen

Table 87   RACIAL PREJUDICE BY CIVIC, MORAL AND INTERPERSONAL VALUES AMONG WHITE NON-JEWISH ADOLESCENTS
(All three communities combined)

	Shouldn't or Don't Care	Should Care	Strongly Should Care	Gamma	Xs
Civic Values:					
Should support equality:	87% (336)	84% (564)	77% (460)	−0.228	0.001
Should let others have power:	87% (395)	82% (604)	77% (358)	−0.205	0.01
Should be a useful citizen:	82% (108)	84% (667)	81% (575)	−0.084	NS
Moral Values:					
Should be honest:	89% (56)	83% (605)	80% (2023)	−0.127	NS
Should follow rules:	84% (286)	81% (1211)	81% (1171)	−0.040	NS
Should be moral:	82% (657)	83% (1209)	77% (793)	−0.107	0.01
Should be hard-working:	82% (270)	81% (1265)	81% (1137)	−0.001	NS
Should be religious:	79% (807)	82% (1030)	82% (836)	+0.052	NS
Interpersonal Values:					
Should respect others:	86% (146)	85% (931)	79% (1608)	−0.198	0.001
Should not be conceited:	91% (129)	83% (734)	79% (1820)	−0.177	0.01
Should not be self-centered:	84% (235)	83% (846)	79% (1596)	−0.123	0.05

NS—Not significant.

Table 88   RACIAL PREJUDICE BY EQUALITARIAN VALUES
AMONG WHITE NON-JEWISH ADOLESCENTS
(All three communities combined)

Percent racially prejudiced for those
whose score on the equalitarian values
scale was:

| Low | | | | High | | |
0	1	2	3	4	Gamma	Xs
88%	88%	83%	76%	76%	−0.241	0.001
(149)	(287)	(435)	(290)	(191)		

in Table 88, the association between the resultant scale and racial prejudice is stronger (gamma = 0.241) than for the two items examined independently, indicating an additive effect.

These results seem to indicate that internalization of equalitarian values has some influence in containing racial prejudice. Moreover, the effect is

Table 89   RACIAL PREJUDICE BY ACADEMIC DEPRIVATION BY
EQUALITARIAN VALUES AMONG WHITE NON-JEWISH ADOLESCENTS
(All three communities combined)

Percent racially prejudiced for those whose
score on the academic deprivation scale was:

And whose score on the equalitarian values scale was:	Low 0	1	2	3	High 4	Total	Gamma	Xs
Low 0	80%	95%	82%	100%	83%	88%	0.076	NS
	(25)	(20)	(28)	(33)	(35)	(149)		
1	88%	86%	93%	88%	89%	88%	0.030	NS
	(41)	(51)	(54)	(65)	(64)	(287)		
2	77%	81%	87%	88%	82%	83%	0.112	NS
	(70)	(83)	(99)	(75)	(84)	(435)		
3	61%	77%	78%	79%	91%	76%	0.326	0.02
	(43)	(56)	(73)	(48)	(54)	(290)		
High 4	67%	76%	81%	82%	77%	76%	0.171	NS
	(36)	(45)	(41)	(33)	(22)	(191)		
Total	74%	81%	85%	87%	86%	83%	0.189	0.01
	(221)	(257)	(296)	(255)	(267)	(1,372)		
Gamma	−0.299	−0.245	−0.201	−0.332	−0.018	−0.241		
Xs	0.05	NS	NS	NS	NS	0.001		

NS—Not significant.

Table 90 RACIAL PREJUDICE AND ANTI-SEMITISM BY COGNITIVE
SOPHISTICATION AMONG WHITE NON-JEWISH ADOLESCENTS

(All three communities combined)

Percent racially prejudiced among those whose
level of cognitive sophistication was:

	Low												High		
	0	1	2	3	4	5	6	7	8	9	10	11	Gamma	Xs
	*	90%	91%	88%	87%	86%	88%	78%	78%	65%	70%	52%	−0.285	0.001
	(1)	(21)	(64)	(175)	(294)	(344)	(396)	(354)	(268)	(207)	(67)	(21)		

Percent anti-Semitic among those whose
level of cognitive sophistication was:

	Low												High		
	0	1	2	3	4	5	6	7	8	9	10	11	Gamma	Xs
	*	71%	68%	66%	64%	58%	56%	43%	39%	34%	24%	10%	−0.317	0.001
	(2)	(21)	(65)	(177)	(293)	(343)	(396)	(354)	(267)	(204)	(67)	(21)		

* Too few cases for stable percentage.

independent, by and large, of academic deprivation. The relationship between scores on the equalitarian values scale and the incidence of racial prejudice is moderate or strong at each level of academic deprivation except the most severe, where no relation is found (Table 89).

We shall check later to determine whether subscribing to equalitarian values also has the power to contain prejudice independently of level of cognitive sophistication. For now, however, the results must be judged as offering some support to a particular specification of enlightened-value theory.

Cognitive Sophistication

It was speculated earlier that the cognitive element may be less significant in racial than in anti-Semitic prejudice. There proved to be a very slight tendency in this direction, but, as Table 90 shows, the association between the summary measure of cognitive sophistication and anti-Semitism is only very slightly stronger than the association between cognitive sophistication and racial prejudice. Of the several factors examined, cognitive sophistication is the most strongly associated with both forms of prejudice.

The test made earlier to discover whether cognitive sophistication provides the link between academic deprivation and anti-Semitism showed that statistically the link does not exist. Each variable—academic deprivation and cognitive unsophistication—was found to be independently related to anti-Semitism and their joint effect was seen to be only slightly greater than their separate effects. We concluded that this was a result of academic deprivation and cognitive unsophistication being measures of the same thing; to be cognitively unsophisticated by our measures is to be academically deprived, and vice versa.

The same test for racial prejudice (see Table 91) produces somewhat different results. Cognitive sophistication continues to produce a reduction in prejudice irrespective of level of academic deprivation except among the most deprived (score 4). This can be seen by examining the gammas across the bottom of the table. Note that they are strong or moderate in strength among those who score 0, 1, 2, or 3 on academic deprivation. Among those scoring 4, however, the association virtually disappears.

As regards the relationship between academic deprivation and racial prejudice controlling for cognitive sophistication (the column of gammas at the right in the table), the pattern is erratic. Insofar as any tendency is revealed, being academically deprived appears to be a source of racial prejudice among cognitively sophisticated youngsters. Among cognitively unsophisticated teenagers, there is, if anything, a slight tendency for academically privileged youngsters to be more racially prejudiced.

Table 91   RACIAL PREJUDICE BY ACADEMIC DEPRIVATION AND
COGNITIVE SOPHISTICATION AMONG WHITE
NON-JEWISH ADOLESCENTS

(All three communities combined)

Percent racially prejudiced among those
whose score on the academic deprivation
scale was:

And whose score on cognitive sophistication was:		Low 0	1	2	3	High 4	Total	Gamma	Xs
Low	0	*	*	*	*	*	*		
		(0)	(0)	(0)	(0)	(1)	(1)	. . .	. . .
	1	*	*	*	*	82%	90%	−1.000	NS
		(0)	(0)	(2)	(8)	(11)	(21)		
	2	*	*	*	93%	94%	91%	−0.302	NS
		(2)	(3)	(5)	(14)	(32)	(64)		
	3	91%	89%	91%	93%	81%	88%	−0.276	NS
		(11)	(18)	(33)	(44)	(63)	(175)		
	4	73%	89%	89%	87%	85%	87%	−0.012	NS
		(15)	(28)	(71)	(68)	(94)	(294)		
	5	84%	87%	85%	84%	85%	86%	−0.011	NS
		(37)	(54)	(82)	(75)	(75)	(344)		
	6	89%	84%	92%	87%	90%	88%	+0.008	NS
		(52)	(54)	(84)	(87)	(67)	(396)		
	7	75%	72%	80%	85%	79%	78%	−0.107	NS
		(72)	(84)	(78)	(61)	(48)	(354)		
	8	67%	81%	80%	78%	89%	78%	−0.046	NS
		(61)	(73)	(55)	(46)	(26)	(268)		
	9	63%	68%	61%	68%	62%	65%	−0.048	NS
		(71)	(57)	(38)	(22)	(13)	(207)		
	10	68%	69%	69%	*	*	70%	+0.068	NS
		(28)	(13)	(13)	(8)	(4)	(67)		
High	11	*	*	*	*	*	52%	+0.060	NS
		(8)	(8)	(2)	(2)	(1)	(21)		
Total		74%	80%	82%	85%	84%	81%	+0.151	0.001
		(415)	(494)	(560)	(511)	(573)	(2,698)		
Gamma		−0.283	−0.332	−0.318	−0.257	−0.033	−0.285		
Xs		NS	0.05	NS	NS	NS	0.001		

* Too few cases for stable percentage.
NS—Not significant.

These results are more vividly portrayed in Table 92, which is a replication of Table 91 except that the scale of cognitive sophistication has been collapsed into a dichotomy. Once again, cognitive sophistication is shown to effect a slight reduction in the incidence of racial prejudice at all levels of academic deprivation except among the most deprived. Academic deprivation, however, continues to have a weak positive association with prejudice only among the cognitively sophisticated. Among the cognitively unsophisticated, academic deprivation and level of prejudice are virtually unrelated.

Table 92   RACIAL PREJUDICE BY ACADEMIC DEPRIVATION AND COGNITIVE SOPHISTICATION AMONG WHITE NON-JEWISH ADOLESCENTS

(all three communities combined)

Percent racially prejudiced whose score on the academic deprivation scale was:

And whose score on cognitive sophistication was:	Low 0	1	2	3	High 4	Total	Gamma	Xs
Low	83% (65)	88% (103)	88% (193)	88% (209)	85% (276)	87% (899)	−0.045	NS
High	72% (292)	76% (319)	80% (270)	82% (226)	83% (159)	78% (1,313)	+0.181	0.01
Total	74% (415)	80% (494)	82% (560)	85% (511)	84% (573)	81% (2,698)	+0.151	0.001
Gamma	−0.314	−0.407	−0.287	−0.226	−0.019	−0.298		
Xs	NS	0.01	0.05	NS	NS	0.001		

NS—Not significant.

Substantively, these results indicate that level of cognitive sophistication is an element in racial prejudice, as it was found to be in anti-Semitism. They also suggest that, among the cognitively sophisticated, the level of academic deprivation further discriminates the level of prejudice. The reason, we suspect, is that which pertained also in the analysis of anti-Semitism—the level of academic deprivation is an indirect indication of the level of cognitive unsophistication. What is enigmatic in these results and contradicts what was found earlier for anti-Semitism is the failure of the level of academic deprivation to discriminate levels of prejudice among the cognitively unsophisticated and, indeed, for the academically privileged to be slightly more subject to prejudice than the academically deprived among those who score

Table 93 EQUALITARIAN VALUES BY COGNITIVE SOPHISTICATION AMONG WHITE NON-JEWISH ADOLESCENTS

(all three communities combined)

Level of Cognitive Sophistication

| | Low | | | | | | | | | | High | | Total | |
	0	1	2	3	4	5	6	7	8	9	10	11		
% high on equalitarian values scale (4–5)	* (1)	* (8)	46% (26)	28% (76)	27% (144)	35% (191)	33% (211)	36% (186)	38% (146)	43% (107)	51% (39)	30% (10)	36% (1,389)	Xs = NS Gamma = −0.090

* Too few cases for stable percentage.
NS—Not significant.

especially low on cognitive sophistication (Table 91). Manifested here, we suspect, is class prejudice on the part of unsophisticated teenagers who are privileged. If this interpretation is correct, the fact that the same result does not apply among the cognitively sophisticated suggests that there is power in cognitive sophistication to contain class as well as racial and anti-Semitic prejudice. It should be kept in mind, however, that in our data none of the relationships are very marked.

Cognitive Sophistication and Equalitarian Values

Still an open question in the analysis is the status of the earlier findings on the association between adherence to equalitarian values and level of prejudice. Is this association sustained once cognitive sophistication is taken into account? Or is it an artifact of cognitive sophistication producing both greater commitment to equalitarian values and to less racial prejudice?

Cognitive sophistication is not associated with adherence to equalitarian values, as can be seen in Table 93. While there is a slight but inconsistent tendency for the more sophisticated to support equalitarian values, the gamma is less than weak (-0.090) and the association is not significant. This suggests that adherence to equalitarian values is related to the level of prejudice independently of the level of cognitive sophistication. To find out,

Table 94   RACIAL PREJUDICE BY EQUALITARIAN VALUES
AND COGNITIVE SOPHISTICATION AMONG
WHITE NON-JEWISH ADOLESCENTS

(All three communities combined)

| And who were: | Percent racially prejudiced among those whose score on the equalitarian values scale was: | | | | | |
	Low	Medium	High	Total	Gamma	Xs
Cognitively unsophisticated (6–11)	93% (150)	87% (150)	83% (140)	88% (444)	-0.299	0.05
Cognitively sophisticated (0–5)	85% (206)	80% (227)	74% (255)	79% (693)	-0.210	NS
Total	88% (356)	83% (435)	76% (481)	82% (1,372)	-0.281	0.001
Gamma	-0.398	-0.273	-0.256	-0.309		
Xs	0.05	NS	0.05	0.001		

NS—Not significant.

we have collapsed in Table 94 the equalitarian values scale into a trichotomy and the cognitive sophistication scale into a dichotomy and then examined how the two are related conjointly to prejudice.[3]

Table 94 tells us essentially that each variable contributes independently to a reduction in racial prejudice. Statistically, cognitive sophistication exerts its most powerful effect among those unenlightened in values. In turn, adherence to equalitarian values makes more of a difference to the level of prejudice of the cognitively unsophisticated, as can be seen by comparing the two gammas. Overall, the leverage of cognitive sophistica-

Table 95 SOCIAL DISTANCE AND FEELINGS OF HOSTILITY TOWARD BLACK TEENAGERS BY COGNITIVE SOPHISTICATION AND COMMITMENT TO EQUALITARIAN VALUES FOR WHITE NON-JEWISH ADOLESCENTS

(All three communities combined)

Social distance to a high-status black teenager:	Percent scoring high on social distance among those whose commitment to equalitarian values was:			Total	Gamma	Xs
	Low	Medium	High			
Cognitively unsophisticated (6–11)	61% (151)	51% (148)	50% (138)	54% (441)	−0.122	NS
Cognitively sophisticated (0–5)	47% (203)	40% (219)	34% (256)	40% (684)	−0.166	0.05
Total	53% (431)	44% (424)	39% (480)	45% (1,359)	−0.165	0.001
Gamma	−0.252	−0.193	−0.302	−0.256		
Xs	0.05	NS	0.001	0.001		
Social distance to a low-status black teenager:						
Cognitively unsophisticated (6–11)	67% (151)	59% (150)	59% (138)	61% (443)	−0.123	NS
Cognitively sophisticated (0–5)	55% (201)	53% (220)	41% (256)	49% (683)	−0.184	0.01
Total	61% (425)	53% (427)	42% (84)	53% (1,354)	−0.178	0.001
Gamma	−0.234	−0.124	−0.291	−0.226		
Xs	0.05	NS	0.01	0.001		

Hostility to black teenagers:	Percent scoring high on hostility among those whose commitment to equalitarian values was:					
	Low	Medium	High	Total	Gamma	Xs
Cognitively unsophisticated (6–11)	28% (154)	23% (151)	15% (137)	22% (446)	−0.182	NS
Cognitively sophisticated (0–5)	20% (208)	15% (223)	8% (261)	14% (698)	−0.228	0.001
Total	23% (445)	18% (432)	11% (485)	17% (1,387)	−0.231	0.001
Gamma	−0.149	−0.190	−0.201	−0.193		
Xs	NS	NS	NS	0.001		

NS—Not significant.

tion appears to be greater than that of enlightened values, but their net effect is shown to be essentially additive. The least prejudice is shown by the cognitively sophisticated who subscribe to equalitarian values and the most prejudice by those unsophisticated teenagers who reject enlightened values.

These results afford more support for an enlightened-values theory of racial prejudice than was found earlier for anti-Semitism. Comparatively, however, the two sets of results are about equally supportive of the importance of the cognitive element in prejudice reduction. In other respects, the two sets of results are also approximately concordant in what they reveal about the social location of prejudice. They are also in agreement in failing to afford any support for frustration–aggression theories of prejudice. Neither set of results suggests that peer group friendships have a strong relation to prejudice. Insofar as there is any effect, it was more evident in the analysis of anti-Semitism than of racial prejudice.

One final matter remains to be addressed, and as at the end of previous chapters we shall now turn to other measures of prejudice to determine whether our conclusions also apply to them. Our interest here is to determine whether cognitive sophistication and adherence to enlightened values are related to other measures of racial prejudice as they were to the summary measure. As can be seen in Table 95, which parallels Table 94 except that the other measures of prejudice have been substituted for the summary measure, the results using the other measures vary slightly in strength but not in direction. Cognitive sophistication and a commitment to equalitarian values are independently associated with an absence of prejudice. Their joint effect is additive.

A further test of these conclusions, which have been based solely on the responses of white non-Jewish teenagers, can be obtained by examining briefly and in comparable fashion racial prejudice among Jewish teenagers.

Racial Prejudice Among Jewish Teenagers

It is not often possible to learn how minority groups view one another. Studies of randomly chosen samples typically do not include enough persons from racial and ethnic minorities to make analysis feasible. In the present study we have been more fortunate in this regard. We have been able to replicate most of our investigation of anti-Semitism to determine how

Table 96   RELATIVE ACCEPTANCE OF STEREOTYPES OF
BLACK TEENAGERS AMONG JEWISH AND
WHITE NON-JEWISH TEENAGERS

(Results reported for Commutertown and Oceanville only)

Stereotypes accepted more often by non-Jewish than Jewish youth	Commutertown	%	Oceanville	%
Difference of 15 or more percentage points:	*Pushy	22	*Pushy	21
	*Conceited	19	*Conceited	15
	*Untrustworthy	15	Different	15
Difference of 6 to 14 percentage points:	School spirit	13	*Vain	14
	*Sloppy	12	*Untrustworthy	13
	Different	12	*Bossy	11
	*Powerful	12	*Immoral	9
	*Selfish	11	*Sloppy	9
	*Immoral	11	*Troublemakers	8
	*Gaudy	11	*Powerful	6
	*Troublemakers	8		
Stereotypes accepted about the same by both groups:				
Difference less than 5 percentage points:	Religious		*Unfriendly	
	Intelligent		*Sly	
	*Vain		Ambitious	
	*Unfriendly		Intelligent	
	Ambitious		School spirit	
	*Sly		*Gaudy	
	*Bossy		*Selfish	
	*Quitters		Athletic	
	Athletic		Religious	
			*Quitters	

* Stereotypes judged to be outrightly negative.

black teenagers view Jewish adolescents and what the sources of anti-Semitism are in the black subcommunity (see Appendix B). It is possible now to turn the question around and to examine briefly the nature and sources of racial prejudice among Jewish teenagers.

The qualities we have found most conducive to prejudice—economic and academic deprivation and a lack of cognitive sophistication—are less prevalent among Jewish than among non-Jewish adolescents, as we saw in Chapter 4. Consequently, if our findings have any generalizability, we should expect to find Jewish youth to be less racially prejudiced on the average than their non-Jewish classmates.

We can make a meaningful comparison only for Commutertown and Oceanville because of the virtual absence of Jews in Central City. Our findings confirm our expectations. In both communities, Jewish youngsters are less prone to racial prejudice than non-Jewish youth, and this is true whatever indication of racial prejudice is used for the comparison. For example, there are no negative stereotypes of blacks which Jewish teenagers accept more often than non-Jews; for most negative items, the acceptance rate by non-Jews is greater by 10 or more percentage points (Table 96).

On the summary measure of racial prejudice, 64 percent of the Jewish teenagers in Commutertown score as racially prejudiced. In Oceanville, 62 percent do. In comparison, substantially higher proportions of non-Jewish teenagers manifest high scores: 82 percent in Commutertown and 73 percent in Oceanville. Measures of social distance toward blacks also reveal less racial prejudice on the part of Jewish adolescents (Table 97).

Table 97   SOCIAL DISTANCE TO LOW- AND HIGH-STATUS BLACKS AMONG JEWISH AND NON-JEWISH ADOLESCENTS

Percent scoring high* on social distance scale:

Social distance to black teenagers	Commutertown		Oceanville	
	Jews	Non-Jews	Jews	Non-Jews
Low-status referent	37% (405)	46% (368)	45% (139)	54% (290)
High-status referent	12% (409)	27% (373)	17% (139)	29% (291)
Social distance to blacks in general				
Low-status referent	31% (371)	42% (366)	46% (129)	58% (298)
High-status referent	19% (376)	33% (368)	30% (129)	50% (301)

* High = score of 4 or 5 on scale from 1 to 5.

These differences notwithstanding, racial prejudice is found especially among less privileged Jewish youth as it was among deprived non-Jewish teenagers. Comparatively, the associations between the measures of economic and academic deprivation are smaller among Jews than among non-Jews. In Commutertown the gammas for the relation between academic deprivation and racial prejudice are 0.141 for Jewish teenagers and 0.207 for non-Jews. In Oceanville, the figures are 0.144 for Jews and 0.232 for non-Jews.

The weaker relationships appear, in part, to be a result of the relatively smaller number of Jews in the lowest status categories. They could also result from a greater cultural homogeneity among Jewish teenagers and a greater sensitivity, by virtue of their minority status, to the problem of prejudice. That such sensitivity exists is suggested by the evidence that at each level of privilege, whether measured by economic or academic status, Jewish youngsters reveal less prejudice than their equally privileged or deprived counterparts. Thus, it is not only because they are more privileged that Jewish youngsters show less prejudice.

When the relation between deprivation and prejudice is probed further to determine the intervening processes at work, the findings for the Jewish adolescent subcommunity prove to be essentially consistent with those for non-Jewish teenagers.

In both subcommunities, racial prejudice and a lack of cognitive sophistication go together although the associations are somewhat stronger for non-Jews than for Jews. In Commutertown, the gammas are 0.285 for Jews as compared to 0.375 for non-Jews, and in Oceanville they are 0.375 and 0.409, respectively.

For non-Jews, it will be recalled, there was no relation between the teenagers' own prejudice scores and the prejudice scores of their friends. The same is true among Jewish teenagers. Moreover, among Jewish as among non-Jewish adolescents, the association betweeen each of the frustration measures and prejudice is at most weak and often nonexistent.

As among non-Jews, adherence to equalitarian values is associated with a reduction in prejudice and once again the association is moderate in strength (-0.227). A moderate association also prevails irrespective of level of cognitive sophistication.

Despite all that they confirm about similarities in the process by which prejudice is nurtured or starved in the two subcommunities, the data leave unexplained just why Jewish youngsters, other considerations being equal, are less prone to racial prejudice than their non-Jewish counterparts. We presume that this is because the victims of prejudice are less likely to manifest it themselves; however, the data afford no basis for testing the truth of the assumption or for exploring its operation if it is true.

Table 98   RACIAL PREJUDICE BY COGNITIVE SOPHISTICATION AMONG BLACK NON-JEWISH TEENAGERS
(All three communities combined)

Percent racially prejudiced among those whose score on cognitive sophistication was:

Low											High	
0	1	2	3	4	5	6	7	8	9	10	11	
*	*	40%	65%	40%	38%	36%	31%	27%	35%	*	*	Gamma = −0.246
(0)	(1)	(15)	(49)	(67)	(85)	(76)	(55)	(34)	(17)	(6)	(1)	Xs = −0.05

*Too few cases for stable percentage.

A Comment on Black Self-Images

Do any of the ideas that have been explored to account for prejudice toward other groups also apply to prejudice toward one's own group? The thesis that adolescent prejudice is to a considerable extent a result of naiveté in recognizing, and simplistic thinking in accounting for, group differences suggests that the more cognitively unsophisticated may also exhibit more prejudice, not only toward other groups, but toward their own group as well. If this is the case, an additional degree of significance is accorded to the role that cognitive factors play in adolescent prejudice. A simple test is readily available in our data because black respondents as well as white teenagers were asked to respond to the black stereotype battery.

The data are moderately confirming of our expectation. As Table 98 indicates, there is a tendency, although not an entirely consistent one, for less cognitively sophisticated black teenagers to hold more negative beliefs about their own group than their more cognitively sophisticated counterparts. The gamma of −0.246 indicates at least a moderate tendency for prejudice to increase as cognitive sophistication decreases.

The implication of this finding is that an increased level of cognitive functioning is likely to be a deterrent, not only against prejudice among majority groups, but also against the debilitating acceptance of negative images among minority groups themselves. Conversely, the cognitively unsophisticated teenager is more likely both to perpetuate stereotypes of others and to accept these simple-minded notions when they are applied to himself. In other words, the significance of cognitively unsophisticated modes of thought appears to lie, not only in the discriminatory behavior toward minority groups by unsophisticated members of majority groups that may result from stereotyped beliefs, but also in the subtle tendency for the unsophisticated minority group member to be more susceptible to these stereotypes and to their immobilizing effects.

Summary

Our examination of racial prejudice was not designed to explore in detail the ways in which racial prejudice and anti-Semitism differ nor to investigate fully the sources of racial prejudice, but to determine the general applicability of our conclusions regarding the nature and sources of adolescent anti-Semitism. With some minor exceptions, we have found the same conclusions applicable to both forms of prejudice.

Both racial prejudice and anti-Semitism are found more characteristically among the economically and academically deprived rather than among privileged youngsters. To the extent that slight differences do occur in the two forms of prejudice, academic deprivation appears relatively less significant as a source of racial prejudice than of anti-Semitism.

A lack of cognitive sophistication appears to be an important reason why both forms of prejudice are relatively more common among the deprived than among the privileged. The importance of cognitive functioning is seen among both non-Jewish and Jewish teenagers, as well as among black teenagers with regard to their self-images. Enlightened values have also been found to have a greater bearing on racial prejudice than on anti-Semitism. However, no support was found for frustration–aggression theories of prejudice, nor did we find, as we did for anti-Semitism, that the teenagers' personal level of racial prejudice is related to that of their friends.

Unfortunately we have been unable to examine either the effect of contact or context upon racial prejudice as we did in Chapter 4 with regard to anti-Semitism. The amount of actual friendship between whites and blacks in our three towns is too small to examine its effects and the virtually identical racial proportions of the three towns precludes comparisons of different contexts. It seems likely, nevertheless, that our conclusion in Chapter 4 that the characteristics of minority groups themselves to some extent nourish prejudice also applies to racial prejudice. Indeed, it is probable that at least part of the extremely high incidence of negative racial stereotypes among these teenagers is due to the fact that they were responding to objective conditions; for example, in agreeing that blacks are frequently in trouble with school authorities.

This consideration again leads us to the position that it is not necessarily the *perception* of racial or ethnic differences which constitutes prejudice, but how these differences are *explained;* e.g., whether black teenagers are understood to be in trouble with school authorities because of racially innate differences or because of institutional, economic, or historical processes. How a person responds both emotionally and behaviorally to a relative difference between racial groups would appear to depend more upon how this difference is understood than on how it is perceived.

To some extent increased cognitive sophistication can undoubtedly mitigate prejudice by creating an aversion to the simplistic generalities inherent in stereotyping. But probably more importantly, increased cognitive sophistication can reduce prejudice by creating a better understanding of *why* racial differences exist. We turn now to a more explicit consideration of the implications of these findings, first for the study of prejudice, and second for the role the schools might play in combating prejudice.

6 The Findings in Broader Perspective

The formal part of our inquiry is now complete. We have mined the data as much as we think they warrant and reported the results in considerable detail. On reflection, however, there are things about prejudice which the inquiry has taught us that were not reported fully in the foregoing chapters. The forest, now that our examination of the trees has given us a glimpse of it, turns out to be something more than the sum of the parts. We report on this view in this brief chapter because we think it puts into broader perspective all that has gone before and because it also affords an appropriate introduction to what will be said in the last chapter on the applied significance of the inquiry.

The main conclusion to emerge from our inquiry is that prejudice is nurtured especially among youths who have not developed the cognitive skills and sophistication to combat it. Judged on purely statistical grounds, level of cognitive sophistication accounts for more of the variance in the incidence of adolescent prejudice than any other factor examined. The amount of variance accounted for is not great—from about 0.09 to about 0.25, depending upon whether anti-Semitism or racial prejudice is to be accounted for and on whether prejudice is examined among our total sample of adolescents or among particular subgroups. Still, as social science findings go, it isn't often that any single factor is found to explain more of the variance than has been accounted for here. Moreover, with the benefit of hindsight, we can see how, if we were to do the study again, our measures of cognitive sophistication and of the two forms of prejudice might be strengthened in ways that would presumably reveal cognitive sophistication to be even more important in determining the incidence of prejudice.

Simply to discover that cognitive sophistication is associated with the absence of prejudice and cognitive unsophistication with its presence says little about the process by which the two variables are linked, however. Just what are the ways in which cognitively sophisticated youngsters come to an understanding of prejudice so that they are led to reject it? In turn, what about a lack of cognitive skill disposes an adolescent to hold prejudiced beliefs?

Because we hadn't anticipated the findings, no attempt to answer these questions was built into the design of our inquiry. Yet it is evident that answers are necessary if the full significance of the relationship between levels of cognitive sophistication and the incidence of prejudice is to be understood and if the possibility of trying to raise the level of teenagers' cognitive capabilities as a means to effect a reduction in prejudice is to be explored.

Reflecting on the matter and building on the clues that the analysis has afforded, especially the analysis in Chapter 4 of the effects of a Jewish presence on anti-Semitism, the following observations emerge by way of elaborating upon and refining a cognitive theory of prejudice.

There are two fundamental reasons, we propose, why the cognitively sophisticated are better able to resist prejudice than their unsophisticated counterparts. First, by virtue of their cognitive capabilities, they are better able to deal with the "truth content" of any stereotype. Second, they are better fortified to resist an intolerant response to "real" group difference.

Stereotypes of group differences that make relative differences absolute are false overgeneralizations, however true the relative differences that inspire them. Prejudice has been associated traditionally with a failure to recognize the distinction between relative and absolute differences and with a response to relative differences as if they were absolute. Falling prey to such overgeneralizing may not be accounted for wholly as resulting from faulty cognition. Yet, that cognitive failure is a necessary, if not sufficient, ingredient for such overgeneralization is an initial assumption we are as disposed to make as we are to suggest that cognitive sophistication is necessary to guard against such overgeneralization.

Overgeneralization of group differences, however, needs to be kept distinct from perceptions of group differences that are recognized as relative and not made absolute. Stated in relative terms, perceptions can be true or false or, more appropriately perhaps, more or less accurate. Unfortunately, the objective evidence necessary to establish the accuracy of a claimed perception is frequently not available. Moreover, what constitutes objective evidence can become ambiguous if group differences observable in one context are not present in another. There is also always the possibility of group differences being true in one's own experience while objectively false.

Given the number of assertions about group differences to which teen-agers are exposed, it becomes a herculean task to sort them out, to make judgments about which ones are grounded in evidence, and to decide about their relative accuracy. Doing these things adequately is beyond the ken of almost anyone, however highly developed one's cognitive skills. Yet, be-cause the task is complex, it can be expected that persons with such skills are most capable of making the attempt and, in consequence, of recog-nizing how inaccurate many stereotypes are and how unsupported by evi-dence. Such recognition affords effective armor against prejudice; to flower, bigotry has to be rationalized and there is no rationalization where negative ascriptions about an outgroup are not believed.

Cognitive sophistication, however, can be a two-edged sword. When group differences are real, it is the cognitively sophisticated youngster once again who is most likely to know that they are. Thus, while we can assume that cognitive sophistication will arm youngsters against overgeneralization about group differences and enable them to be more discriminating in judg-ing the accuracy of alleged relative differences, it does not necessarily follow that these teenagers will be led thereby to be more tolerant and unprej-udiced. On the contrary, if group differences are real, which, as we have seen in the analysis, they sometimes are, the cognitively sophisticated may be more prone to a hostile response because the reality of the differences will be more visible to them.

That it doesn't happen this way is because cognitive sophistication makes possible not only more accurate perception of group differences but also more sensitive understanding of how existing group differences have come about. Arriving at some explanation of group differences is not called for, of course, where allegations about them are rejected as inaccurate and wrong. Where group differences are real or believed to be real, however, some accounting for them inexorably follows, albeit sometimes implicitly and often simplistically.

The explanatory component has been almost entirely neglected in past research on prejudice, and our inquiry did not deal with it head on. From what we have learned indirectly, however, it seems reasonable to conclude that it may have a stronger bearing on prejudice than does accuracy of perception. This is because the mode of explaining group differences is decisive in whether the potential for prejudice in negative stereotyping is activated or neutralized. Some modes of explanation rationalize an intol-erant response; others effectively derail it.

Judging from clues offered by the analysis, explanations rationalizing intolerance characteristically conceive of negatively evaluated group differ-ences as resulting from deficiencies inherent to the group itself. Jewish teen-agers, where they exhibit or are thought to exhibit conceit, or pushiness, or clannishness, are understood to do so because that is the way Jews are or choose to be. In effect, Jewishness itself becomes the explanatory factor. Similarly, where black youngsters are believed to do less well on intelligence tests or to be more prone to rob and steal, the reason they do so is that blacks are inherently that way. Simply being black is the fault.

Such explanations effectively rationalize prejudice because they say, in effect, that there are grounds for it. Moreover, they afford no reason not to be prejudiced. They also encourage the overgeneralization of stereotypes. This does not mean that such explanations do not allow exceptions to be countenanced. However, the exceptions are of the "some of my best friends are . . ." kind that prove the rule. In effect, the *modus operandi* of such explanations is to presume guilt unless proved innocent, rather than the other way around.

In contrast to those explanations of group differences that rationalize prejudice are those that reveal its irrationality. Explanations that are sensitive to the historical circumstances which gave rise to group differences and that recognize the cultural, social, and psychological forces which sustain them guard against relative differences being made absolute. More importantly, such reasoning makes it clear that the group itself is not at fault. The net effect of such explanations will not necessarily be approval of the negative trait manifested by a group. Rather, their product is understanding —a comprehension of the way group differences can and do come about that allows for dealing with them on their own terms.[1]

Youngsters in Commutertown and Oceanville who are able to recognize the conceit of Jewish teenagers to be a derivative of their being successful rather than of their being Jewish are not led to admire conceit. Indeed, their response to the teenagers they perceive to be conceited might well be somewhat hostile. What their explanatory mode arms them against is having their dislike of conceited teenagers blossom into a dislike of all Jewish teenagers.

Cognitive sophistication enters into the equation because it leads to nongeneralizing explanations rather than the rationalization of prejudice. The kind of comprehension necessary simply calls for greater cognitive skill. Thus, cognitive sophistication prevents acceptance of false allegations of group differences and prevents a hostile response to allegations having a basis in fact.

These remarks about cognition and prejudice are not intended to deny that other factors also play a role in the nourishing or starving of prejudice. We are inclined to see that role as more inextricably linked with the cognitive factor than the analysis *per se* has perhaps suggested. The remaining pages are devoted to speculating about what some of these links might be.

The analysis revealed enlightened values to be mildly associated with the absence of prejudice. In part, this was an artifact of cognitive sophistication being predisposing both to enlightened values and to being unprejudiced. Especially with reference to racial prejudice, however, enlightened values were found to be related to a reduction in the incidence of prejudice independently of level of cognitive sophistication. The question may be raised, as we have raised it for the relationship between level of cognitive sophistication and prejudice, as to what process underlies this relationship.

Our earlier surmise was that the effect was the result of enlightened values making prejudice taboo. In effect, not being prejudiced becomes one more enlightened value to which one may be socialized. We are not led to deny that such a process may be operative; however, our theorizing about cognitive sophistication suggests that the process may operate only as long as no evidence has been confronted that appears to be a plausible justification for prejudice. Once the relative possession of a negatively evaluated trait by an outgroup is demonstrated, enlightened values may not by themselves enable the kind of understanding necessary to neutralize the potentially hostile response.

An effect that enlightened values can have, of course, is to be blinding of real group differences, especially differences that cast the outgroup in a negative light. That this can and does happen is demonstrated over and over again in research on prejudice. There are always some persons who, when asked, will either deny any group differences or acknowledge only differences whose affect is neutral or positive. In past research such persons have been judged to be unprejudiced and in our own analysis we have so judged them, too. Assuming the reliability of the data, no other judgment is warranted since they are, at the moment at least, unprejudiced. However, our measure of prejudice would have been stronger had we been able to distinguish those who avoid being prejudiced by denying group differences from those whose understanding of group differences leads them to being unprejudiced.

The data afforded virtually no support for psychological theories of prejudice, which suggests that psychological factors may also have very little to do with cognitive modes of explaining prejudice. As we noted previously, the absence of relationships may be due to the inappropriateness to teenage samples of the standard psychological measures we used or adapted to our use, rather than to theoretical inadequacies. Consequently, it would be premature to conclude the irrelevancy of psychological factors in prejudice formation.

If psychological factors do play a role, we suspect that they are likely to be influential indirectly through affecting teenagers' cognitive functioning rather than to be a direct influence on the ways in which group differences are perceived and understood. Our study, for all its demonstration of a cognitive theory of prejudice, has contributed little to account for the achievement of the appropriate level of cognitive sophistication. Presumably, such sophistication is learned since it occurs more frequently among teenagers with educated parents and who do well at school. Just how the learning takes place and whether it is generalizable so that to be cognitively sophisticated is something that everyone can be taught are questions that future research must address (we'll have something to say about the possible value of such research in the next chapter).

If it is found that cognitive sophistication cannot be universally taught, it would still have to be demonstrated how much, if at all, and in what ways, psychological factors are the obstacles to such learning. It is conceivable that they may not be. However, it is at the point of accounting for variation in cognitive functioning rather than in accounting for prejudice directly that psychological factors are potentially important.

As to the significance of context and contact for how group differences come to be understood, no simple generalizations are possible, if we are to believe our data, since so much depends on the nature of the context and the character of the contact. Being in a context where an outgroup is present heightens the opportunity for negative stereotypes to be confirmed or denied effectively. Confirmation, as we have seen in Commutertown and Oceanville, is a challenge to cognitive capabilities which many are unable to meet, with the consequence that they become victims of prejudice, a state they might not have reached had they not been challenged. By the same token, however, those whose cognitive capabilities enable them to meet the challenge are undoubtedly made stronger to withstand becoming prejudiced.

In sum, the role that factors other than cognitive sophistication play in influencing the incidence of prejudice is likely to be significantly influenced by whether they operate in the presence or absence of cognitive sophistication. Their power to effect a reduction in prejudice, we would suggest, is enhanced the higher the sophistication. Enlightened values seem less likely to be compartmentalized where there is a sufficient level of cognitive sophistication regarding the sources of group differences to make tolerance, equality, and brotherhood not only proper but also reasonable responses. Psychological troubles, particularly frustration, seem less likely to be displaced onto innocent minority groups when the reasons for group differences are understood. And contact is more likely to generate tolerance rather than hostility when there is sufficient cognitive ability to understand why the outgroup is the way it is.

A cognitive theory may afford new understandings of the nature of prejudice and of the processes by which it is produced. There remains the question, however, whether the understanding gained gives promise of greater control over the incidence of prejudice. This question is addressed in the final chapter.

7 The Schools and Prejudice

Our inquiry combined an intellectual interest to advance under-standing about the sources and nature of adolescent prejudice with a practical concern to find more effective ways to combat it. In previous chapters, we have been preoccupied with satisfying intellectual curiosity. In this one, we want to consider what use may be made of what has been learned. The findings, if they have any use at all, ought to be most inform-ing of what more and what different the schools might do in efforts to control prejudice.

By and large, the problem of prejudice has not had high priority on the agendas of the nation's schools. Rarely do school districts mobilize them-selves in an all-out effort against prejudice. More significantly, perhaps, prejudice is not included usually among the subjects requiring pedagogical attention. Courses on prejudice are not offered in the majority of schools. Indeed, there is no textbook for such a course below the college level. Inso-far as the subject is treated in more general social studies courses, it is dealt with briefly and mostly without the course being required of all students.

This relative neglect of prejudice is surprising in light of the enormous involvement with the problem of discrimination, especially racial discrimin-ation, since the Supreme Court decision on school desegregation twenty years ago. A natural complement to efforts to bring about racial integration would seem to have been a parallel effort to teach black and white young-sters how to get along with each other. Yet, except in more progressive school districts, no systematic effort was made to deal with the human relations side of racial integration. More often than not, youngsters were not prepared for the new situation, and in many instances, neither was there any preparation of teachers. To be sure, courses in black culture and history were introduced into school curricula. This came about late in the game, however, and mostly as a result of pressure from black parents rather than as an analytically arrived at strategy for dealing with prejudice. The policy generally followed, more by default than by design, has been to rely on culture contact to somehow solve the problem of prejudiced attitudes, with overt incidents of prejudiced behavior being dealt with on an *ad hoc* basis as they arise.

The net effect is that racial harmony has not been a product of racial integration. Prejudice is rampant in school populations, and judging from our own inquiry, not only racial prejudice but anti-Semitism and a virulent but especially neglected class prejudice as well.

Just why the schools have dealt with the problem of prejudice mostly through a policy approximating benign neglect is not entirely clear. Implicit in the question is the assumption that the schools should be doing something more. Certainly there is precedent for looking to the schools as an instrument of social reform, though some observers have suggested that, being a creation of society, schools are bound more to reflect than to lead it. There are built-in constraints on an institution whose constituency controls the purse strings.

Timidity rather than boldness certainly characterized the response of most of the school districts asked to cooperate in our study. Admittedly, there were legitimate pedagogic reasons to turn us down since cooperation meant some considerable disruption of class schedules. From what we were told, however, and from our experiences before at least one school board, it was also evident that our study made school administrators nervous about how their constituencies would react. It was easier to say no than to face the prospect of controversy. School officials in the cooperating districts also found it the better part of discretion to be cautious, as is made evident by our agreement that the names of the school districts would not be revealed.

Aside from structural constraints, the failure of schools to do anything very much about prejudice is also apparently a result of prejudice not being perceived to be a serious problem. The prejudice youngsters harbor is made highly visible by a study such as ours. However, unless there is such research or unless prejudice is so severe as to lead to open conflict, it is not visible in the ordinary course of events. Prejudice is harbored in silence and when it is displayed it is likely to be displayed privately rather than publicly. Youngsters are especially more likely to conceal their prejudice from teachers and school officials than to reveal it.

The truth in these observations was brought vividly home to us in our own inquiry through the discovery that teachers in Commutertown, Oceanville, and Central City were mostly of the opinion that prejudice did not constitute much of a problem in their schools. In response to brief question-naires administered to all teachers but returned by only a minority, 11 per-cent in Commutertown, 4 percent in Oceanville, and 1 percent in Central City reported that problems occur in their schools which might be interpreted as Jewish-Christian conflict. There was somewhat more awareness of black–white conflict. Still, only a minority of teachers—22 percent in Com-mutertown, 11 percent in Oceanville, and 27 percent in Central City—reported that there had been problems between black and white youngsters in their schools.

A third and perhaps the crucial reason for the schools' neglect of prej-udice is that it has simply not been clear what could or should be done if the obstacles to doing something weren't there. Scholars are not agreed about the sources of prejudice and, if some of the theories are correct, there isn't very much the schools can do about prejudice anyway. Thus, it isn't as if blueprints for prejudice control were available but not being used. A school district with convictions (and the courage to act on them) that prejudice control is a school responsibility that ought to be actively pursued would have to start almost from scratch to develop a comprehensive pro-gram. Since no school district has the resources to do that, it is not sur-prising that not very much is being done.

The leverage necessary to turn the situation around and to involve schools actively and creatively in the struggle against prejudice is not likely to be provided by a single research project, especially one whose results fly in the face of some prevailing suppositions about prejudice. Still, in the absence of other stimuli, it becomes important to nourish all possible sources of leverage; consequently, these final remarks are offered on what may be implied by way of application of what has been learned.

Our inquiry has least to contribute directly to relieving the structural constraints on schools that rightly or wrongly limit their capacity to act. That our study was pursued without incident in three diverse communities and involved about 5,000 youngsters in a study process to which there was no parental approval suggests that schools are more timid than they need to be. If school board members and school officials see the con-trol of prejudice as an act of social reform and do not conceive that to be an appropriate school function, our research can demonstrate to them the cost of their neglect but it has nothing really to say about the issues of educational philosophy involved.

Our study does contribute to making the problem of prejudice visible. There will undoubtedly be those who respond to the virulent prejudice revealed to exist in these three communities by denying that it is happening or could happen where they are. National studies of prejudice gainsay such a response, of course, but still it can be expected that some will feel comfortable keeping their heads in the sand. The more general response we hope the study will elicit is that the results hold up a mirror to all school districts in America, not just to those in Commutertown, Oceanville, and Central City.

It seems likely that the structural constraints would not loom so large and that lack of saliency would prove so much an obstacle if it were clearer what the schools might do to exert leverage on prejudice. Our study has not produced a formula for action, tried, tested, proved worthy, and ready for immediate application. It has not even demonstrated that the schools have the capacity to do anything about prejudice. The study does, however, suggest some ideas worthy of being tried, and if they work, it will not only have been demonstrated that schools have leverage to apply but a formula for applying that leverage will have been found.

The findings suggest that the best way for the schools to combat prejudice is simply for them to do their fundamental job of education more effectively. This at least appears to be the message of the consistent finding that the most effective armor against prejudice is cognitive sophistication. Presumably, if the general level of cognitive sophistication were raised, without necessarily any specific instruction about prejudice, the incidence of prejudice would be reduced.

No school official or teacher is likely to disagree that the quality of education in America can stand improvement. Most would also probably feel that they are doing about the best possible with the resources available. Any simple suggestion that schools try harder is likely, not only to fall on deaf ears, but also, as the principal practical suggestion of an extensive research project, to look somewhat ridiculous. Still, the evidence cannot be denied that some leverage on prejudice would be the product of more effective general education, especially if the schools could find a way to make up for the disparity in the educational input provided by home environments and carried over into school environments.

An unanswered question, of course, is how many youngsters are inherently capable of gaining even under the most favorable educational conditions the cognitive sophistication necessary to an understanding of prejudice. It seems doubtful that everyone has the necessary innate capacity. At the same time, there is every reason to believe that there are more with the necessary capabilities than are learning how to use them.

For all that might be achieved through raising the general quality of education, though, such educational reform may be not only unrealistic and impractical but perhaps not even necessary to deal explicitly with the problem of prejudice. There is some reason to believe, given our findings, that it may be possible through appropriate didactic instruction to teach young-sters to be cognitively sophisticated about prejudice, even in the absence of their becoming cognitively sophisticated generally.

The research does not tell us what form this instruction should take. For example, would it be better offered in a single course devoted exclusively to the subject of prejudice or provided at appropriate places throughout the school curricula? Nor do the results indicate at precisely what age levels instruction should be provided. It is reasonably clear from the study's find-ings, however, what the content of such instruction ought to be.

To begin, it is evident that instruction should not begin and end with simply pronouncing prejudice to be bad. To teach enlightened values can do no harm and may be reinforcing when accompanied by additional in-struction to enable the youngsters to deal with prejudice intellectually. Alone, enlightenment has little or no leverage; in fact, relying upon it may only create the dangerous illusion that it is effective.

Instruction must obviously contend with the many false stereotypes about group differences that nourish prejudice. That prejudice prevails is clearly due in part to false beliefs never being challenged and their falsity and irrationality revealed. This is not an easy thing to do, however. The chal-lenge cannot be made effectively where there is absolutely no objective evidence for judging the truth of a stereotype. Also, when there is evidence demonstrating a stereotype to be erroneous, for the prejudiced person there is often subjective evidence to refute the objective. What a teacher has to say is unlikely to be disconfirming of what a youngster has experienced personally. As we have seen, all stereotypes are not false, not in particular settings nor in general.

The answer to the instructional dilemma is not, as is frequently thought and practiced, to deny or to overlook the existence of group differences, especially differences that appear to reflect negatively on one group in comparison to another. Such instruction is undoubtedly well motivated and practiced because it is thought that the acknowledgment of group differ-ences may breed prejudice, but its more likely consequence is to compro-mise the integrity of the teacher and, in the process, either mute his or her potential to be effective or produce a boomerang effect by making it seem to the discerning youngster that there is some justification after all for prejudice.

The pedagogical solution pointed to by the research is for the existence of group differences to be forthrightly acknowledged and discussed, whether they appear to reflect on a group positively, negatively, or neutrally. If any-thing, negative attributions are especially to be acknowledged to ensure that there are no grounds for a youngster to feel deceived. It will be discovered, if a systematic effort is made to find out, that there is not that much known about group differences that is grounded in solid evidence. Still, to teach youngsters how to distinguish the facts about group differences from the surmises and the fiction appears crucial to forestalling the too ready acceptance of sweeping and false ascriptions.

The honest acknowledgment of group differences will inevitably confirm rather than deny the validity of some allegations that the prejudiced make about the deficiencies of an outgroup. No group has a monopoly on virtue and, if there are group differences, some individuals will favor one group over the other and some will do the opposite. Left to their own devices, as we have seen, many youngsters will not be sensitive to nuances and, confronted with evidence of the grain of truth in a stereotype, they are ill equipped to draw any other conclusion than that prejudice is justified.

Our findings suggest three kinds of educational input are needed to teach youngsters not to fall victim to simplistic thinking. First, instruction in the logic of inference is called for so that youngsters can come to recognize when group differences are being falsely accounted for, as was the case with those teenagers in Commutertown and Oceanville who falsely attributed the conceit of Jewish peers to their Jewishness rather than to their success. Learning the logic of inference requires instruction in the notion of causality; that is to say, the necessity of looking beyond surface characteristics, beyond easy explanations, to discover more subtle reasons for human behavior. It also requires instruction in the rules of evidence. Just as a teenager learns to inspect a chemical solution to judge its properties, he needs to be able to examine human situations and decide what conclusions he reasonably can and cannot infer. To do this, of course, involves training in the social sciences beyond the specific problem of prejudice. But it is perhaps a necessary pedagogical task if youngsters are to be made capable intellectually of coping with prejudice.

Second, specific instruction is needed about how group differences come about. This means going into the historical background of group differences to reveal their cultural and social sources. Why black teenagers are less successful in school and why Jewish teenagers and their parents are prone to clannishness, for example, have to be explained so that their historical roots are understood and the social forces making for their persistence in contemporary society comprehended. Especially necessary, it seems, is instruction showing that group differences are not exclusively the result simply of genetic traits or attributable simply to the acts of individuals without respect to social, cultural, and historical pressures.

Third, instruction is required to make clear the size of group differences so as to guard against the common tendency for relative differences, which virtually all group differences are, to be generalized. For example, it needs to be made clear that all Jewish teenagers are not successful in school, nor are all non-Jewish teenagers unsuccessful. The differences are, as most human differences, matters of degree. Instruction is required which makes it evident that this is the case even though stereotypes and generalizations are often used as shorthand ways of describing group differences.

Our data suggest that instruction pursued along these lines, presuming it could be carried out successfully, would make prejudice so indefensible intellectually as to render it inoperative even for youngsters surrounded by prejudiced peers. Making prejudice inoperative would not necessarily result in friendliness and approval being substituted for intolerance. Comprehension of the way group differences can and do come about does not mean that traits previously reacted to negatively will now be thought of positively. Such comprehension does forestall, however, an intolerant response and allow for group differences to be dealt with on their own terms.

For example, recognition that clannishness manifested by teenage peers of the Jewish faith and their parents has historical roots and is associated with past persecution of Jews by non-Jews is unlikely to result in admiration of clannishness. However, contrary to an understanding of clannishness as as innate deficiency of Jewish character, the effect will not be prejudice.

Such a pedagogical effort as is proposed constitutes a tall order and, admittedly, the research does not demonstrate that if it were tried, it would work. It is conceivable, first of all, that the number of youngsters who could absorb and learn from such instruction would be no more than the number who now learn the irrationality of prejudice more indirectly because, through whatever means, they learn how to think. It is also conceivable that our research, by virtue of inadequacies in measurement, has grossly underestimated the emotive element in prejudice. Even if it has, of course, it would not necessarily mean that dissonance between one's cognitive understanding of prejudice and one's emotional feelings about an outgroup would necessarily be resolved emotionally. Nevertheless, it is evident that if the psychological factors are paramount, instruction devoted to developing only cognitive understanding of prejudice has much less chance to be effective than if such factors are not significant, as the present research suggests.

These cautions notwithstanding, the idea that it may take no more than instruction, although of a special kind, to effect a substantial reduction in the incidence of prejudice seems sufficiently compelling to justify some effort to test it out. The test could be made nominally by individual school districts introducing some formal instruction about prejudice into their curricula, using whatever resources and materials are now current. Such testing, however, would be inconclusive and not be conducive, if the idea has merit, of the most effective educational package being produced.

If it is to be made at all, the test ought to be made seriously. This would require an investment in the development of an educational package including the preparation of written, audio-visual, and other materials informed by the pedagogical strategy suggested by the research. Some experimentation would be called for to try out alternative educational models and to discover at what age levels the instruction might be begun most effectively (the earlier probably the better, given the evidence that by adolescence prejudice is as widespread as it is). Ultimately, field tests would be required to judge the merit of the fundamental idea and of the devices developed to implement it.

There is no obvious place in the nation's educational structure for such a test to be taken up and pursued. Leadership might come from a school of education, from one of the national educational associations, an agency of the federal government, from a private foundation, or from some combination of these. The structural constraints referred to earlier may be enough to forestall anyone taking the lead. That would be unfortunate, for prejudice remains the nation's most virulent social disease and the schools, of all institutions, are the most likely to supply the long needed remedy.

Prejudice emerges from our inquiry as a more complex phenomenon than previous research has suggested or our conception of it before we began our inquiry. The complexity is not recognized by most teenagers and because it is not we have put the major burden of these remarks on a possible means to make the complexity known. A complementary question which arises has to do with teachers' understanding of the complexity.

Schools operate more or less on the assumptions that teachers are unprejudiced, that they are equipped to deal with prejudice when it arises as a problem, and that even teachers who have no explicit responsibility for instruction about prejudice will in informal ways make a positive contribution to such instruction. Our tiny study of teachers made no effort to test these assumptions. We suspect it probably would have been thought unbecoming of us had we tried. Yet, even presuming the best of goodwill on the part of teachers, it seems unlikely that many of them will have made prejudice a special subject of study or have thought through its subtleties. Consequently, it is possible that teachers, rather than being the positive force in combating prejudice they are thought to be, may be exercising no leverage at all or on occasion be inadvertently doing harm.

Clearly, any effort to deal with the problem of prejudice through an innovative instructional program such as has been proposed would of necessity have to make sure that teachers are qualified to do their parts whether they are to be involved directly in the formal instruction or not. It also seems desirable that school districts, in the more ordinary course of events, take steps to assure themselves that their teachers have a sophisticated understanding of prejudice and know how to deal with it constructively in classroom situations.

Understandably, teachers don't like to be checked up on and there would undoubtedly be resistance to any proposal that teachers take a test to judge their comprehension of such things as stereotyping, the nature of group differences, and how group differences come about, and their ability to recognize prejudice in students and to respond effectively to contain it. Still, presented in a constructive way and with responses submitted anonymously, such a test might be acceptable to teachers. If so, it could become a fundamental tool in prejudice control, usable not only with teachers but with other occupational groups such as the police, clergy, probation officers, and social workers, for whom dealing with prejudice and discrimination is an everyday occurrence.

So far, we have been talking about the more practical implications of the findings, things the schools could do given the will to do them. The results of our inquiry suggest one additional point at which the schools might exercise leverage although in this instance it is not so clear that the leverage is in the schools' control.

It is evident from the findings that there is a significant class element in prejudice and that a substantial net reduction in prejudice would be achieved if this class component were removed. Racial prejudice especially is aggravated by the class factor and apparently would not be nearly so virulent if it were grounded in race alone.

Like other forms of prejudice class prejudice is subject to being muted and contained through coming to understand its nature and the forces that bring it about. Simply learning that there is a class structure in America, for example, and that one's class is not something the adolescent chooses for himself has, in itself, a certain power to mute hostility to someone because of class differences. Thus, the proposals for teaching youngsters not to be prejudiced and for upgrading teachers' knowledge and understanding of prejudice ought to effect some reduction in class bias as well as other forms of prejudice. In addition, schools can conceivably do about class prejudice something they are unable to do about religious or racial prejudice. The schools can't make Jews into Christians nor blacks into whites. They might, however, be able to reduce the social inequality that breeds class prejudice.

Our results and those of other investigations indicate that the schools have not been very effective in bringing about the equality espoused in the

American dream. The high correlation between adolescents' socioeconomic status and their academic status is indicative that the schools are perpetuating rather than making up for the deficiencies which some youngsters bring with them to school. This means also, of course, that the schools are contributing to the perpetuation of prejudice.

Here again, structural constraints, the problem's lack of saliency, and not knowing what to do anyway all contribute to the *status quo* being maintained. Our study affords no special advice about how the schools might break the roadblocks, but it does make evident that anything that the schools can do to eliminate *arbitrary* privilege would redound in the reduction of prejudice. This does not mean that merit should not be recognized and rewarded. It does mean doing everything possible to ensure that students are not excluded from the full cognitive benefits of the school merely because they are poor, black, or something else. In sum, if the schools could break down the correlation between socioeconomic status and academic success, they would also be reducing the correlation of socioeconomic status and prejudice.

A byproduct of raising levels of cognitive sophistication about prejudice could be greater acceptance of schools taking the initiative in breaking down arbitrary privilege and in innovating programs to make up for past inequities. Prejudice, it is evident, remains a major obstacle to such things getting done.

Appendix A: Construction of Scales

In this section details are presented on the methods used for constructing scales found in the foregoing analysis. Where it was possible to do so without unduly encumbering the analysis, scales were briefly described in the body of the book. Others which require more detailed comment are discussed here. For ease of reference, the scales are described in the order in which they appear in the discussion and are arranged by chapter. Footnotes within the chapters give the page upon which the construction of a specific scale is described.

Chapter 1: Attitudes, Feelings, and Patterns of Friendship

Social Distance

Summary measures of social distance to both high-status and low-status Jews were constructed as follows: One point was given for each activity teenagers were *unwilling* to countenance. The activities included in the scale are the nine discussed in Chapter 1 plus a tenth item about living in an apartment building with Jews (this item proved to be somewhat contaminated by differences in the three towns regarding living in apartments in general). The scale ranged from a low of 0 to a high of 10. It was then collapsed to a five-point scale, where a score of 1 (low social distance) equals 0 to 2, a score of 2 equals 3 to 4, a score of 3 equals 5 to 6, a score of 4 equals 7 to 8, and a score of 5 (high social distance) equals 9 to 10.

Nicholls Homophily–Heterophily Index

The Nicholls index for the analysis of ingroup–outgroup choice is independent of the proportion of the total population made up of each group. The index bears certain similarities to a chi-square, as it is calculated as a discrepancy of the observed frequency of choices given to a group from an expected frequency. Because this expected value takes account of the proportion of the group being chosen in the total population, the index may be compared across populations that differ in their proportions of various groups. The index runs from a value of $+1.0$, indicating that all of the choices given by group Z were to group Y, to -1.0, indicating that none of the choices given by group Z were to group Y. An index of 0.0 indicates that the members of group Z were choosing the members of group Y at the level to be expected by chance from their distribution in the population. An index close to 0.0 implies that the chooser is not taking the group membership by which the chosen group is classified into account in his choices.

TERMS USED IN THE FORMULA.

H = the index

Total = total number of choices given to all Y groups by group Z (choosing group)

$Obs._Y$ = number of choices given to group Y by group Z (Y runs from 1 to number of ETHGRPS)

$Exp._Y$ = expected frequency of choices to be given to group Y

N_{Total} = total number of people in all Y groups

N_Y = number of people in the Yth group

CALCULATION OF THE INDEX.

Formula for the expected frequency:

(1) When Z = Y, and members cannot logically choose themselves:
$$Exp._Y = Total \times (N_Y - 1) / (N_{Total} - 1)$$

(2) In all other cases:
$$Exp._Y = Total \times N_Y / N_{Total}$$

Formula for the index:

(1) When $Obs._Y - Exp._Y = 0$ or positive:
$$H = \frac{Obs._Y - Exp._Y}{Total - Exp._Y}$$

(2) When $Obs._Y - Exp._Y$ is negative:
$$H = \frac{Obs._Y - Exp._Y}{Exp._Y}$$

Chapter 2: The Social Context of Adolescent Prejudice

Summary Index of Anti-Semitism

Eight stereotype items comprise the summary anti-Semitism measure: selfish, unfriendly, gaudy, conceited, pushy, immoral, vain, and trouble-makers. The table reports the results of the factor analyses that were performed for the two forms of the questionnaire in each of the three towns. As the principal component scores indicate, each of the eight items receives a factor loading of at least 0.500 (except for "troublemakers" on the teen-age form in Commutertown). The results of oblimax and varimax rotations also confirmed the assumption that the items are measures of a single rather than several underlying phenomena.

PRINCIPAL COMPONENT SCORES

	Teenage Form			Adult Form		
	Commuter-town	Ocean-ville	Central City	Commuter-town	Ocean-ville	Central City
Vain	0.768	0.789	0.758	0.780	0.747	0.737
Conceited	0.770	0.773	0.670	0.787	0.720	0.757
Selfish	0.697	0.722	0.681	0.692	0.716	0.657
Pushy	0.594	0.681	0.670	0.670	0.701	0.690
Unfriendly	0.619	0.668	0.590	0.678	0.668	0.618
Gaudy	0.533	0.598	0.670	0.659	0.598	0.660
Immoral	0.575	0.623	0.644	0.593	0.580	0.715
Troublemakers	0.476	0.517	0.613	0.548	0.599	0.632

It will be recalled from the discussion that the eight items included in the index are worded the same or nearly the same on the two forms of the questionnaire, thereby making it possible to combine the forms throughout the analysis.

To construct the scale, points were first assigned for responses to each of the eight items according to the following formula:

	Score
Disagree strongly	1
Disagree moderately	2
Disagree a little	3
Check mark placed between or on both agree and disagree responses	4
Agree a little	5
Agree moderately	6
Agree strongly	7

Each teenager's responses to the eight items were then averaged, yielding an average anti-Semitism score that ranges between 1 and 7. Average scores not resulting in whole numbers are rounded, those between 0.01 and 0.50 being rounded down to the nearest whole number, those of 0.51 to 0.99 rounded up. Teenagers who answered at least four of the eight items were assigned an average score based on the items answered. Those answering less than half the eight items were excluded from the scale.

As Chapter 2 reports, teenagers with average scores of 4 or more are considered anti-Semitic; those with scores of less than 4, not anti-Semitic.

Exactly the same procedures are used in the construction of the summary index of racial prejudice upon which the analysis in Chapter 6 is based.

Father's Socioeconomic Status

Four items were available in the questionnaires as measures of family socioeconomic background: father's education, mother's education, father's income, and father's occupational status. The latter two items, considered more precise indicators of economic deprivation or privilege, were combined to form a summary index of father's socioeconomic status with scores assigned as follows:

Father's Annual Income	Scores on Index of Father's Socioeconomic Status
$20,000 or more	3
$10,000 to $20,000	2
$5,000 to $10,000	1
Less than $5,000	0
Father's Occupational Status	
Very high (e.g., doctors, lawyers, high-level executives)	3
High (e.g., teachers, owners of small businesses, accountants)	2
Average (e.g., skilled workers, salesmen, protective-service workers)	1
Low (e.g., operatives, unskilled workers)	0

Adding the scores of the two items produced a scale ranging from 0 (low status) to 6 (high status). Respondents failing to answer any of the items were excluded from the index. This procedure is followed throughout the analysis.

For purposes of comparison, an index was also constructed using the other two available indicators of socioeconomic status: father's and mother's education. Two points were assigned for each having at least some college education, one for at least some high school education, and zero for less education. The gammas for the relation between this scale and anti-Semitism in the three towns are 0.272, 0.126, and 0.076 respectively.

Economic Deprivation

The economic deprivation index was constructed as follows:

Father's Socioeconomic Status Scale Score	Score on Economic Deprivation Index
6	0
4, 5	1
1–3	2
0	3
Teenager's Economic Status	
High	0
Medium	1
Low	2

Scores were added to create a scale ranging from 0 (low economic deprivation) to 5 (high economic deprivation).

Academic Deprivation

Three items were included in this index, with points assigned for each item as follows:

School Performance Scale Score	Score on Academic Deprivation Index
0	3
1, 2	2
3, 4	1
5	0
Likelihood of Attending College	
Low	2
Medium	1
High	0
Like School	
Not at all	3
Not much	2
Some	1
Very much	0

To conserve cases, this scale which ranges from 0 to 7 was subsequently collapsed as follows: 0 and $1 = 0, 2 = 1, 3 = 2, 4 = 3, 5-7 = 4$.

Chapter 3: Causes of Adolescent Anti-Semitism

F Scale

The ten items from the Christie reversed version of the F scale were presented in a battery of items that also included Rosenberg's self-esteem items. Respondents were asked to circle one of six answers for each item: disagree strongly, disagree moderately, disagree a little, agree a little, agree moderately, agree strongly. Five of the items were worded so that agreement indicates high authoritarianism and five so that it means low F. For purposes of the scale, degrees of agreement and disagreement were disregarded and 1 or 0 point was assigned simply for agreement or disagreement, depending on the item. The scale ranges from 0 (low authoritarianism) to 10 (high authoritarianism).

Flexibility

Respondents were presented Gough's ten flexibility scale items and asked to say whether each is a true or a false statement. All but one of the items is worded so that answering "true" indicates *low* flexibility. A score of 1 was assigned for each answer indicating flexibility and 0 for each indicating a lack of flexibility, thus creating a scale ranging from 0 to 10. To conserve cases, this scale was then collapsed to run from 0 to 3, where 0 (low flexibility) $= 0-4, 1 = 5-7, 2 = 8-9$, and 3 (high flexibility) $= 10$.

Chapter 4: The Effects of a Jewish Presence

Combined Scale of Deprivation/Unsophistication

This scale combines scores on the academic deprivation scale with those on the cognitive sophistication scale as follows:

Academic Deprivation	Score on Scale
4	4
3	3
2	2
1	1
0	0

Cognitive Sophistication	Score on Scale
0–4	3
5–6	2
7–9	1
10–11	0

Adding the scores produces a scale ranging from 0 (low deprivation/unsophistication) to 7 (high deprivation/unsophistication).

Chapter 5: Adolescent Racial Prejudice

Summary Index of Racial Prejudice

The procedures for constructing this scale are the same as those described earlier for the summary index of anti-Semitism. As the following principal component scores indicate, each of the eight items included in the scale loads highly on a single factor—all are above 0.500.

PRINCIPAL COMPONENT SCORES

	Teenage Form			Adult Form		
	Commuter-town	Ocean-ville	Central City	Commuter-town	Ocean-ville	Central City
Vain	0.729	0.753	0.790	0.799	0.775	0.803
Conceited	0.654	0.677	0.674	0.735	0.713	0.756
Selfish	0.734	0.768	0.783	0.786	0.727	0.780
Pushy	0.560	0.590	0.750	0.720	0.655	0.799
Unfriendly	0.598	0.587	0.516	0.587	0.574	0.535
Gaudy	0.637	0.645	0.634	0.681	0.700	0.637
Immoral	0.746	0.767	0.805	0.760	0.788	0.801
Troublemakers	0.783	0.797	0.787	0.805	0.713	0.790

Appendix B: Anti-Semitism Among Black Adolescents

An unanticipated finding in Chapter 1 was the discovery of less anti-Semitism among black than among white teenagers in each of the three communities studied. This violation of the theory that prejudice is characteristically more common among the relatively more deprived members of society aroused the suspicion, as have several other studies in the present series on prejudice, that perhaps different processes may be operating in the black community to produce or to prevent anti-Semitism than in the white subculture. This suspicion led us to decide, it will be recalled, to pursue the main analysis on white teenagers only. The comparable analysis for black teenagers is presented here.

Until now, sociological and psychological theory about prejudice has been grounded primarily in white experience. Inductively, theory has been produced from case studies, experiments, and surveys with predominantly white subjects; deductively, from ideas stimulated by reflections on white-dominated Western culture.

This parochial epistomology of social theory does not mean, of course, that it is necessarily appropriate only to accounting for white behavior. But if there is one lesson to be learned from the perceptive writings of W. E. B. DuBois, Frantz Fanon, and Kenneth Clark, among others, it is that theoretical monism is engaged in only at the risk of critically oversimplifying the diverse richness of social reality.

It is easier, however, to assert the potential for bias in generalizing beyond one's data than it is to overcome it. Hypotheses derived from the observation of white experience may be shown not to apply to blacks at all, or to explain less about black than about white behavior. To account for the discrepancies, however, requires special existential knowledge of black society that some have asserted is accessible only to black social scientists and that in any case has still largely to be accumulated.

189

In the present analysis no attempt will be made to develop special theories to account for prejudice among black teenagers. Our inquiry was not designed with that purpose in mind, and the nature of the data collected does not allow the task to be pursued retrospectively. What we can and will do is to seek to demonstrate the extent to which the same mechanisms operate or fail to operate among both whites and blacks and, in so doing, we hope to distinguish the areas in which present theory is adequate and the areas where new theory is required.

The main propositions which informed and were found confirmed in the analysis of the white data were that prejudice would be found especially among more socially deprived subgroups in teenage society and that its social location there is the result of the relative absence in such groups of the cognitive sophistication necessary to understand the nature of prejudice and, thereby, to avoid taking it up. To judge how informing these propositions are of the black data, we shall replicate in its essentials the analysis pursued for whites in Chapters 2, 3, and 4. Because the results for blacks do not differ significantly by town, tabulations will be presented for all three towns combined with significant variations between towns being reserved for marginal treatment.

Deprivation and Prejudice

In Chapter 2 a variety of characteristics indicative of deprivation or privilege, including economic status, academic performance, and expected future social status, were examined and found to be associated with prejudice among white non-Jewish adolescents. When the joint influence of these factors on prejudice was investigated, it was learned that academic forms of deprivation (school performance, school satisfaction, and college plans) were more closely associated with anti-Semitism than was economic deprivation (of parents and of teenagers) and, in fact, constituted the reason why economic factors were related to prejudice. The first question of interest here, then, is whether deprivation is also a source of prejudice for black adolescents.

Table B-1 reports the relation between anti-Semitism and economic deprivation among black teenagers. Respondents from all three towns are combined in this table. Figures are also presented for total white non-Jewish respondents in the three towns for purposes of comparison. Looking first at parents' socioeconomic status, which is measured by father's income and occupational status, a relationship with anti-Semitism just as strong as, if not somewhat stronger than, that for whites is observed for blacks, although in both cases the relationships are only slight. Fewer blacks than whites score high on socioeconomic status, but at every successive level of privilege there exists a correspondent decrease in the likelihood of anti-Semitism, just as among whites. Unfortunately, the confidence that can be placed in this relationship is limited by the fact that a large number of black teenagers (approximately one-third) did not know or were not willing to reveal the socioeconomic statuses of their fathers. For those who answered the question, however, the relationship is clearly in accordance with our previous findings. It is noteworthy also that within each status category black teenagers continue to manifest less prejudice than their white counterparts. Although socioeconomic factors do not account for the lower levels of negative attitudes among blacks, they are one of the social conditions that affect prejudice in both racial groups.

Table B-1 ANTI-SEMITISM BY ECONOMIC DEPRIVATION FOR
BLACK AND WHITE NON-JEWISH ADOLESCENTS

Parents' socioeconomic status:	Percent anti-Semitic among those whose status was:								
	High						Low		
	6	5	4	3	2	1	0	Gamma	Xs
Black	* (7)	* (9)	31% (13)	31% (26)	40% (141)	41% (56)	50% (145)	+0.174	NS
White	38% (79)	46% (70)	51% (263)	51% (172)	49% (1,107)	55% (238)	51% (399)	+0.045	NS

Teenagers' economic status:	High	Medium	Low		
Black	43% (231)	42% (256)	39% (100)	−0.049	NS
White	46% (1,133)	50% (1,005)	60% (501)	+0.158	0.001

* Too few cases for stable percentage.
NS—Not significant.

Teenagers' economic status, measured by receiving an allowance and not having to work after school at a parttime job, does not show similar relations for blacks and whites, however. Instead of there being an increase in prejudice with lower status, there is essentially no difference or, if anything, a slight decrease in anti-Semitism among blacks. Separate analysis of the two items included in the economic status scale also indicates essentially no variation in anti-Semitism, at least between those who have to work and those who do not. There is a slight tendency, however, for black teenagers who receive an allowance to be more prejudiced than those who do not, a reversal of the comparable relationship among white teenagers.

These findings in themselves do not necessarily contradict the theory that prejudice is more typical of the deprived, however. A more likely interpretation is that the indicators used to measure economic status among white adolescents do not function in the same manner for blacks. One or both of the items used to measure economic deprivation may not be a sign of status within the black teenage subcommunity. Still, the possibility cannot be ruled out entirely that the absence of a relationship may, indeed, indicate that this form of deprivation bears no connection with the attitudes of black adolescents toward Jews.

Some evidence is available, then, for suggesting that among both blacks and whites economic deprivation, at least that acquired from parents, is one of the conditions associated with being more highly prejudiced.

The relationships between anti-Semitism and measures of academic status for blacks and whites are compared in Table B-2. In Chapter 2 five items indicating relative academic privilege or deprivation were examined: grades, homework time, school satisfaction, wanting to go to college, and planning to go to college (expectations and preparatory programs). Each of these factors, it was argued (although reservations were also acknowledged), is indicative either directly or indirectly of how well an adolescent is functioning objectively or subjectively relative to his peers in the competition to which they are subject as high school students. Each is also a sign of students' access to or achievement of the social and intellectual rewards offered by their school environments.

When these factors are analyzed to discover their relationship to prejudice, similar patterns occur among blacks and whites. Making better grades and devoting more time to homework, for example, are associated with a lower incidence of anti-Semitism. Similarly, black youngsters who like school and both want and expect to go on for further schooling are less prejudiced than those disliking school and without college aspirations. Generally speaking, however, measures of academic deprivation are not so strongly associated with prejudice among blacks as they were among white non-Jewish high school students. Although school satisfaction and college aspirations produce about as much variation in anti-Semitism in one group as in the other, blacks show less variation on the other three items than whites.

It is also important to note that blacks persistently continue to score lower on anti-Semitism than their white classmates even when students ranking similarly on all the measures of academic status examined are compared. Clues other than academic deprivation, then, must be sought to account for the relatively lower level of anti-Semitism among black adolescents.

In sum, except for teenage economic status of blacks, the direction of the associations with anti-Semitism of each individual indicator of both economic and academic deprivation is the same for black and for white teenagers. The strengths of the relationships are also comparable though weaker for blacks on some of the measures of academic deprivation.

It was found that among whites the effects of deprivation on prejudice were additive. That is to say, the greater the number of ways in which white youngsters experience economic or academic deprivation, the more anti-Semitic they are likely to be. In light of the absence of a relation between

Table B-2   ANTI-SEMITISM BY ACADEMIC DEPRIVATION ITEMS FOR BLACK AND WHITE NON-JEWISH ADOLESCENTS

(All three communities combined)

Percent anti-Semitic among those whose grades were:

Grades:	B+ to A	B	B− to C	C− to D	Gamma	Xs
Black	33% (58)	40% (104)	41% (360)	40% (71)	0.118	NS
White	35% (522)	45% (588)	56% (1,270)	65% (305)	0.299	0.001
Homework time:	2 hours per day or more	1 hour or 1½ hours	½ hour or less		Gamma	Xs
Black	38% (130)	39% (312)	48% (156)		0.131	Ns
White	41% (749)	51% (1,340)	62% (602)		0.252	0.001
School satisfaction:	Like school very much	Some	Not very much	Not at all	Gamma	Xs
Black	34% (260)	48% (286)	45% (42)	46% (11)	0.217	0.02
White	42% (988)	53% (1,351)	67% (253)	68% (100)	0.279	0.001
College aspirations:	Like to go	Not like to go	Don't care		Gamma	Xs
Black	39% (497)	56% (66)	49% (37)		0.277	NS
White	48% (2,131)	61% (383)	65% (176)		0.275	0.001
College plans:	High	Medium	Low		Gamma	Xs
Black	31% (110)	43% (313)	46% (142)		0.120	NS
White	42% (938)	52% (959)	60% (678)		0.189	0.001

NS—Not significant.

teenage economic status and prejudice, the same result would not be anticipated for blacks with respect to economic deprivation. As can be seen in Table B-3, the summary index of economic deprivation is not consistently associated with prejudice. Parental economic deprivation alone is more strongly related to anti-Semitism than is the summary scale (gamma = 0.174 rather than 0.136).

Table B-3 ANTI-SEMITISM BY SUMMARY MEASURES OF DEPRIVATION
FOR BLACK AND WHITE NON-JEWISH ADOLESCENTS
(All three communities combined)

Percent anti-Semitic among those
whose scores on economic deprivation were:

| | Low | | | | | High | | |
	0	1	2	3	4	5	Gamma	Xs
Black	*	29%	43%	38%	56%	36%	0.136	0.10
	(6)	(21)	(91)	(147)	(97)	(25)		
White	32%	47%	47%	47%	58%	61%	0.126	0.001
	(47)	(255)	(746)	(728)	(434)	(69)		

Percent anti-Semitic among those
whose scores on academic deprivation were:

| | Low | | | | High | | |
	0	1	2	3	4	Gamma	Xs
Black	33%	36%	34%	46%	48%	0.167	0.10
	(49)	(83)	(155)	(140)	(124)		
White	32%	43%	49%	55%	67%	0.322	0.001
	(413	(491)	(559)	(512)	(578)		

* Too few cases for stable percentage.

The summary measure of academic deprivation is related to attitudes toward Jews. As among white teenagers, blacks who are most deprived academically exhibit the most anti-Semitism and its amount progressively decreases as academic deprivation is reduced. Whereas the gamma for whites is moderate (0.322), that for blacks is weak (0.167), however. Thus, although academic deprivation is associated with prejudice in both racial groups, it does not provide as much understanding about the social location of prejudice in the black as in the white community.

To complete the analysis of deprivation as it is related to prejudice, the joint effects of economic and academic status must be examined. The summary measure of economic status developed for whites will not be used, however, since it did not prove to be significantly associated with anti-Semitism. Rather, parents' socioeconomic status will be substituted since it alone is more strongly associated with prejudice. Testing the joint effects of parental status and academic status, then, permits a judgment to be made about the relative importance of background factors and school factors in the maintenance of prejudice. Table B-4 presents this information.

The small number of cases, especially in the higher categories of socio-economic status, make it difficult to obtain an entirely clear portrait from Table B-4. Generally speaking, however, when socioeconomic and academic status are examined simultaneously, both continue to affect anti-Semitism scores. The influence of academic deprivation seems to be somewhat the stronger of the two, but academic factors do not "interpret" the relation between economic background and prejudice as clearly and as completely for blacks as they did for whites. Instead, each form of deprivation shows sufficiently independent association with anti-Semitism to reveal that teen-agers deprived on both counts manifest more hatred and hostility than those deprived on one or the other measure, and youth ranking as most privileged on both types of deprivation score lowest on prejudice.

In sum, among black as among white teenagers, anti-Semitism is located especially in those subgroups which are the most deprived economically, socially, and academically. It is least present among the most privileged teenagers in both communities. However, congruent with results found previously in studies of adults, privileged and deprived black teenagers differ relatively less in their anti-Semitism than do privileged and deprived white adolescents.

Why this is the case is not immediately self-evident. The analysis pursued so far also does not reveal why in the white subculture the process at work linking the several forms of deprivation to anti-Semitism is one which proceeds from economic deprivation in the home to academic deprivation to anti-Semitism, whereas in the black subcommunity the two forms of deprivation are more independently associated with prejudice. We shall probably not be able to resolve these discrepancies with the data at hand. However, an exploration of the various connecting processes examined in Chapter 3 for white teenagers will shed some light on why deprivation is less powerfully and somewhat differently related to anti-Semitism among adolescent blacks.

Intervening Variables

Four possible interpretations of the relationship between deprivation and anti-Semitism were subjected to test in the earlier analysis of white prejudice. These were that (1) the deprived project hatred and aggression onto minority groups out of frustration and anxiety about their status, (2) the

Table B-4 ANTI-SEMITISM BY PARENTS' SOCIOECONOMIC STATUS AND ACADEMIC DEPRIVATION FOR BLACK NON-JEWISH ADOLESCENTS

(All three communities combined)

Percent anti-Semitic among those whose parents' socioeconomic status was:

And whose academic deprivation score was:	High 6	5	4	3	2	1	Low 0	Total	Gamma	Xs
Low 0	* (2)	* (2)	* (7)	* (6)	40% (10)	* (3)	36% (11)	33% (49)	+0.356	NS
1	* (3)	* (2)	* (2)	* (3)	33% (24)	* (7)	48% (25)	36% (83)	+0.194	NS
2	* (1)	* (4)	* (3)	* (6)	36% (42)	43% (14)	44% (34)	34% (155)	+0.116	NS
3	* (1)	* (1)	* (1)	* (6)	47% (34)	* (8)	46% (41)	46% (140)	−0.116	NS
High 4	* (0)	* (0)	* (0)	* (1)	52% (21)	58% (19)	60% (25)	48% (124)	+0.150	NS
Total	* (7)	* (9)	31% (13)	31% (22)	40% (131)	41% (151)	50% (136)	42% (551)	+0.174	NS
Gamma	−0.556	+1.000	+0.538	+0.538	+0.186	+0.455	+0.140			
Xs	NS	NS	NS	NS	NS	NS	NS			

*Too few cases for stable percentage.
NS—Not significant.

deprived are more likely to be anti-Semitic because they associate with peers who are more prejudiced, (3) "enlightened" values that are in opposition to hatred and hostility are less likely to be held by deprived groups, and (4) prejudice is more common among deprived teenagers because of a more general lack of cognitive sophistication. Subjecting the data on black teenagers to the same tests produces the following results.

Frustration

The three scales used as indicators of the kind of psychological impairment conducive to frustration, anxiety, and presumably aggression are shown in Table B-5 as they relate to anti-Semitism among black youngsters. It will be recalled that the F scale is the Christie revised version, which is a modification of the original scale developed by the authors of *The Authoritarian Personality*; the index of self-acceptance is composed of four

Table B-5   ANTI-SEMITISM BY MEASURES OF FRUSTRATION FOR
BLACK NON-JEWISH ADOLESCENTS
(All three communities combined)

Percent anti-Semitic among those
whose score on the F scale was:

Low									High			
0	1	2	3	4	5	6	7	8	9	10	Gamma	Xs
*	*	*	35%	50%	44%	45%	46%	47%	*	*	+0.013	NS
(0)	(0)	(6)	(20)	(28)	(95)	(98)	(56)	(15)	(6)	(0)		

Percent anti-Semitic among those whose score
on the self-accepance scale was:

Low			High			
0	1	2	3	4	Gamma	Xs
39%	39%	43%	40%	37%	−0.003	NS
(31)	(112)	(181)	(142)	(35)		

Percent anti-Semitic among those whose score
on the self-esteem scale was:

Low				High			
0	1	2	3	4	5	6	Gamma Xs
*	*	39%	46%	40%	45%	46%	+0.016 NS
(0)	(3)	(26)	(108)	(88)	(69)	(44)	

* Too few cases for stable percentage.
NS—Not significant.

items taken from Gough's scale of the same name, and the measure of self-esteem is that developed by Rosenberg. As the table demonstrates, no association exists between any of these scales and anti-Semitism. These findings are entirely consistent with those already found for white teenagers. The disclaimers made earlier about the possible invalidity of the scales when employed with teenagers must also be registered here, with perhaps double emphasis to recognize added difficulties that black youngsters may have experienced in responding to the items making up the scales. If the meaning of the items was ambiguous to white teenagers, then there is reason to believe that they may have been even more uninterpretable to blacks both because of cultural differences and because of their generally lower level of academic functioning. On two of the scales, F and self-esteem, almost half of the black respondents, in fact, failed to answer enough of the items to be included in the analysis, providing clear reason for hesitation in basing conclusions on the results of these scales. As for whites, however, the possibility does remain that frustration is simply not an important source of prejudice at this stage of life.

Interaction with peers

Just as among whites, how anti-Semitic one's friends are is related to how anti-Semitic one is oneself. The relation isn't as strong for blacks as it is for whites, but as Table B-6 shows, the general tendency is for anti-Semitism scores to increase the higher the average of friends' anti-Semitism scores. Unfortunately, the small number of cases makes it impractical to try to ferret out the three-variable relation between anti-Semitism, academic deprivation, and friends' anti-Semitism.

Table B-6   ANTI-SEMITISM BY FRIENDS' ANTI-SEMITISM FOR
BLACK NON-JEWISH ADOLESCENTS
(All three communities combined)

Percent anti-Semitic among those whose friends'
anti-Semitism scores were:

Low						High		
1	2	3	4	5	6	7	Gamma	Xs
37%	38%	41%	49%	63%	*	*	0.128	NS
(38)	(164)	(220)	(98)	(16)	(6)	(0)		

* Too few cases for stable percentage.
NS—Not significant.

Enlightened values

The proposition that anti-Semitism is more likely among deprived youth because they are less likely to subscribe to democratic values that run counter to hatred and discrimination was tested for whites in three ways. First, it was tested for civic values on the supposition that commitment to equalitarian and civil libertarian ideals would be effective armor against prejudice. Second, it was tested for moral values. Here, the expectation was that adherence to too rigid and intolerant moral standards would mean ostracizing groups perceived as not sharing or meeting these standards. Third, it was tested for interpersonal values on the assumption that beliefs in prejudice and brotherhood ought not to go together. Among whites, the proposition gained support only when tested for interpersonal values. Civic and moral values, if held, are apparently sufficiently compartmentalized so as not to influence orientations to minority groups.

Making the same tests for black adolescents produces the results reported in Table B-7. Like whites, most blacks agree with all the values though with varying strength. How much agreement there is, however, has no consistent relation to levels of anti-Semitism. This is true for all three sets of values—civic, moral, and interpersonal. The results for whites and blacks, then, are discrepant with respect to interpersonal values but in accord on the other two sets of values.

As we remarked earlier, there has been some tendency in the literature on prejudice to conceive enlightened values and cognitive sophistication as operating in concert in prejudice reduction. These results do not have anything to say about the role of cognitive sophistication in relation to enlightened values, but they afford little support to the belief that the enlightened-values thesis is operative among white teenagers and none at all to the belief that enlightened values or their absence is informing of black attitudes toward Jews.

Lack of cognitive sophistication

The last proposition—that prejudice is rooted in cognitive failure to understand its nature and, therefore, in being unarmed against it—was tested for white teenagers by examining the association between anti-Semitism and three indicators of level of cognitive sophistication or unsophistication. One measure—involvement in intellectual activities—sought to test teenagers' exposure to cognitively sophisticated viewpoints. A second measure—cynicism—afforded an indirect indication, at least in part, of teenagers' vulnerability to oversimplified (i.e., cognitively unsophisticated) understandings of human nature. The third measure—flexibility—distributed teenagers according to their ability to deal with complexity and ambiguity in thinking. Table B-8 reports the relations between these three scales and anti-Semitism for black adolescents. Since prejudice was found to be associated with these scales for whites in Chapter 3, these relations are also reported on here to make possible comparisons between blacks and whites.

Table B-7   ANTI-SEMITISM BY CIVIC, MORAL, AND INTERPERSONAL VALUES FOR BLACK NON-JEWISH ADOLESCENTS

(All three communities combined)

Percent anti-Semitic among those whose response to the values items was:

Civic Values:	Disagree or Don't Care	Mildly Agree	Strongly Agree	Gamma	Xs
Should be useful citizen	63% (27)	44% (127)	38% (154)	−0.222	NS
Should support equality	50% (24)	44% (80)	41% (202)	−0.186	0.05
Should let others have power	47% (66)	42% (112)	41% (128)	−0.062	NS
Moral Values:					
Should be religious	38% (144)	39% (218)	47% (227)	+0.124	NS
Should be honest	56% (16)	46% (134)	40% (443)	−0.134	NS
Should follow rules	48% (60)	39% (265)	43% (266)	+0.005	NS
Should be moral	45% (170)	41% (280)	41% (138)	−0.055	NS
Should be hardworking	54% (48)	42% (250)	40% (286)	−0.099	NS
Interpersonal Values:					
Should not be self-centered	44% (82)	46% (203)	38% (305)	−0.112	NS
Should respect others	57% (35)	42% (185)	40% (374)	−0.093	NS
Should not be conceited	52% (23)	44% (135)	41% (437)	−0.089	NS

NS—Not significant.

Two of the three measures of cognitive sophistication are clearly related to prejudice. Each increment in level of flexibility and intellectual interests is associated with a correspondent decrease in anti-Semitism. The results for blacks are not strong, yet they are roughly equivalent to and about as strong as those for whites. The association between cynicism and anti-Semitism, however, is virtually nil in the black sample.

To prove the credibility of the proposition that academically deprived teenagers are relatively more susceptible to anti-Semitism because they are less sophisticated cognitively, it must first be demonstrated that academic deprivation and a lack of cognitive sophistication go together. In Table

Table B-8 ANTI-SEMITISM BY COGNITIVE SOPHISTICATION ITEMS
FOR BLACK AND WHITE NON-JEWISH ADOLESCENTS
(All three communities combined)

Percent anti-Semitic among those
whose intellectual activity was:

	Low					High		
	0	1	2	3	4	5	Gamma	Xs
Black	55% (11)	57% (37)	46% (136)	40% (145)	36% (127)	25% (65)	−0.231	0.02
White	64% (67)	66% (265)	59% (629)	49% (733)	41% (584)	36% (258)	−0.267	0.001

Percent anti-Semitic among those
whose flexibility was:

	Low		High		Gamma	Xs
	0	1	2	3		
Black	* (6)	46% (120)	43% (254)	26% (62)	−0.197	NS
White	71% (41)	56% (495)	52% (1,263)	41% (520)	−0.191	0.001

Percent anti-Semitic among those
whose cynicism was:

	Low			High		Gamma	Xs
	0	1	2	3	4		
Black	37% (38)	36% (75)	44% (117)	43% (143)	39% (103)	+0.020	NS
White	35% (393)	45% (594)	52% (651)	60% (506)	62% (312)	+0.250	0.001

* Too few cases for stable percentage.
NS—Not significant.

B-9, it can be seen that they do so for blacks just as they do for whites. The more deprived teenagers are on measures of academic standing, the lower they score on indicators of cognitive functioning. It remains still to be demonstrated that it is principally a lack of cognitive sophistication that accounts for anti-Semitism being especially located among the academically deprived. This requires an examination of the joint effect of academic deprivation and cognitive sophistication on anti-Semitism.

Table B-9   ACADEMIC DEPRIVATION BY COGNITIVE SOPHISTICATION ITEMS FOR BLACK AND WHITE NON-JEWISH ADOLESCENTS

(All three communities combined)

Percent with high cognitive sophistication whose level of academic deprivation was:

Intellectual	Low				High		
activity (% high)	0	1	2	3	4	Gamma	Xs
Black	64%	47%	39%	31%	17%	−0.294	0.001
	(47)	(75)	(145)	(127)	(113)		
White	59%	48%	29%	26%	14%	−0.415	0.001
	(407)	(483)	(530)	(492)	(544)		
Cynicism (% low)							
Black	39%	31%	23%	21%	12%	−0.218	0.01
	(44)	(74)	(134)	(114)	(97)		
White	57%	50%	42%	33%	26%	−0.239	0.001
	(390)	(465)	(521)	(480)	(521)		
Flexibility (% high)							
Black	24%	14%	16%	11%	11%	−0.117	NS
	(41)	(70)	(119)	(102)	(93)		
White	30%	24%	22%	20%	19%	−0.130	0.001
	(378)	(445)	(492)	(454)	(474)		

NS—Not significant.

When this examination was done for white adolescents, both factors were found to be associated with anti-Semitism with approximately equal strength and independently of one another. Statistically speaking, cognitive sophistication did not "interpret" the relation between academic status and anti-Semitism as we had expected it would. In reflecting on this result, we concluded that probably the measures rather than the underlying proposition were at fault. That is to say, white teenagers' academic standing, rather than being a source of their cognitive powers, is an indicator of them. Consequently, anti-Semitism turns out to be related to both of the indices simultaneously because each is a measure of cognitive functioning.

As can be seen in Table B-10, the same result is obtained for black teenagers. Each factor, academic deprivation and cognitive sophistication, continues to have a relationship to anti-Semitism with the other factor controlled, and in combination the effect of the two factors on anti-Semitism is additive. Thus, for black and for white teenagers, prejudice is in large measure the result of a failure to develop the powers of reasoning necessary to recognize it, to comprehend it, and in the final analysis, to avoid taking it up.

Table B-10 ANTI-SEMITISM BY ACADEMIC DEPRIVATION AND COGNITIVE SOPHISTICATION FOR BLACK NON-JEWISH ADOLESCENTS
(All three communities combined)

Percent anti-Semitic among those whose level of academic deprivation was:

And whose level of cognitive sophistication was:	Low 0	1	2	3	High 4	Total	Gamma	Xs
Low	27% (22)	30% (26)	31% (35)	33% (18)	25% (8)	30% (114)	0.031	NS
Medium	30% (10)	33% (21)	37% (44)	49% (39)	40% (35)	41% (157)	0.122	NS
High	* (5)	33% (15)	39% (33)	38% (32)	61% (36)	47% (128)	0.225	NS
Total	33% (149)	36% (83)	34% (155)	46% (140)	48% (124)	42% (604)	0.167	NS
Gamma	0.322	0.044	0.111	0.006	0.436	0.224		
Xs	NS	NS	NS	NS	NS	0.05		

* Too few cases for stable percentage.
NS—Not significant.

Context and Contact

It remains to examine for black teenagers the effect of a Jewish presence on anti-Semitism. White teenagers, as seen in previous chapters, are influenced in their attitudes toward Jews, not only by their social position and by the sophistication they bring to interpreting social life, but also by the extent and nature of their exposure to Jewish adolescents. Other things being equal, being in a context where Jews are present has the effect of increasing the gross amount of white anti-Semitism. At the same time, forming friendships with Jews in such contexts is associated with a reduction in prejudice.

The contextual effect also prevails among black adolescents although to a lesser degree. Whereas the proportion anti-Semitic in Central City, with only a few Jewish teenagers, is 28 percent for blacks, it is 34 percent in Oceanville and 37 percent in Commutertown. Respectively, the figures for whites are 41 percent, 53 percent, and 66 percent. Thus, the range for whites is 25 percentage points, but only 9 percentage points for blacks.

Relatively, black teenagers are considerably less likely than white non-Jewish youth to have Jewish friends. In Commutertown, for example, only 16 percent of the black teenagers included a Jewish youth in the list of five people with whom they go around most often, in comparison with 41 percent of the white non-Jewish teenagers. In Oceanville, only 6 percent of the blacks but 36 percent of the whites mentioned Jews. And in Central City with only a few Jewish teenagers available to make friends with, 3 percent of the white students, but none of the blacks, listed Jewish friends.

Given the paucity of black/Jewish friendships, there are only a few black teenagers whose attitudes toward Jews are subject to being influenced by friendship with them. Nevertheless, as the gammas in Table B-11 show, friendship is associated with less anti-Semitism. In both Commutertown and Oceanville, black teenagers who have one or more Jewish friends are less anti-Semitic than those without such friends.

There is no direct evidence to account for the smaller contextual effect of a Jewish presence on black than on white prejudice. We suspect that, in part, it is due to blacks being in less direct competition with Jewish teen-

Table B-11   ANTI-SEMITISM BY NUMBER OF JEWISH FRIENDS FOR BLACK NON-JEWISH ADOLESCENTS

| | Percent anti-Semitic among those whose Jewish friendships number: | | | | | | | |
	0	1	2	3	4	5	Gamma	Xs
Commutertown	54%	46%	*	*	*	*	−0.356	NS
	(195)	(28)	(3)	(4)	(2)	(1)		
Oceanville	43%	*	*	*	*	*	−0.390	NS
	(133)	(6)	(2)	(0)	(0)	(0)		
Central City	32%	*	*	*	*	*	−1.000	NS
	(229)	(1)	(0)	(0)	(0)	(0)		

* Too few cases for stable percentage.
NS—Not significant.

agers than are non-Jewish whites. Negative attributions of Jewish success, it will be recalled from Table 7 in Chapter 1, were much more frequently made by white than by black youngsters in the two towns having a substantial Jewish presence. The differences do not appear in Central City.

It also seems likely that Jewish clannishness is less likely to be of concern to black than to white youngsters. The increased clannishness expressed by Jewish parents as their children enter into the age of dating is likely to be perceived and felt more by non-Jewish whites than blacks simply because the occasions for interracial dating, given prevailing racial barriers, are so rare. Black parents also apparently feel that the threat of interfaith involvements is so remote as to warrant little concern. In Table B-12, for example, black parents, as measured by the reports of their children, do not increase pressure for endogamous dating as their teenagers become older (except among the seventeen Oceanville seniors), in comparison with white parents who significantly increase their ethnocentrism.

That blacks are less prone than non-Jewish whites to forming Jewish

Table B-12   PARENTS' RELIGIO-CENTRISM FOR BLACK AND WHITE NON-JEWISH ADOLESCENTS

Percent anti-Semitic who said their parents wanted their dates to be of their own religion:

	Eighth	Grade Tenth	Twelfth	Difference*	Xs
Commutertown					
Black	32% (108)	31% (78)	32% (51)	0	NS
White	48% (259)	58% (298)	60% (198)	12	0.001
Oceanville					
Black	33% (76)	26% (49)	47% (17)	14	NS
White	50% (203)	52% (240)	67% (168)	17	0.001
Central City					
Black	34% (98)	20% (91)	27% (53)	−7	NS
White	43% (466)	42% (483)	55% (391)	12	0.001

* From 10th to 12th grades.
NS—Not significant.

friendships is scarcely surprising given the racial barriers in the one instance and not in the other. Since friendships with Jews reduce white anti-Semitism, however, it would appear that the relative absence of black/Jewish friendships ought, at least in Commutertown and Oceanville, to result in greater black anti-Semitism. That it doesn't is due probably to the effects of Jewish success and clannishness being muted in the black samples.

It was not to be expected, given differences in the opportunities for black/Jewish interaction as against non-Jewish white/Jewish interaction, that the effect of context and contact would be precisely the same in the two subcommunities. The fact that the results are as concordant as they are suggests that the underlying processes at work transcend differences attributable to race.

Summary and Conclusions

The results for blacks are not so different from those for whites as our decision to undertake separate analyses anticipated. By and large, the same prejudice-producing system appears to be operative in both groups. Anti-Semitism tends to be especially located among the socially deprived. Psychic impairment characterized by frustration and anxiety, as measured by authoritarianism, low self-acceptance, and low self-esteem, does not seem to be an important factor in the maintenance of prejudice for either blacks or whites, nor do enlightened values play a significant role in reducing prejudice. Lack of cognitive sophistication appears to be the major reason for the higher incidence of prejudice among the deprived in both racial groups. The gross amount of anti-Semitism is greater among both blacks and whites in settings where Jews are present, but, in such contexts, having friends who are Jewish is associated with less anti-Semitism.

The differences we found bore primarily on the relative strength of the associations between the several causal factors and anti-Semitism. The relation between deprivation and prejudice is not so strong among blacks as among whites, and economic conditions seem to be more significant relative to academic deprivation in the former group than in the latter. Interpersonal values are unrelated to prejudice among blacks where they are associated with slightly higher levels of tolerance among white non-Jewish teenagers. As for whites, cognitive sophistication is found for blacks to be more strongly associated with anti-Semitic prejudice than any other factor examined. Moreover, the combined effect of academic deprivation and cognitive sophistication is once again additive. The size of a Jewish presence makes less difference in the anti-Semitism of blacks than whites. Blacks, however, are less likely than whites to have Jewish friends.

Throughout, blacks express less anti-Semitism than whites even with factors such as deprivation, cognitive sophistication, and friendship with Jews controlled. In the communities where Jews are present, this appears to be partly the result of the different potential for intergroup interaction. Blacks are less likely to have Jewish friends but are less likely also to come into direct academic competition with Jewish youth. Thus, there is perhaps less resentment about the relatively greater success of Jews. Also, because of racial barriers, blacks are possibly less likely to experience Jewish clannishness as distinct from white clannishness generally or to express religious clannishness themselves. The data afford no clues as to why black teenagers should also be less anti-Semitic in settings where Jews are absent. However, blacks and whites differ less in the amount of anti-Semitism they express in Central City than in the other two communities.

Black teenagers, it is evident from these results, are caught up in the same social processes as whites. Still, unique factors are operating in the black adolescent community which cannot be wholly understood from a perspective informed primarily by research on white subjects. The analysis has enabled us to point to what some of these unique factors are, but our theory has not enabled us wholly to account for them. Clearly, more work is needed to fully comprehend prejudice as it is manifested in both adolescent subcultures, but most especially the black one.

Appendix C: Supplementary Tables

Table C-1   ANTI-SEMITISM BY ACADEMIC DEPRIVATION BY SEX
FOR WHITE NON-JEWISH ADOLESCENTS
(All three communities combined)

Percent anti-Semitic among those whose
score on the academic deprivation scale was:

	0	1	2	3	4	Total	Gamma	Xs
Boys	35%	49%	54%	59%	68%	56%	0.288	0.001
	(179)	(249)	(290)	(278)	(321)	(1,389)		
Girls	29%	37%	45%	50%	66%	46%	0.344	0.001
	(234)	(242)	(269)	(234)	(257)	(1,309)		

Table C-2   ANTI-SEMITISM BY ACADEMIC DEPRIVATION BY
RELIGION FOR WHITE NON-JEWISH ADOLESCENTS
(All three communities combined)

Percent anti-Semitic among those whose score
on the academic deprivation scale was:

	0	1	2	3	4	Total	Gamma	Xs
Protestant	30%	41%	45%	46%	57%	44%	0.226	0.001
	(311)	(353)	(378)	(295)	(291)	(1,722)		
Catholic	39%	52%	57%	72%	77%	64%	0.387	0.001
	(80)	(108)	(154)	(173)	(234)	(791)		

Table C-3   ANTI-SEMITISM BY COGNITIVE SOPHISTICATION BY SEX FOR WHITE NON-JEWISH ADOLESCENTS
(All three communities combined)

Percent anti-Semitic among those whose score on
the cognitive sophistication scale was:

	Low											High		Total	
	0	1	2	3	4	5	6	7	8	9	10	11	Total	
Boys	*	60%	76%	65%	68%	59%	60%	45%	43%	45%	19%	*	56%	Gamma = −0.273
	(0)	(10)	(37)	(100)	(153)	(187)	(208)	(168)	(114)	(83)	(21)	(7)	(1,389)	Xs = 0.001
Girls	*	82%	57%	66%	59%	55%	51%	41%	35%	26%	26%	7%	46%	Gamma = −0.341
	(1)	(11)	(28)	(77)	(140)	(156)	(188)	(186)	(153)	(121)	(46)	(14)	(1,309)	Xs = 0.001

* Too few cases for stable percentage.

Table C-4 ANTI-SEMITISM BY COGNITIVE SOPHISTICATION BY RELIGION FOR WHITE NON-JEWISH ADOLESCENTS

(All three communities combined)

Percent anti-Semitic among those whose score on the cognitive sophistication scale was:

	Low											High		
	0	1	2	3	4	5	6	7	8	9	10	11	Total	
Protestant	*	55%	63%	59%	59%	52%	47%	37%	35%	30%	23%	*	44%	Gamma = −0.302
	(0)	(11)	(38)	(107)	(200)	(227)	(260)	(245)	(174)	(136)	(48)	(0)	(1,722)	Xs = 0.001
Catholic	*	88%	79%	76%	74%	68%	75%	56%	46%	46%	33%	*	64%	Gamma = −0.333
	(1)	(8)	(19)	(58)	(77)	(102)	(114)	(89)	(80)	(56)	(15)	(5)	(791)	Xs = 0.001

* Too few cases for stable percentage.

Table C-5 PATH COEFFICIENTS USING ORDINAL STATISTICS

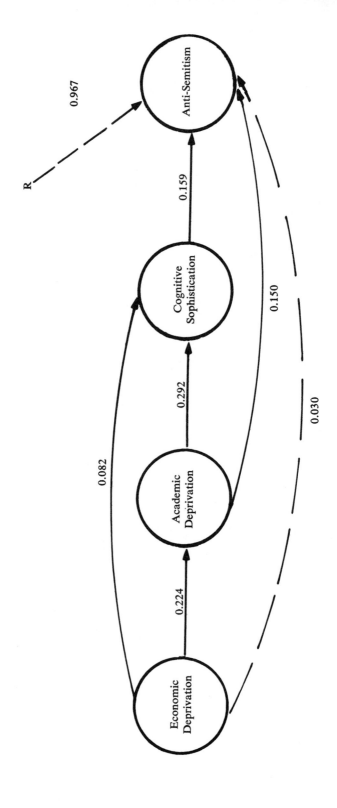

Notes

Introduction

1. Other studies in the Patterns of American Prejudice Series, all published by Harper & Row, have investigated: religion and prejudice in *Christian Beliefs and Anti-Semitism*, by Charles Y. Glock and Rodney Stark (1966); prejudice and public opinion about the Eichmann trial in *The Apathetic Majority*, by Charles Y. Glock, Gertrude J. Selznick, and Joe L. Spaeth (1966); prejudice in the black community in *Protest and Prejudice*, by Gary T. Marx (1967); prejudice in the nation-at-large in *The Tenacity of Prejudice*, by Gertrude J. Selznick and Stephen Steinberg (1969); prejudice and politics in *The Politics of Unreason*, by Seymour M. Lipset and Earl Raab (1970); and prejudice and the clergy in *Wayward Shepherds*, by Rodney Stark, Bruce Foster, Charles Y. Glock, and Harold Quinley (1971).

2. R. E. Goodnow and R. Taiguri, "Religious Ethnocentrism and Its Recognition Among Adolescent Boys," *J. Abnormal Soc. Psych.*, 47:316–20, 1952; C. A. Insko and J. E. Robinson, "Belief Similarity versus Race as a Determinant of Reactions to Negroes by Southern White Adolescents: A Further Test of Rokeach's Theory," *J. Per. Soc. Psych.*, 7: 216–21, 1967; G. D. Mayo and J. R. Kinser, "A Comparison of the 'Racial' Attitudes of White and Negro High School Students in 1940 and 1948," *J. Psych.*, 29:397–405, 1950; J. D. McNeil, "Changes in Ethnic Reaction Tendencies During High School," *J. Ed. Res.*, 53:199–200, 1960; H. H. Remmers and N. Weltman, "Attitude Inter-relationships of Youth, Their Parents, and Their Teachers," *J. Soc. Psych.*, 26:61–68, 1947; M. Rosenberg, *Society and the Adolescent Self-Image* (Princeton: Princeton University Press, 1965); D. H. Russell and I. V. Robertson, "Influencing Attitudes Toward Minority Groups in a Junior High School," *School Rev.*, 55:205–13, 1947; W. C. Wilson, "Development of Ethnic Attitudes in Adolescence," *Child Devel.*, 34: 247–59, 1963; R. Zeligs, "Training Racial Attitudes Through Adolescence," *Sociology Soc. Res.*, 23:45–54, 1938.

3. James Coleman et al., *Equality of Educational Opportunity* (Washington: Government Printing Office, 1966); Samuel Bowles and Henry Levin, "The Determinants of Scholastic Achievement—An Appraisal of Some Recent Evidence," *J. Human Resources*, 3:1, 3–25, 1968; Alan B. Wilson, *The Consequences of Segregation* (Berkeley: Glendessary Press, 1969).

4. Richard D. Lambert and Marvin Bressler, "The Sensitive-Area Complex: A Contribution to the Theory of Guided Culture Contact," *Am. J. Soc.*, 60:

583–92, 1955; Irwin Katz, *Conflict and Harmony in an Adolescent Interracial Group* (New York: New York University Press, 1955); Barbara K. MacKenzie, "The Importance of Contact in Determining Attitudes Toward Negroes," *J. Abnormal Soc. Psych.*, 43:4, 417–41, 1948; John Mann, "The Effects of Inter-racial Contact on Sociometric Choices and Perceptions," *J. Soc. Psych.*, 50:1, 143–152, 1959; Muzafer Sherif, *Intergroup Conflict and Cooperation: The Robber's Cave Experiment* (Norman, Okla.: Oklahoma University Press, 1961); Marx, *op. cit.*, 154–59.

5. We chose to use as the final sample only those students who were present for all three administrations of the questionnaire.

6. The administration of the teacher questionnaire was informal. Questionnaires were left in teachers' mail boxes with a request that they be filled out and returned. School principals were requested to urge teachers to fill out and return the questionnaires. Return rates varied widely by school and by town, ranging from 21 percent from one school in Commutertown to 94 percent from a school in Central City. The variety in the return rate makes it necessary to be cautious in generalizing from the responses of the teachers to the school districts at large. However, as will be seen, only very limited use is made of responses to the teacher questionnaire in the following analysis and the cautionary note is repeated at the appropriate point.

Chapter 1: Attitudes, Feelings, and Patterns of Friendship

1. The classification of prejudice into three components was first suggested, so far as we have been able to discover, by Bernard Kramer in "Dimensions of Prejudice," *J. of Psych.*, v. 27–28, pp. 389–451, 1949. See also Isador Chein, "Notes on a Framework for the Measurement of Discrimination and Prejudice," Appendix C in Marie Jahoda, Morton Deutsch, and Stuart Cook, *Research Methods in Social Relations*, Part One (New York: Dryden Press, 1951).

2. Also motivating this decision was a desire to include the same item in the battery asking about attitudes toward Jews as in the battery of items asking about blacks.

3. See Charles Herbert Stember, "The Recent History of Public Attitudes," in C. H. Stember, *et al.*, *Jews in the Mind of America* (New York: Basic Books, 1966); Gertrude J. Selznick and Stephen Steinberg, *The Apathetic Majority* (New York: Harper & Row, 1966).

4. See Gary T. Marx, *Protest and Prejudice* (New York: Harper & Row, 1967); Selznick and Steinberg, *op. cit.*; Stember, *op. cit.*

5. Stereotype questions were asked in a form to allow teenagers to report that they agreed strongly, agreed moderately, agreed a little, disagreed a little, disagreed moderately, or disagreed a lot. In Table 2 and in subsequent tables in Chapter 1, we report the population expressing agreement irrespective of the strength with which it was espoused. Examination of the full range of responses indicated that this was the most appropriate cutting point for conveying the meaning of the responses economically.

6. Selznick and Steinberg, *op. cit.*

7. Generally speaking, the incidence of anti-Semitism and other forms of prejudice has been found to be less in the North Atlantic region than in other sections of the country. See Selznick and Steinberg, *op. cit.*, 170–71, 176, 181, 182; Marx, *op. cit.*, 126–67.

8. See Marx, *op. cit.*, 146–48, 167; Selznick and Steinberg, *op. cit.*, 117–31; Louis Harris and Bert E. Swanson, *Black–Jewish Relations in New York City* (New York: Praeger Publishers, 1970).

9. See Marx, *op. cit.*, 186.

10. Another item, "Live in the same apartment house," was also asked about but we did not include this item in the analysis. Upon examination, it was discovered that many who responded negatively did so, not to indicate social distance, but to express their dislike for living in an apartment house.

11. However, as will be seen in Chapter 2, the more the hostility, the greater the social distance.

12. See p. 181.

13. See p. 181.

Chapter 2: The Social Context of Adolescent Prejudice

1. Detailed reference to extant theories will be made in Chapter 3.

2. The extent to which the findings for white adolescents are repeated for black teenagers is reported in Appendix B.

3. By the time the child is four to seven years of age he or she has often already learned some of the culturally available concepts and phrases used to describe other ethnic groups, although he may not know yet what these concepts and phrases mean. See Mary E. Goodman, *Race Awareness in Young Children*, 2d. ed. (New York: Crowell-Collier, 1964).

4. See p. 183.

5. Moderately agree was scored 6; agree a little, 5; no feelings either way, 4; disagree a little, 3; and moderately disagree, 2.

6. For a comprehensive treatment of the statistical properties of gamma, see Linton C. Freeman, *Elementary Applied Statistics* (New York: John Wiley & Sons, Inc., 1968). A brief, clear description is available in Earl R. Babbie, *Survey Research Methods* (Belmont, Calif.: Wadsworth Publishing Co., Inc., 1973), 303–4.

7. James S. Coleman, *The Adolescent Society: The Social Life of the Teenager and Its Impact on Education* (New York: Free Press, 1961).

8. Selznick and Steinberg, *op. cit.*, 69–93; see especially Table 20, p. 75.

9. See p. 184.

10. This cutting point was decided upon because scores of 4–7 on the anti-Semitism scale consistently increase with each increase of prejudice on validating items; scores of 1–3 consistently decrease. This can be seen by re-examining Table 16, p. 32. Note that the tendency for Commutertown teenagers to

score highest and for Central City teenagers to score lowest on the anti-Semitism scale is maintained at each point on the scale from 7 down to 4. In turn, however, Commutertown youngsters are least likely and Central City youngsters most likely to score 1, 2, and 3 on the scale. In effect, those who are in the middle of the scale, score 4, are more like those who are more anti-Semitic than those who are less anti-Semitic.

In using this cutting point and for shorthand purposes calling those with scores of 4 to 7 "anti-Semitic," we shall assume that this designation is understood to mean all those who don't clearly reject anti-Semitism; that is, either those who answer the questions used to form the scale in an outrightly anti-Semitic way on the average or those who are as likely to answer in an anti-Semitic as in a non-anti-Semitic way.

Several alternative conventions might have been adopted in pursuing the analysis. We could have chosen to present all the tabulations with all seven categories on the anti-Semitism scale shown in full. We decided against doing so simply because the tables would have been overly complex and virtually impossible to comment upon. Another alternative was to use a mean score, that is, simply present the average scores on the anti-Semitism scale of the subgroups of teenagers in whom we are interested. This procedure would have been an acceptable substitute for the convention adopted, but our choice was governed by *gamma* affording a more suitable measure of the strength of relationships than the measures appropriate for use when mean scores are being compared. In addition, mean scores allow for less clarity and ease of presentation than percentages.

Since either choice is to some extent arbitrary, we have checked the results presented in the text, substituting mean scores for percentages. The results using both procedures are essentially equivalent.

11. The inverse relationship between prejudice and higher education is discussed from this perspective in Robert C. Angell, "Preferences for Moral Norms in Three Problem Areas," *Am. J. Soc.*, 67:6, 650–60, May 1962.

12. Comparing the differences between those planning to attend college and those not planning to attend college with the differences between high school graduates and college graduates found by Selznick and Steinberg (*op. cit.*, p. 72) suggests that it may not be unreasonable to assume that at least half of the difference in prejudice between the college trained and the non-college trained may exist before persons ever reach college age.

13. Pages 185 and 186.

14. For a more detailed discussion of the logic of examining three variables simultaneously using cross-tabular analysis the reader is referred to Herbert Hyman, *Survey Design and Analysis: Principles, Cases and Procedures* (New York: Free Press, 1955), especially Chapter 7, and Morris Rosenberg, *The Logic of Survey Analysis* (New York: Basic Books, Inc., 1968).

15. Prejudice is also associated with academic deprivation among both boys and girls and among both Protestants and Catholics; see Tables C-1 and C-2 in Appendix C, p. 209.

Chapter 3: Causes of Adolescent Anti-Semitism

1. One of the early works in which this theory gained clearest expression, albeit with regard to racial prejudice rather than anti-Semitism, is John Dollard's *Caste and Class in a Southern Town* (Garden City: Doubleday & Company, 1937). This theory was then formalized by John Dollard, Neal Miller, Leonard Doob, *et al.*, in *Frustration and Aggression* (New Haven: Yale University Press, 1939).

2. T. W. Adorno, Else Frenkel-Brunswik, D. J. Levinson, and R. N. Sanford, *The Authoritarian Personality* (New York: Harper & Row, 1950).

3. Michael Banton, *Race Relations* (New York: Basic Books, Inc., 1967), 298.

4. Gertrude J. Selznick and Stephen Steinberg, *The Apathetic Majority* (New York: Harper & Row, 1966), 167–69.

5. For example, Robin M. Williams, Jr., *Strangers Next Door* (Englewood Cliffs, N.J.: Prentice-Hall, Inc., 1964), especially p. 180.

6. Some evidence on the effect of parental influence, at least as perceived by the adolescent, is presented in Chapter 4, however.

7. James S. Coleman, *The Adolescent Society: The Social Life of the Teen-ager and Its Impact on Education* (New York: Free Press, 1961).

8. Williams, *op. cit.*

9. John Harding, Harold Pvoshansky, Bernard Kutner, and Isador Chein, "Prejudice and Ethnic Relations," in Gardner Lindzey, ed., *Handbook of Social Psychology*, 2d ed. (Reading, Mass.: Addison-Wesley, 1969), 1–76.

10. Probably the best known exposition of this thesis remains that of Gunnar Myrdal, *An American Dilemma* (New York: Harper & Row, 1944). A recent empirical examination is provided by Selznick and Steinberg, *op. cit.*

11. Samuel A. Stouffer, *Communism, Conformity, and Civil Liberties* (New York: Doubleday & Co., Inc., 1955).

12. Myrdal, *op. cit.*

13. Frank R. Westie, "The American Dilemma: An Empirical Test," *Am. Soc. Rev.*, 30:527–38, 1965.

14. Recent data from a national sample, for example, shows that "simplism" is common among at least half the uneducated but common among less than 10 percent of those fortunate enough to have college educations (Selznick and Steinberg, *op. cit.*, 141).

15. *Ibid.*, especially pp. 135–69.

16. T. W. Adorno, Else Frenkel-Brunswick, D. J. Levinson, and R. N. Sanford, *The Authoritarian Personality* (New York: Harper & Row, 1950).

17. For a review, see John P. Kirscht and Ronald C. Dillehay, *Dimensions of Authoritarianism: A Review of Research and Theory* (Lexington, Ky.: University of Kentucky Press, 1967).

18. Roger W. Brown, *Social Psychology* (New York: Free Press, 1965), 477–546.

19. Besides the research reported in the original volume, see also especially Else Frenkel-Brunswik, "Further Explorations by a Contributor to 'The Authoritarian Personality,' " in R. Christie and M. Jahoda, eds., *Studies in the Scope and Method of "The Authoritarian Personality"* (Glencoe, Ill.: Free Press, 1954).

20. The Christie reversed version of the F scale is used. For details regarding scale construction see the Appendix, p. 186. For present purposes, scoring high is defined as 7 through 10.

21. R. Christie, J. Havel, and B. Seidenberg, "Is the F Scale Irreversible?," *J. Abnormal Soc. Psych.*, 56:143–59, 1958.

22. The items for this scale were taken from the California Personality Inventory with specific items being selected with the advice of Prof. H. G. Gough. Ten of the original 26 items were selected.

23. Morris Rosenberg, *Society and the Adolescent Self-Image* (Princeton: Princeton University Press, 1965).

24. *Ibid.*, Appendix.

25. The time order we have been assuming is that having anti-Semitic friends is a source of anti-Semitism. It is equally plausible, of course, that the causal sequence is in the opposite direction: being anti-Semitic oneself is a stimulus to seeking out friends who share one's prejudices. With cross-sectional data it is not possible to learn which of the two processes is operating.

26. Stouffer, *op. cit.*; Selznick and Steinberg, *op. cit.*, 143–48.

27. Seymour M. Lipset and Earl Raab, *The Politics of Unreason* (New York: Harper & Row, 1969).

28. Lipset and Raab, *op. cit.*; Selznick and Steinberg, *op. cit.*, 53–66.

29. Items were scored 0 where response was "shouldn't" or "don't care," 1 where response was "should," and 2 where response was "strongly should."

30. H. G. Gough, *California Psychological Inventory Manual* (Palo Alto, Calif.: Consulting Psychologists Press, 1957).

31. See Appendix A, p. 186.

32. These items are taken from the Gough personality scale and were originally part of a measure of tolerance.

33. See Appendix C, p. 212, for a replication of the interrelationships between socioeconomic status, academic deprivation, cognitive sophistication, and anti-Semitism using path analysis. The method used is that developed by Robert E. Smith for ordinal data. See Robert B. Smith, "Neighborhood Context and College Plans: An Ordinal Path Analysis," *Social Forces,* 51:199–217, 1972; Robert B. Smith, "Do Path Analysis: Instructions for the Dichotomous-Ordinal Path Analysis Program" (mimeo).

34. The data also show that cognitive sophistication and anti-Semitism are related independently of sex and of religion. See Appendix C, Tables C–3 and C–4. It will be noted in these tables that, in all comparisons, girls show less prejudice than boys and Protestants less prejudice than Catholics. The relationships between sex and prejudice and religion and prejudice are not pursued further in the text, since the more general findings apply for boys as well as girls and for Protestants as well as Catholics.

Chapter 4: The Effects of a Jewish Presence

1. For a review of the literature on intergroup contact and prejudice, see Y. Amir, "Contact Hypothesis in Ethnic Relations," *Psych. Bul.*, 71:319–42, 1969. See also J. J. Preiss and H. J. Ehrlich, *An Examination of Role Theory* (Lincoln, Neb.: University of Nebraska Press, 1966) and Robin M. Williams, Jr., *Strangers Next Door* (Englewood Cliffs, N.J.: Prentice-Hall, 1964).

2. At least judging from teenagers' responses about their parents.

3. A reader of our manuscript has called our attention to Donald T. Campbell's article, "Stereotypes and the Perception of Group Differences" (*Am. Psychologist*, 22:817–29, 1962). Campbell, we belatedly learn, has preceded us in discovering both the importance of the "truth" content of stereotypes and of the explanatory factor in judging prejudice. We regret that we were unaware of this article before pursuing our own analysis, but are happy to acknowledge here that these ideas are not unique to us.

4. For construction of the combined deprivation/unsophistication scale, see Appendix A, p. 186.

5. Campbell, *op. cit.*

Chapter 5: Adolescent Racial Prejudice

1. In light of the fact that the adolescent and adult forms of the questionnaire produced virtually similar results, we will not consider responses to the adult form.

2. The factor analysis was conducted the same as for anti-Semitism stereotypes and produced much the same results. These results (see also Table 81) suggest that there is a common core of negative stereotypes that are indiscriminately applied to both blacks and Jews. This in no way denies, however, that some stereotypes tend to be ascribed more often to blacks, also probably because of some "truth content," although we are not in a position to test this assertion as we did regarding anti-Semitism in Chapter 4.

3. The equalitarian values scale was collapsed as follows: 0 and 1=low; 2= medium; 3 and 4 = high. The cognitive sophistication scale was collapsed as follows: 0 to 5 = low; 6 to 11 = high.

4. Campbell, *op. cit.*

Chapter 6: The Findings in Broader Perspective

1. Donald T. Campbell also makes this point in his article previously cited ("Stereotypes and the Perception of Group Differences" in *Am. Psychologist.* 22:817–29, 1962).

Index

Schools and prejudice (*cont'd*)
  education quality and, 174
  instruction on prejudice, 171, 174–76
    historical background of group differ-
      ences, 176
    on logic of inference, 176
    psychological factors and, 177
    size of group differences, 176–77
  perception of problem, 172–74
  racial prejudice, 171–72, 173
  teachers
    competence for instruction in preju-
      dice, 178–79
    recognition of problems, of preju-
      dice, 172–73. *See also* Academic
      deprivation and anti-Semitism;
      Academic deprivation and racial
      prejudices
School-spiritedness, Jewish, 107
  stereotype of, 5
    acceptance by non-Jewish adoles-
      cents, 14
Self-acceptance
  academic deprivation and, 71
  anti-Semitism and, 72
  Gough scale, revised, 70–71
  racial prejudice and, 145
Self-esteem
  academic deprivation and, 73–75
  anti-Semitism and, 73
  racial prejudice and, 145
  Rosenberg scale of, 72–74
Selfishness, stereotype of
  of blacks, summary index of racial
    prejudice and, 140–41
  of Jews, 3, 8, 9, 14
    summary index of anti-Semitism, 30
Sloppiness of Jews, stereotype of, 4–5,
  8, 11
    summary index of anti-Semitism and,
      34
Slyness of blacks, stereotype of, 134
Slyness of Jews, stereotype of, 5, 110
  acceptance
    by blacks, 14
    Jewish presence and, 14, 109–13
    by Jewish youth, 111
    by non-Jewish whites, 8, 14–15,
      107–9

Social deprivation. *See* Deprivation
Social distance
  anti-Semitism
    academic deprivation and, 59–60
    blacks and, 21–22
    cognitive sophistication and, 102
    feelings about Jews and, 16–22
    friends' anti-Semitism and, 100
    hostility, attitudinal, and, 17–18
    intimacy of relationship and, 17,
      19
    presence, Jewish, and, 18, 22
    status and, 16–22, 26
    utility of measurement, 22
  racial prejudice and, 136–9, 141
    Jewish and non-Jewish whites com-
      pared, 159
  scales, construction of, 181
Socialization, anti-Semitism and
  to enlightened values, and reduction of
    prejudice, 65
  to unenlightened values, as cause of
    prejudice, 61
Status, economic, teenage, and anti-Semitism, 42–43
Status, social
  anti-Semitism and
    cognitive sophistication and, 65–66
    deprivation, prejudice and, 38–39.
      See also Deprivation
    social contact and, 17, 19
    social distance and, 17–22, 26
    teenage status and, 43–45
  racial prejudice and, 136–39, 141
    Jewish and non-Jewish whites com-
      pared, 159
Status, socioeconomic
  class prejudice and. *See* Class prejudice;
    Deprivation
  of family, anti-Semitism and, 50, 51
    blacks and, 194–95
    scale for determination of father's
      status, 184–85
    summary index and, 54–58
  Jews, in general, 107. *See also* Aca-
    demic deprivation; Deprivation;
    Economic deprivation
Stereotypes of blacks, 133
  acceptance

Until now, little has been known about adolescent prejudice. In this pivotal study the authors shed much light on the basic questions that account for prejudice and also for its absence.

Focusing primarily on anti-Semitism—and contrasting it to racial prejudice—the authors examine the prevailing belief that inter-religious and interracial contact breaks down prejudices and religious and racial stereotypes, creates opportunities for friendship across religious and racial lines, and generates norms of tolerance. Toward that end, a total of 4631 students in the eighth, tenth, and twelfth grades, in three separate Eastern Seaboard communities, were given questionnaires. Teachers, too, in each school system were given questionnaires. The findings show that prejudice is nurtured especially among youths who have not developed the cognitive skills and sophistication to combat it. Indeed, the authors believe that "Prejudice is rampant in school populations . . . not only racial prejudice but anti-Semitism and a virulent but especially neglected class prejudice as well."

To enable youngsters to avoid falling victim to simplistic thinking, the authors recommend education in

—the logic of inference so that youngsters can recognize when group differences are being falsely accounted for;

—how group differences come about;

—the degree of difference within a group so as to avoid generalizations about the group members.

This book is the result of a grant to the University of California from the Anti-Defamation League of B'nai B'rith for a study of anti-Semitism and other forms of prejudice in America.

9950